STOP WASTING YOUR YARD!

100 Edible Plants You Can
Probably Grow at Home

STOP WASTING YOUR YARD!

100 Edible Plants You Can Probably Grow at Home

Kate Russell

solificatio

San Francisco, California

Stop Wasting Your Yard!
100 edible plants you can probably grow at home
Kate Russell

Published by Solificatio
2021 Trade Paperback Edition
First Edition, June 2021
Copyright © 2021 Kate Russell

The Daily Garden
https://www.thedailygarden.us/

ISBN: 978-0-9977619-6-2

I dedicate this book to my dear husband, Stuart,
for all his hours of encouragement
and proofreading The Daily Garden blog.

PREFACE

I have loved growing plants for as long as I can remember.

It all started with a plastic cup, a black sponge, and four hard, dry kernels of corn. The sponge fit snugly into the cup and each kernel was turned a different direction, wedged between the cup and the sponge. Three-year-old me added water and I was hooked!

Travel forward 50+ years and you find me studying for the Master Gardener certification test. As a fun study aid, I started writing a garden word of the day in my Facebook feed. After passing the exam, I stopped the posts but friends and family urged me to continue. And continue I did, writing a Garden Word of the Day for nearly five years.

This book is part of the knowledge I gained in that process.

As you read and use this book, please keep in mind that I have taken certain liberties, making generalizations that may or may not be technically accurate. The important thing here is that the information is accurate enough to help you successfully grow food at home.

ACKNOWLEDGMENTS

I would like to thank my husband Stuart, my children Sarah and Joshua, and the many friends and fellow gardeners who have provided encouragement in this project.

I would also like to thank The Proclaimers for their song about walking 500 miles—it kept me walking across Spain, and it kept me writing this book.

Contents

INTRODUCTION

You have a yard and you buy groceries. But you can often produce better tasting groceries for a fraction of the cost in your own yard. All you need is a warm, sunny spot to grow food. And gardening is good for you. It gets you outside and active. It puts you back in touch with natural cycles, improving your sleep, and burning calories. Working the soil has even been shown to reduce stress and anxiety. Who doesn't need that?

Gardening is good for the environment, too. Instead of shipping products halfway around the world, all you have to do is go outside and collect the freshest, sweetest produce you've ever eaten. No gas stations required.

Imagine opening your back door onto a space filled with attractive herbs, melons, climbing peas and beans, and perennial rhubarb or asparagus. Where a pinch of basil, a basket of fresh tomatoes, and an onion bulb are free for the taking.

Unless you live on a rock pile, you probably already have plants in your yard. Most or all of those plants are not edible, and yet you probably water them, feed them, and clean up after them. For what? Instead, over time, you can replace many of those ornamental plants with edibles. You can also add edible plants to an existing landscape.

Stop Wasting Your Yard! gives you the tools you need to transform your greedy, mostly unproductive ornamental landscape into an edible sanctuary, without losing curb appeal or your sanity. *Stop Wasting Your Yard!* helps you see what you can grow, what can go wrong, and how to fix it. And you don't have to tear out your landscape and start hoeing rows. It's easier than that. In fact, the plants that are already growing in your yard provide clues about which edible plants will grow best.

This book may not change the world, but it just might help you make the most of your yard. And the bragging rights are amazing.

Let's get gardening!

Another day's harvest!

P.S. Don't let the Latin scare you off. Those fancy words can come in handy when shopping for seeds and seedlings.

Chapter One

HOW TO START GARDENING

Fresh, sun-ripened tomatoes are one of the most common reasons people start gardening, but don't let that be your only reason. With just a little space and water you can grow your own lettuces, radishes, beets, herbs, and so much more! But start small. Gardeners are in it for the long haul.

As tempting as it may be to order everything that looks good from the glossy pages of a seed and plant catalog, don't do it. Start small. Taking on too much in the beginning can be discouraging. Pick just a few plants to start and learn about what works for you and your garden. You can expand over time, as you learn more. And you probably will. You may decide you have the space for a fruit cocktail tree or an artichoke bush. Maybe rhubarb and asparagus are better suited to your space.

Will your garden be perfect? Will it look like the cover of a magazine?

No, it won't. Real gardens rarely do. And that's okay. What I can tell you is that when those first seeds germinate, when you harvest your first tomato, when you give a friend a jar of home-grown dried oregano, you will feel amazing. And the easiest way to get food plants to grow is to pick plants from families that are already growing in your yard.

Once you know what will grow in your yard, you can run with it. But not at first. Taking care of a garden requires effort and water. Speaking of water, as a rule, avoid overhead watering.

Overhead watering often translates into several plant diseases that are difficult to get rid of once they take hold. Instead, let the hose run at ground level, use soaker hoses, or install a drip system.

Lifelong gardeners know that there is always more to learn. But what if you've never gardened before? You don't have any seeds or garden tools and you have no idea where to start. That's okay. All you need is a sunny spot in your yard, some water, and a little patience.

Fresh basil, tomatoes, and more!

Starting to garden is a lot like painting the bathroom. The actual painting is one of the last things you do. Good preparation is key to success. Gardening is the same way. Before you start digging, it's a good idea to prepare by learning more about what you have to work with:

- How much sunlight do you have?
- What is your Hardiness Zone?

- What kind of soil is in your yard?
- What's already growing well?
- How do plants grow?
- What about raised beds and containers?

By answering these questions, you will be able to pick the easiest food plants to grow in your yard.

And once you get started, since seed packets nearly always contain far more seeds than you will ever need or use, swap with friends and neighbors!

How much sunlight reaches your yard?

Sun-loving tomatoes will never produce abundant fruit if they don't get enough light, while tender lettuces may bolt (go to seed) before producing much in the way of salad greens if they get too much sun.

The amount of sunlight that reaches your yard and the time of day it shines on your soil largely determine which plants will grow well. And putting plants in the wrong location is a waste of time and money. Plant labels and seed packets will tell you how much sunlight a plant needs, and some plants grow in more than one type of exposure to the sun.

TYPES OF SUN EXPOSURE

Full sun means an area gets 8 or more hours of direct sunlight every day. Full sun is usually found on the south side of your house (assuming you live in the northern hemisphere). Most summer crops prefer full sun. These are your go-getters. Partial sun is for the late sleepers of the plant world. They need time to wake up and may not be ready to deal with direct sunlight until later in the day. These plants grow best when they get 3-6 hours of afternoon sunlight. Partial sun is usually found on the west side of your house. Partial shade is for our early risers. These plants grow best when they get 3-6 hours of sunlight in the morning, and are then protected from more intense midday and afternoon sun. Full shade can be dappled or deep, but very few edible plants can grow in shade.

So how much sun is in your yard? It might surprise you.

If you were to set up a time lapse camera in a strategic position in your yard, you would be able to see how shaded areas move across your landscape. Neighboring deciduous trees create huge pockets of shade in summer, and less in winter. The angle of the sunlight changes through the seasons, too. It's a good idea to identify which areas of your yard get full sunlight, partial sun, and partial shade before buying and planting seeds and seedlings.

If you want a truly accurate record of what type of sunlight is reaching your yard, you can create a sun map.

HOW TO MAKE A SUN MAP

Making a sun map of your yard is not hard, but it does take some time—a full year, in fact. That's because the angle of the sun changes from season to season, trees drop their leaves, and you will need information from each season, at different times of day, to make an accurate sun map. But today is as good a day as any to get started.

Follow these steps to create your own sun map:

- Make a map: Draw a rough sketch of your property or trace a satellite image of your yard.
- Create a key: You can simply pencil in the places where shade occurs, making areas that get the most shade the darkest, or you can use different colors for full sun, partial sun, partial shade, and full shade.
- Mark your map: Walk around your property and mark where sunlight and shade occur, or take photos and transfer the information onto your map.

Once you have a map of where and when sunlight appears in

your yard, you will be able to make better choices about which plants will thrive and where to put them.

What's your Hardiness Zone?

Your USDA Hardiness Zone is a number or number-letter combination that identifies how cold your winters get. This is important when it comes to plant selection. Most plant labels and seed packets will tell you if a specific plant will perform well in your zone. Of course, each yard is different. As you garden, you will learn more about your yard and which plants are best suited to it.

If you live in the U.S., you can use this map to identify your USDA Hardiness Zone. Other countries have similar maps. You can also look online for a more detailed view of your Hardiness Zone.

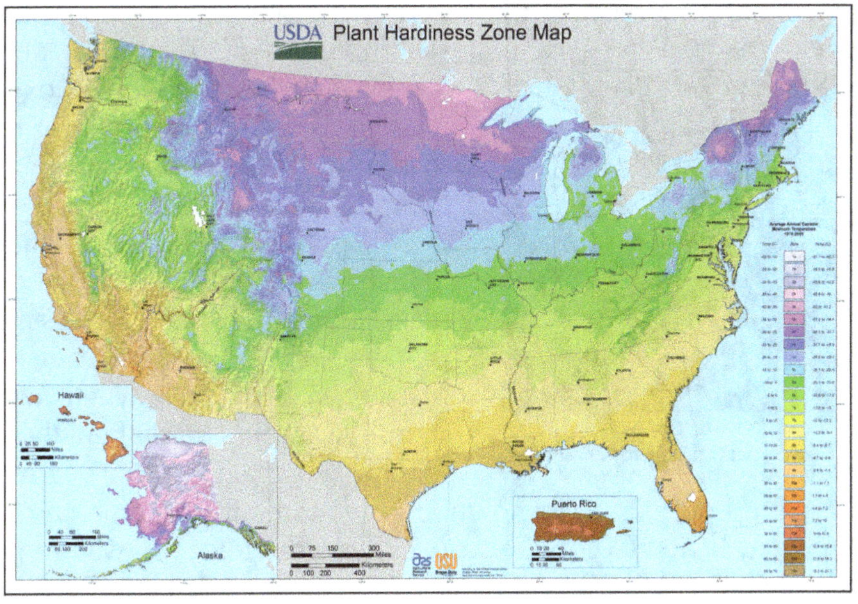

In this book, I've listed specific Hardiness Zones, ideal soil temperatures, and sun exposures. Hardiness Zones will tell you how much cold a plant can handle. Ideal soil temperatures mostly apply to seed germination, but also to optimal plant health. In some cases there are two sets of numbers, for plants that can be grown as either an annual or a perennial.

Even if you live in a zone where something might not grow well, I hope you still enjoy learning about these amazing edible plants. And sometimes, you can coax plants to grow where they shouldn't be able to.

What's in your soil?

Dirt is the stuff that gets on your clothes and in your carpet. Soil is something else entirely. Soil has value. But what is it, really?

WHAT IS SOIL?

Soil is a highly complex natural body that scientists call the pedosphere. Some call it the Earth's living skin. Soil stores water and nutrients, filters our drinking water, helps break down toxic wastes, and is a critical player in carbon cycling, nitrogen cycling, and, let's face it, life on Earth.

Cutaway view of soil from a raised bed

Ideally, you want soil that is rich in nutrients and friable, or easy to work. Very few yards start out that way. More often, residential soil was trucked in when your house was built and then thoroughly compacted. That's great for your house, and not so good for your plants. In some cases, that may be not so good for you, either, since toxic soil was commonly used in residential construction many years ago. But, you can't improve your soil until you know what it already holds.

Soil is 25% air, 25% water, 45% minerals, and 5% organic matter, give or take a few percentage points. Different types of soil are described by their texture, structure, and nutrient content.

Soil Texture

Soil minerals come in three sizes: small, medium, and large. We call them clay, silt, and sand, respectively. The ratio of those different-sized minerals is what makes up your soil's texture. If your soil's texture is too sandy, nutrients and water will wash away before plants

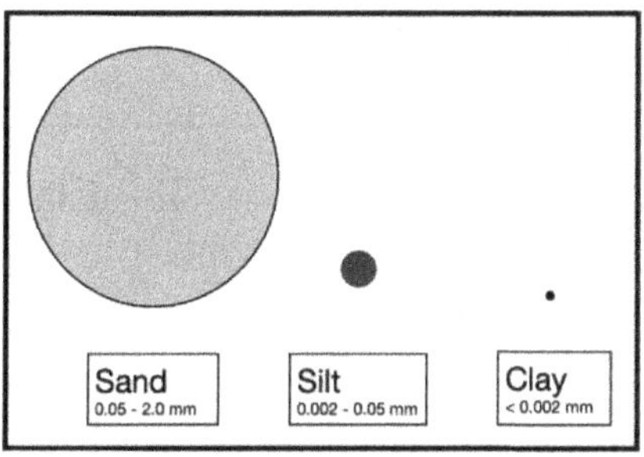

Relative soil texture sizes (Kate Russell)

can grab them. If your soil is mostly clay, it will hold so tightly to water and nutrients that plant roots will have a hard time doing their job. (Did you know that any organic particles surrounded by clay are protected from the microorganisms that break them down into nutrients that can be used by plants? I didn't either.)

Great soil is a balanced combination of all three mineral sizes and has lots of different-sized spaces between the bits of minerals. These spaces, called macropores and micropores, hold and allow water and gases to flow, carrying nutrients to your plants. They allow roots to move around, too. Two of the best ways to improve soil texture are to add compost and apply mulch.

Soil Structure

The bits of organic material and minerals found in soil are called aggregates. Soil aggregates are held together by dead things in various stages of decomposition, earthworm and insect poop, chemical excretions of nearby plant roots, and a fungal coating called glomalin. The arrangement of aggregates within your soil is called its structure. Good soil structure makes for healthier plants because it offers a variety of spaces for roots to move around in, with access to plenty of food and water.

The only way to have a variety of aggregates in your soil is by adding organic material. By organic, I mean things that used to be (or still are) alive. Of course, organic gardening is a good idea, too. We will get to that. For now, we need to learn how to create the best possible soil for your garden.

> **The Clay-Sand Myth**
> Gardeners who struggle with heavy clay often believe that adding sand will solve their problem.
> It makes sense. Sand is big, clay is small, mixing them together will put the soil somewhere in the middle, right?
> Wrong. What ends up happening is all those tiny clay particles fill all the spaces between the grains of sand, creating something very similar to concrete.
> Don't do it.

WATER IN THE SOIL

As we all know, if it has holes in it, water will find a way through it. This is true for your tent, your roof, and your garden.

The rate at which water flows through something is called permeability. If you've ever tried buying a home, you were probably required to pay someone to conduct a perc

Water droplet

test. Real estate percolation tests are done to make sure that your house won't wash away when it rains and that your septic system won't back up into the living room. A percolation test in the garden can give you the information you need to make informed decisions about improving your soil and helping plants get the water and nutrients they need without drowning.

In the garden, water and air flow in and out of soil, leaves, and plant cells. For a plant, this is the Stuff of Life. The water and air that flow through a plant's cell walls carry sugars, minerals, oxygen, carbon dioxide, hormones, waste products, and chemicals that allow your plants to thrive.

How water behaves in your yard will have a big impact on plant health. If you see standing water after it rains or mud that takes a long time to dry, there may be a permeability problem. Soil that repels water, the same way an overly dry sponge lets water roll off rather than being absorbed, may need drainage help.

So, how can you, as a gardener, improve the permeability of your soil? First, avoid overwatering and don't walk on wet soil. If your soil is compacted, aerate it. Applying aged compost and mulch go a long way toward improving soil permeability.

ORGANIC MATTER IN SOIL

Organic matter is all the bugs, plants, and microorganisms, alive and dead, found in soil. You may be surprised to learn that each tablespoon of healthy soil contains more microorganisms than there are humans on Earth. And those microorganisms are very important to your plants' health because they help convert and carry nutrients to plant roots.

You can add organic matter to your soil with these tips:

- Mulching with untreated chipped wood
- Amending with composted kitchen and yard scraps
- Incorporating aged manure from local farms (just make sure they are chemical-free)
- Raising chickens and composting their soiled bedding
- Protecting bare soil with ground cover crops
- Applying organic top dressings

Soil organic matter can range from 1% to 8%. As living things die and begin to breakdown, they add nutrients and improve soil structure. They also alter the electrical charge of soil. This makes a difference for your plants because the minerals they use as food also have electrical charges. Those charges determine how difficult or easy it is for plants to pull mineral nutrients from the soil.

QUICK CHEMISTRY REVIEW

Molecules can be stable, with no charge, positively charged cations (cat-ions), or negatively charged anions (an-ions). Calcium, potassium, and many other plant nutrients are cations, while organic matter tends to be made up of anions. Plants need both. Ensuring that there is enough organic matter in the soil also improves porosity, aeration, and biological activity.

MULCHING

Until it is time to plant, one of the best things you can do for your soil is to cover it with a 4-inch layer of mulch. Mulch blocks weeds, stabilizes soil temperatures, retains moisture, improves soil structure, and (eventually) adds nutrients to the soil. You can buy bagged mulch from a store or you can contact local tree trimmers for free wood chips.

Until recently, people were encouraged to put cardboard down to block weeds before covering an area with mulch. It sounded like a good idea. Now we know that it's a terrible idea. Studies have shown that cardboard and layers of newspaper attract termites and voles. Don't do it.

Another bad idea is regular use of a rototiller. As tempting and satisfying as it may be, regularly using a rototiller destroys valuable soil microorganisms, and it can create a hardpan layer that prevents plant roots from

> **A Rototiller Tale**
> My grandmother once told me how her mother had complained about having to ask her son do the rototilling that year.
>
> "I just can't do it the way I could in my 80s."
>
> She was a hard woman.

growing as deeply as they need to.

If you think you have poor soil, give it a bed of mulch and some water. Mulching can be made even more productive by applying a top-dressing of aged compost on top of the soil before mulching. Earthworms and other critters will do all the work for you, and they do it better, improving your soil while you relax on the patio.

So save your back and stop digging.

Treat your soil with the respect it deserves. Tread lightly, especially when the soil is wet. Stepping stones and permeable paths are good for the soil, preventing compaction and other structural problems.

NITROGEN

Once you've identified your soil's texture, improved its structure, and increased the amount of organic matter, you will want to add nitrogen. Nitrogen is the single most limiting factor in most gardens. Organic matter can help your plants access the nitrogen that is already present, but you will still need to add it on a regular basis. Nitrogen is a highly mobile nutrient and it is easily lost. Most soils contain less than 1% nitrogen, while 2%-5% is ideal. But it is not simply a matter of adding more nitrogen.

Nitrogen comes in many forms. Which one will you use?

Inorganic nitrogen can be found as nitrites or ammonium. When roots take up nitrates, they increase the pH of the immediate area, making it more alkaline. The opposite is true when plants take up ammonium, making the soil more acidic. Organic sources of nitrogen include blood meal and cottonseed meal, both of which will acidify soil. We'll find out why that matters in just a moment.

Before you start adding nutrients and other amendments to your soil, you need to know what's already there. These tests will help.

Soil tests

Some soil tests you can do at home, but others must be done in a lab.

And you can forget those colorful plastic tube kits you see in stores. They may look like a great idea but they are not (yet) accurate enough to be useful. Sending out a sample for testing every three to five years can save you countless hours and dollars by telling you what is missing from your soil and what is in excess. All too often, new gardeners create more problems than they resolve by automatically adding fertilizer every time things don't look the way they do in magazines and seed catalogs. Adding unnecessary fertilizer can create nutrient imbalances that make it difficult for plants to absorb the nutrients they need.

I urge you to use all of these soil tests, starting with the soil structure jar test and the perc test found in the Resources section.

LAB-BASED SOIL TESTS

An inexpensive soil test from a reputable, local lab is one of the best investments you can make in your garden. By local, I mean on whichever side of the Rocky Mountains you reside—the tests used are different for each region. The Olson test is better for the West Coast, while the Brays test is better on the East Coast. Simply contact your local Cooperative Extension, Master Gardeners, or Department of Agriculture for a list of soil labs, or look online. These tests cost about the same as a large bag of fertilizer and they provide a wealth of information, including whether any toxic chemicals are present.

When your results arrive, you may be a little confused by the information. That's to be expected. Most of us do not read lab results on a regular basis. My soil is heavy clay that is highly prone to compaction. Aeration is frequently needed. Clay soil tends to contain plenty of most of the necessary minerals, and too much salt and phosphorus. Iron and nitrogen deficiencies are common where I live. Other areas and soil types have other strengths and weaknesses. Your soil test results should include percentage ratings for each of the major plant nutrients. They may also tell you how much organic matter is in your soil.

Analysis	Value Found	Optimum Range	Analysis	Value Found	Optimum Range
Soil pH (1:1, H2O)	6.2		Cation Exch. Capacity, meq/100g	22.4	
Modified Morgan extractable, ppm			Exch. Acidity, meq/100g	3.7	
Macronutrients			Base Saturation, %		
Phosphorus (P)	75.7	4-14	Calcium Base Saturation	58	50-80
Potassium (K)	225	100-160	Magnesium Base Saturation	23	10-30
Calcium (Ca)	2586	1000-1500	Potassium Base Saturation	3	2.0-7.0
Magnesium (Mg)	642	50-120	Scoop Density, g/cc	0.95	
Sulfur (S)	60.6	>10	Optional tests		
Micronutrients *			Soil Organic Matter (LOI), %	7.6	
Boron (B)	1.7	0.1-0.5	Nitrate-N (NO3-N), ppm	25	
Manganese (Mn)	6.8	1.1-6.3			
Zinc (Zn)	17.4	1.0-7.6			
Copper (Cu)	0.2	0.3-0.6			
Iron (Fe)	1.1	2.7-9.4			
Aluminum (Al)	3	<75			
Lead (Pb)	2.0	<22			

Excessive fertilizer use can cause long-term problems

A soil test will also tell you the soil's pH, and that's important, too.

SOIL pH

Soil pH is a measure of how acidic or alkaline soil is and it has a big impact on plant health. Most plant nutrients can only be absorbed when soil pH is between 6.0 and 7.5. If your soil is outside of that range, you may need to acidify or add lime to it.

These things are not difficult, but you need to know if they need doing and a soil test will tell you.

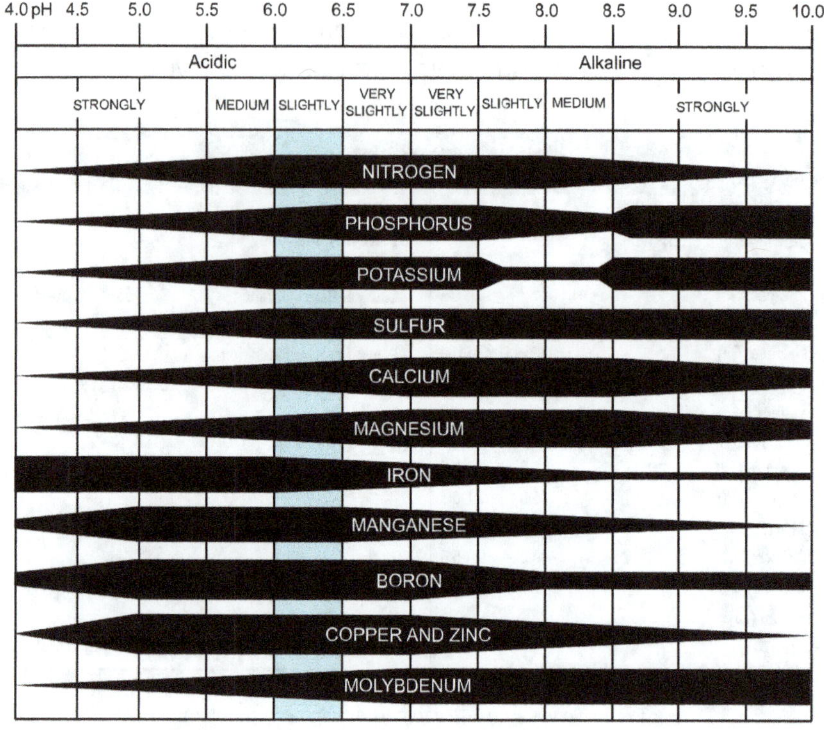

Soil pH and nutrient absorption

Creating healthy soil

Soil creation is called pedogenesis. You can create great soil in your garden and landscape when you:

- Learn what you already have, using reliable soil tests.
- Regularly incorporate organic matter with compost, mulch, and even coffee grounds.
- Analyze your soil structure and aerate, as needed.
- Only add needed amendments, and in the proper form for your soil.
- Determine your soil's pH.

Other ways you can improve your soil's health include

growing cover crops, using crop rotation, installing foot paths to reduce compaction, and avoiding irrigation run-off and urban drool. Creating healthy soil is the best way to grow healthy plants. Healthy plants need less protection from pests and diseases, produce more flowers and food, and require less work.

Chapter Two

HOW DO PLANTS GROW?

Roots go down and stems go up, no matter which way a seed is turned. And once they start growing, plants have a one-track mind. It's all about reproduction.

Everything they do to convert sunlight into sugar is about the next generation. All the water and minerals they suck out of the ground are used to help them create the fruits, nuts, and seeds we love to eat. This is important information for a gardener.

When we cut dead flowers off a rose bush, we trick the plant into making more flowers. When we keep taking tomatoes or melons from our plants, they produce more. If a plant thinks it's going to die, it starts producing seeds. The bottom line in fruit and vegetable gardening is the more you take, the more they make.

Plants have three basic ways of fulfilling their reproductive mission: they can do it in one growing season, two growing seasons, or spread out over several years. The sprinters in this race are the annuals. Annuals work fast, putting all their energies into a single growing season. Basil, melons, and corn are annuals.

Perennial plants settle in for the long haul, creating big root systems that help them come back every year. Fruit and nut trees, asparagus, and rhubarb are popular perennials. Another group falls in the middle, using their first year to build a root system and the second year to create seeds. These are the biennials. Celery, parsley, and carrots are biennials.

How do plants grow?

Before you start putting seeds in the ground, you should look at your yard with an eye to the future. Trees grow taller, fences need replacing, things change. Putting a long-lived plant in the wrong place can create years of headaches. Putting the same plant in the right place can make life easier for both of you.

Annuals are a great way to start gardening. If it doesn't work out the first time around, you can always try again next year. On the other hand, perennial plants don't have to be planted each year and they generally need less care. Modern fruit and nut trees are very productive and you can often find dwarf varieties that fit nicely into even the smallest yards.

> **Tomato Trivia**
>
> Some common edibles, such as tomatoes and peppers, are actually perennial plants grown as annuals. Under the proper conditions, these plants can continue producing food year round for several years.

As tempting as it may be, resist the urge to use grocery store plants and seeds in your garden. While it seems convenient and inexpensive, these plants are not certified disease-free or pathogen-free. They may be safe to eat, but planting them in your garden can introduce pests and diseases that may take years to be resolved.

When you plant seeds, not all of them will grow. Some never start. Some seeds will germinate and then wither and die. That's okay. We expect it.

Whatever you are growing, start by planting seeds as close together as the seed packet says. Then add water and wait. After the soil dries out, add a little more water. Seeds need to be damp but not soggy. Generally speaking, those seeds will all start sprouting at the same time, within a few days of each other. Make sure they have enough light and are protected against strong winds, birds, slugs, and other threats. Once those seedlings all look like they are going to survive, you need to thin them.

Thinning refers to spacing plants based on their expected mature size. If you let plants grow too closely together, they will be more likely to get sick or infested with bugs. You can thin plants by cutting the extras off at ground level with a pair of scissors or gently scooping out the extras and replanting them someplace else.

Many people assume they can't garden because they live in an apartment, rent a room, or have a tiny yard. Nothing could be further from the truth. Nature finds a way to put plants everywhere except Antarctica, and you can, too. Container gardening is an excellent way to work around space limitations (or grumpy landlords).

Raised beds and containers

Raised beds and containers help you make the most of a growing space. Being taller, they are easier on your back, and they give you more control over where your plants are growing.

Raised beds make gardening easier

Raised beds can be nothing more than mounded soil, or

they can be areas framed in with boards, bricks, or stones. Cinderblocks and other forms of cement eventually release salts into the soil, so they are not your best choice. Redwood and cedar boards are insect resistant and will last longer than pine, but they cost more.

Selecting containers for growing food plants can be a lot of fun, but it is critical that your containers are safe for food. Unless you know a container is safe, you have to assume that it isn't. Shipping pallets, for example, are often used to make raised beds. The problem with these materials is that they are nearly always sprayed with chemicals to minimize the transfer of pests and diseases. You

Netted panels keep birds out of raised beds

might not want those chemicals on your food. Also, some pottery is decorated with lead-based glaze or other materials that can be toxic. Make sure your planters are safe before filling them with potting soil.

Plants can be grown in practically anything that isn't toxic. Broken toilets, truck beds, and old leather boots can all be used as planting containers. You can hang a net over a sunny window and plant climbing nasturtiums, peas, or beans in a nearby pot. Transform an old bookcase into a vertical garden or hang pots from your fence. Be creative! Just be sure that all containers have drainage holes. And you can forget adding stones to the bottom of the container. That space is better filled with soil. Also, if you will be moving plants indoors during winter, be sure they are not too heavy to lift, or use a plant stand with wheels.

SOIL, NUTRIENTS, AND WATER

Generally, there are two types of soil you can use for raised beds and containers: planting soil and potting soil. You can also dig up soil from your yard, but that doesn't generally work as well, unless you have really healthy soil.

Planting soil is designed for use in the ground. It can also be used in raised beds. Potting soil works best in containers because it holds water and nutrients better. Potting soil is the best choice for starting seeds.

Avoid using any packaged soil that contains sedge peat—it interferes with drainage. You may be surprised to learn that potting soil isn't really soil at all. Potting soil, also known as potting mix and potting compost, has been used by gardeners since the 1800s, and there are many good reasons for doing so.

First, let's find out what, exactly, is in potting soil.

Potting soil is a manmade recipe that may contain composted bark, sand, perlite, peat, recycled mushroom compost, and mineral nutrients. These mixes are treated to create the best growing conditions for plants. Some potting mixes contain slow-release fertilizers. You can find organic potting soil and you can find potting mix that includes ground up old car tires. It's one of those cases where you really do get what you pay for. If you are committed to organic gardening, be sure to look for the Organic Materials Review Institute (OMRI) label.

Potting soil is designed to retain moisture and nutrients. Because of this ability, fungus gnats are often attracted to pots filled with potting soil—it's the moisture. Sprinkle some ground-up mosquito dunks on top of the soil to control these pests.

Potting soil is also sterilized to kill off pathogens and weed seeds. This is what makes it so useful in container gardening. Some potting soil mixes are designed for specific plant species, such as African violets or cactus. Fresh potting soil is also what keeps your windowsill garden and holiday plants healthy and productive. Stale potting soil…not so much.

Over time, your container plants will use up nutrients in the soil. You can supplement with aged compost, fertilizer, or by changing out the potting soil every few years. That last one is pretty traumatic to root systems, so I don't recommend it unless necessary.

Overwatering and under-watering are the biggest sources of problems for container plants. It is important to let the soil dry out between waterings. Hanging plants and unglazed ceramic pots will need to be watered more often in hot weather. Some plants will become root bound in containers. You can repot these plants into a larger container, or trim the roots.

Whether you grow edible plants in the ground or in containers, you need to know that some of your plants are going to get sick. Some of them will die. And some of them will end up covered with aphids or damaged by other insects.

Before you grab a canister of toxic fumes, you need to know that we have better options these days.

Chapter Three

WHAT CAN GO WRONG?

At first glance, most yards look peaceful.

When my husband and I bought our home, the backyard held us in awe. It was four times the size of most Silicon Valley yards and had been well cared for by its previous owner.

"It's so tranquil," he murmured.

"Oh, no it's not," I replied, shaking my head. "It's a battleground out there, you just don't see it."

Of course, we were both right.

You may not see them right away, but pests, diseases, and poor soil can cause all sorts of problems in the garden. The nice thing is, in most cases, these problems can be corrected or overcome.

Weeds

Shakespeare gave us some excellent gardening advice in his play Richard II, when he told us, "One year's seeds is seven year's weeds." Once a weed takes hold and starts reproducing, your work level will compound exponentially!

These plants are tough and prolific. A dandelion can produce over 2,000 seeds in a single growing season. A single creeping woodsorrel plant produces 5,000 seeds each year. That's a lot of weed seeds! Warm temperatures and moist soil are all it takes to help weeds invade your garden, lawn, and landscape. Fighting weeds is a constant battle, but it is much easier while they are young and vulnerable.

WHY GET RID OF WEEDS?

Getting rid of weeds is work, so why bother? There are many reasons for getting rid of weeds:

- Weeds take up valuable real estate, nutrients, and water.
- Weeds can block sunlight.
- Weeds can carry plant diseases.
- Weeds can provide food and shelter for common plant pests.
- Weeds may release chemicals that slow the growth of nearby plants (allelopathy).
- Climbing vines, such as bindweed, can choke out other plants.
- Some weeds, such as dodder, parasitize host plants.
- Some weeds, such as foxtail, can harm pets.
- Invasive weeds can push native plants, insects, birds, and animals to extinction.

So, getting rid of weeds helps your plants stay healthy. Most of the time.

BENEFITS PROVIDED BY WEEDS

Before trying to rip out every weed on your property, you may be surprised (and relieved) to learn, as I was, that some weeds actually provide benefits. Because they grow and go to seed so fast, weeds reduce erosion and the loss of topsoil. Weeds can also be used to support soil microorganisms and add organic material back into the soil. Weeds absorb carbon, keeping it out of the atmosphere, increase biodiversity, and provide food and shelter for native insects and animals. In some cases, weeds act as trap crops, luring pests away from favorite plants.

Looking at the sunny dandelion in this new light, we see it has a taproot that grows in even the most compacted soil, provides nectar and pollen for beneficial insects, new greens can be used in a salad, and flowers can be used to make wine. So, not all weeds are bad. But most of them are not what we want in our gardens.

WHAT IS A WEED?

Before we start learning about some of the more common weeds, let's be clear about what a weed is and what it isn't. According to Gallagher, "If you pull it out and it grows back, it's a weed." I've always said, "A weed is a plant that grows after you try to kill it." So, how do we get rid of unwanted weeds?

WEED CONTROL

Weeds are some tenacious opponents. They have evolved to go to seed only days after emerging from the soil. Their stems and roots tend to be brittle, so part of them is left behind to continue after you try to pull them out. There are only two ways to get rid of weeds: the Hard Way and the Hard Way.

All too often, we opt for the quick fix. Spray some herbicides on it and its gone, right? Well, that's mostly true. The Hard Truth about this method is that it can also mean those sprays leave behind a residue that can take years to go away. These chemicals may end up in your food and the water supply. Bad plan.

The other Hard Way simply means taking the time to remove every bit of each weed you come across and to check for weeds every single day. The only way to do that is to spend time in the garden and to learn about the most common weeds in your area.

COMMON WEEDS

Each region has its own collection of common weeds. The more you learn about weeds in your garden, the better you will be at getting rid of them!

- Annual sowthistle (*Sonchus oleraceus*). Like dandelions, sowthistle seeds travel on the wind, so they will always be back. Learn to recognize these weeds while they are young, before they go to seed.
- Burning nettle (*Urtica urens*) and stinging nettle (*U. dioica*), have tiny hairs along the stem that sting for several minutes and can itch for hours.
- Common lambsquarters (*Chenopodium album*) may be edible, but these weeds can also carry beet curly top, potato viruses M, S, and X, tomato ringspot, and several mosaic diseases of alfalfa, barley, beans, beets, cucumber, eggplant, hops, lettuce, squash, and watermelons.
- Field bindweed (*Convolvulus arvensis*) may have pretty flowers, but that root system can go down 20 feet or more! Also, bindweed frequently plays host to viruses, such as tomato spotted wilt, vaccinium false bottom, and potato X disease that impact beans, potatoes, and cereals. If you discover bindweed in the garden, your best bet is to monitor the area frequently and pull new growth as soon as you see it. You can also use sheet mulching.
- Pigweeds (*Amaranthus spp.*) provide overwintering sites for disease-ridden green peach aphids and beet armyworms, which negatively affect beans, buckwheat, celery, cilantro, citrus, cole crops, cucurbits, lettuces, parsley, peppers, strawberries, and tomatoes.
- Spotted spurge can reach a surprisingly large size. Mature plants can be several feet in diameter!

Of course, poison ivy, poison hemlock, and crabgrasses are commonly referred to as weeds, as are the many invasive plants being installed haphazardly. Kudzu, ice plant, purple nutsedge, and English ivy are wreaking havoc on local environments wherever they occur. Once established, they are difficult to get rid of.

Common plant diseases

Plant diseases can be confusing. Is a plant wilting because it needs more water or because a fungal disease has blocked its arteries? It might be too much water or something else entirely. It can be hard to tell.

Over time, you will learn to recognize some of the more common plant diseases, if you don't know them already. Once you have identified a disease, you can break the cycle of infection. Sometimes, plants will cure themselves. The most common plant diseases found in gardens include Alternaria, anthracnose, blights, crown rot, damping off, downy mildews, Fusarium wilt, leaf spot, molds, mosaics, powdery mildew, rots, rusts, and Verticillium wilt. As you read and garden, you will become familiar with these diseases and how to respond to them.

THE THREE SIDES OF PLANT DISEASE

Do you remember the fire safety lesson from elementary school where they told you that three things had to be in place for fire to occur? (The answer is fuel, heat, and oxygen.) Take any one of those components out of the equation and behold! No fire. Well, plant diseases work much the same way.

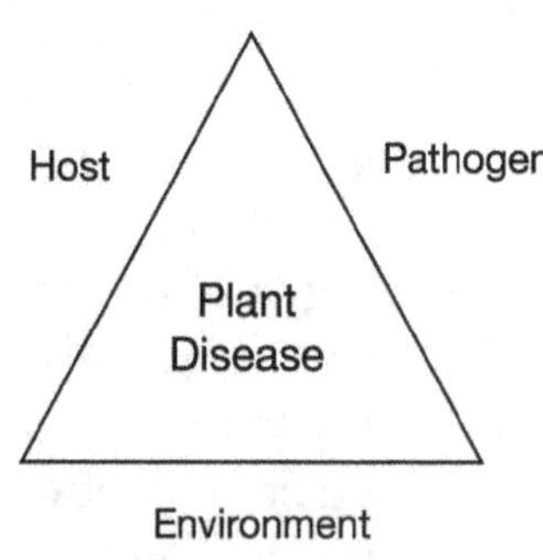

Plant disease triangle

For a disease to take hold in your garden, the environment has to be right, there has to be a host, and the disease (or pathogen) has to be present. Disrupt any one of those three and any diseases that do occur will be much less severe and less frequent. Remove one of those three and there won't be a disease at all. Since prevention is far easier than treatment, the disease triangle is a handy tool for you to use in the garden.

HOW HEALTHY PLANTS DEFEND THEMSELVES

You may be surprised to learn that many pathogens are already present in your garden. New arrivals are unusual and notable. That's why quarantines are used. So, if all the disease-carrying pathogens are already present, why doesn't everything just die a horrible death the moment it appears?

Like us, plants have evolved to protect themselves, though not in the same way. Unlike us, plants do not have immune systems. What they do have is chemical warfare that has developed in tandem with pathogens. Plants use these steps to protect themselves, when they are able:

- Detection - Invaders trigger a chemical messaging system that tells nearby cells (and sometimes other plants) to start protecting themselves, either by thickening their walls or secreting chemicals that are harmful to the pathogen.
- Hypersensitive response - If initial responses are not enough, the cells surrounding the invaded area will self-destruct, creating a barrier to further infection. This is why your plant is not always in trouble when you see dead areas on leaves.
- Systemic acquired resistance - After dealing with a pathogen, plant cells enter a heightened awareness status; commercial growers artificially stimulate this status with chemicals called plant activators, which are less toxic than fungicides and antibiotics, and their effects last longer.
- RNA silencing - After being attacked, plants can use the pathogen's genetic information as a defense mech-

anism - DNA strands are broken down into less harmful versions. Symptoms may still appear, but they won't last as long and plants are able to recover.

(And all this time, you probably thought that plants were relatively passive!)

SYMPTOMS AND DISEASE IDENTIFICATION

Symptoms of plant disease include wilting, stunting, deformed leaves or other growths, cankers, and chlorosis, just to name a few. If you notice disease symptoms, use that information to figure out what is making your plants sick. There are several online resources and you can always contact your local Master Gardeners for advice. Once you know what your plants are up against, you can use the disease triangle to break the cycle.

PATHOGENS

Pathogens are disease-carrying bacteria, viruses, or other microorganisms. Many times, if they are not already present, these pathogens catch a ride into a landscape on flying insects, tools, shoes, scrounged firewood, and newly acquired plants. Chewing insects may simply leave behind a point of entry for disease, or they may be infected themselves, transferring viruses or bacteria to the host plant as they feed. You can interrupt the pathogen side of the triangle with these tips:

- Plant disease-free seeds and plants.
- Sanitize tools regularly.
- Eliminate insects that carry the pathogen (vectors).
- Interrupt pathogen life cycles with crop rotation and cover crops.

ENVIRONMENT

The way you manage your garden and landscape are called cultural practices. Good cultural practices go a long way toward preventing and minimizing disease. If you get nothing else from this book (besides knowing you can grow food at home), commit these practices to memory and put them to use every day.

> **Good Cultural Practices in the Garden**
> - Select plants suited to your microclimate and soil pH.
> - Install plants in a location conducive to their good health.
> - Reduce humidity by improving air flow with judicious pruning and effective drainage.
> - Reduce surface moisture by using drip-emitters and soaker hoses instead of overhead watering.
> - Water early in the morning to give plants time to dry out.
> - Allow soil to dry out between waterings.
> - Ensure good soil structure and fertility with compost.
> - Control pest populations with beneficial insects, weed removal, and good sanitation.
> - Space plants properly.

HOSTS

Host can be the plants that get sick or the plants that don't catch a particular disease but give the pathogen a couch to sleep on for a while. Some diseases affect only a single host, while others can infect many different types of plants. This is where knowing more about your plants and their relations can really help. (Did you know that lilacs grown near apple trees are more likely to get bacterial blight? Or that cedar apple rust can only occur when apples are grown within a couple of miles of Eastern red cedar trees?)

Help prevent disease by looking for naturally disease resistant plants. You may see VFN on the tag: Verticillium wilt (V), Fusarium wilt (F), and destructive nematodes (N). If you select and install plants that are less likely to attract, feed, and/or shelter common pests and diseases in your area, you'll have less to worry about. And reduce disease susceptibility by keeping plants healthy enough to protect themselves.

Time

Many botanists have added time as a plant disease factor, converting our triangle into a pyramid. They do this because time can be a critical factor in disease development. Diseases take time to infect a plant and to reproduce. Water sitting on a leaf for a few minutes may do nothing, while several hours of surface water on the same leaf may be deadly. Regularly monitoring plants for signs of disease can put time in your favor.

Each microclimate has its own set of problems. Learning about your plants and what they are facing puts you in control. There are some diseases that appear in practically every garden, so it is a good idea to familiarize yourself with them.

Most garden-variety plant diseases can be prevented by installing clean, disease-free seed, selecting resistant varieties, spacing plants for good air flow, avoiding overhead watering, and using crop rotation. If you keep leaves dry and do not handle plants while they are wet, you can significantly reduce the spread of disease. Diseased plants should be thrown in the trash.

If you want that extensive, oh-my-goodness list of plant diseases that I am aware of, just look on the next page. Some of the names are hysterical. Where else can you find conditions such as butt rot, karnal bunt, or zebra chip?

Plant diseases

alfalfa mosaic	blight	cucurbit yellow stunting disorder	monosporascus root rot	southern blight
almond leaf scorch	blossom blight	curly dwarf	mosaic virus	spotted wilt
Alternaria leaf blight	blossom brown rot	curly top	mottles	spur blight
Alternaria rot	blossom end rot	currant cane blight	mucor rot	squash mosaic
American gooseberry mildew	blue mold	curvularia blight	mummies	stem blight
angular leafspot	blueberry stunt disease	*Cycloconium oleaginum* fungus	mummy berry	stem canker
anthracnose	Botrytis blight	Cytospora canker	net blotch	stem end rot
aphid borne yellows	Botrytis fruit rot	damping off	olive knot	stem gall
apple measles	bottom rot	dieback	onion rust	stem rot
apple scab	branch canker	diplodia collar rot	onion white rot	stem rust
apricot gummosis	branch necrosis	dodder	panicle and shoot blight	stemphylium rot
Armillaria root rot	branch wilt	dog vomit slime mold	parsnip canker	strawberry crinkle
artichoke curly bottom rot	broad bean mottle	dothiorella canker	pea enation mosaic	strawberry mild yellow edge
Ascochyta blight	broad bean stain	downy mildews	pea seed borne mosaic	strawberry mottle
ashy stem blight	brown bud	dwarf virus	pea streak	strawberry pallidosis
asparagus rust	brown rot	early blight	peach leaf curl	strawberry vein banding
aster yellows phytoplasma	brown stalk	Eutypa dieback	phoma blight	stripe rust
avocado root rot	burr knots	exocortis	phyllosticta	stylar end rot
bacterial blight	butt rot	felt fungus	Phytophthora fruit and crown rot	sudden wilt
bacterial brown spot	buttoning	fig mosaic	Phytophthora root and crown rot	sunblotch
bacterial canker	calico	fire blight	Phytophthora tentaculata	tip dieback
bacterial fruit rot	cane blight	foamy bark canker	Pierce's disease	tobacco mosaic
bacterial head rot	canker	fruit rot	pink disease	tomato bushy stunt
bacterial leaf blight	canker rot	fruitlet core rot	pink root	tomato ringspot
bacterial leaf blotch	carrot motley dwarf	Fusarium crown and foot rot	plum pox	tomato spotted wilt
bacterial leaf scorch	carrot thin leaf	Fusarium dieback	potato blight	tomato yellow leaf curl
bacterial leaf spot	catfacing/cracking	Fusarium wilt	potato scab	transit rot
bacterial soft rot	cavity spot	Fusarium yellows	potyviruses	Tristeza disease complex
bacterial soft spot	cedar apple rust	galls	powdery mildew	trunk rot
bacterial speck	ceratocystis wilt	garlic mosaic	*Pseudomonas syringae actinidiae*	turnip mosaic
bacterial spot	cercospora leaf blight	grey mold	*Pythium* stalk rot	twig blight
bacterial wilt	charcoal fruit rot	halo blight	*Pythium* wilt	Verticillium wilt
barley yellow dwarf	charcoal root rot	heart rot	raspberry leaf curl	virus decline
basal stem rot	chocolate spot	hendersonia rot	Rhizoctonia blight	walnut blight
basil downy mildew	citrus blast	hollow stem	Rhizoctonia limb rot	watermelon mosaic
bean common mosaic	citrus fruit split	huanglongbing	rhizopus rot	web blotch
bean leaf roll	clubroot	Johnson spot	ringspot	white druplet
bean mosaic	collar rot	karnal bunt	root rot	white mold
bean rust	conks	late leaf rust	rust	white rot
bean yellow mosaic	corky ringspot	leaf and cane spot	scab	white rust
belly rot	corm rot	leaf blight	sclerotium stem rot	white sooty blotch
bitter fruit	corn stunt	leaf blotch	seed rot	wilt
black banded disease	cottony soft rot	leaf rot	*Septoria* leaf spot	witches' broom
black mildew	crater rot	leaf scald	shade tree decline	wood rot
black mold	crown gall	leaf spot	shoestring rot	X-disease
black root rot	crown rot	leafroll	shot hole disease	yellow rust
black rot	cucumber green mottle mosaic	lower limb dieback	shot hole fungus	yellow spot virus
black spot	cucumber mosaic	macrophoma rot	smut	yellows virus
blackleg	cucumber vein yellowing	maize dwarf mosaic	soft rot	zebra chip
bleeding canker	cucurbit aphid-borne yellows	measles	sooty mold	zucchini yellows mosaic

Common garden pests

Insects and other pests are an on-going battle in the garden. Some pests are found pretty much everywhere, attacking everything. These are the pests you will be up against most of the time.

Common Pests		
ants	earwigs	scale insects
aphids	flea beetles	slugs
armyworms	grasshoppers	snails
beetles	leafhoppers	spider mites
borers	leafminers	thrips
caterpillars	loopers	weevils
crickets	mealybugs	whiteflies
cutworms	nematodes	

If I listed every pest that may appear in your garden, you might just give up before you start, or run from the room screaming. (If you enjoy that sort of thing, look on the next page for a list of all the pests that I've encountered.)

While the army of pests that may attack your garden looks overwhelming, do not despair! In most cases, there are only a few insect and other pests that will frequent your particular landscape.

Learning how to identify these pests, when to expect them, and how to reduce the damage they cause can help your garden stay healthy and productive. But don't expect to learn all this right away. It takes time. You will learn, as you come across damaged leaves, moldy fruit, and pockmarked stems, which insects are in your neck of the woods. Once you see them, you need to learn about them. There are plenty of online resources, as well as your local Master Gardeners and County Extension Office.

When you find a destructive pest in your garden, try to catch it. Small plastic containers work well. If capturing a pest isn't your cup of tea, try to get some photos of it. This will help you to identify it and learn about how to best respond.

Keep in mind that each yard is unique. So is each year. Some years, aphids will be a major problem. Other years, your normally docile sowbugs will start eating everything in sight. The trick is to be observant and take it as it comes. Over time, you will learn about your garden's pests. You may even discover that you find some of them fascinating!

As a rule, you will want to avoid using broad spectrum pesticides. These chemicals kill off just as many beneficial insects as pests (and they probably aren't good for us, either).

Garden pests

ants	Colorado potato beetles	gooseberry fruitworms	navel orangeworms	southern fire ants
aphids	corn earworms	gophers	nematodes	spider mites
apple maggots	corn maggot larvae	grasshoppers	onion eelworms	spittle bugs
armyworms	crickets	harlequin bugs	onion flies	spotted wing drosophila
artichoke plume moths	crown borers	hornworms	onion maggots	squash bugs
Asian citrus psyllid	cucumber beetles	katydids	orange tortrix moths	squash ladybugs
Asian longhorn beetles	currantworms	leaf rollers	pear psylla	squirrels
avocado lace bugs	cutworms	leaf-footed bugs	plum curculio	stink bugs
bagrada bugs	darkling beetles	leafhoppers	quinoa plant bugs	sunflower bud moths
birds	deer	leafminers	rabbits	swede midge
borers	diaprepes root weevil	leek moth	raspberry horntail wasps	thrips
boxelder bugs	earwigs	light brown apple moth	rats	tomato fruit worms
cabbage maggots	Eugenia psyllid	light masked chafer	red berry mites	tomato psyllids
cabbage root maggots	fall webworms	loopers (inchworms)	redhumped caterpillars	treehoppers
cabbageworms	false chinch bugs	lygus bugs	rhizoctonia parasites	voles
carrot flies	flea beetles	mealybugs	root maggots	walnut husk flies
celery flies	fruit flies	melonworm moth	sawflies	walnut twig beetles
clearwing moth	fruitworms	millipedes	scale insects	weevils
click beetles	garden centipedes	mites	seedcorn maggots	whiteflies
codling moth	glassy-winged sharpshooters	moles	slugs and snails	wireworms

Integrated Pest Management

Gardening has changed in recent years. Behind us, hopefully, are the days of ravaging rototillers and cascading chemicals. We have learned a lot about microorganisms that live in the soil.

These microscopic creatures feed our plants and improve our mood. Extensive digging and plowing kill these tiny helpers, so save your back and your plants by keeping digging to a minimum.

We have also learned that it is far better to encourage beneficial insects that kill and parasitize garden pests, rather than spraying chemicals. Instead of poisoning our food and our soil, we now add a few umbrella-shaped flowers and let Mother Nature do most of the work.

This combined program of least damaging chemicals, beneficial insects, and selecting plants best suited to your yard creates a sustainable system.

Beneficial hoverfly on carrot flower

Chapter Four

WHAT'S ALREADY GROWING WELL?

Do you have trees that need little or no care? Do the same weeds keep coming back, year after year?

Instead of looking at weeds as the enemy, you can look at them as the forward guard. They've already scouted the area. For them, conditions are good enough for growing. And you don't have to be a plant expert to recognize most of them. Which weeds are growing in your yard? Dandelions? Spurge? Thistles? These plants are all from different plant families and you can use that information to make gardening in your yard easier.

FAMILY GROUPS

Have you ever been to a family reunion and wondered how that one cousin could possibly be related to everyone else? Well, it happens in plant families, too. Perfectly respectable peas and beans must cringe in shame, knowing they're related to kudzu and burr clover. And those demure tomatoes and peppers? They're stuck with wild jimsonweed and deadly thorn apples at the reunion picnic.

Knowing more about a plant's family can help you be a better gardener. In many cases, you can generalize about plant care, problems, and best practices based on which family a plant is in. It also makes you sound really smart when talking with others about their garden struggles and successes.

Understanding more about plant families also lets you take advantage of your weeds. Knowing which weeds are growing in your yard can help you pick edible plants that will grow more easily. Is burr clover a problem? Peas and beans should grow well. If your weeds are more of the mustard variety, then the cabbage family will love your yard. Dandelions in the lawn? Salad greens and sunflowers will grow just as well.

So, which plant families do we eat? And which weeds are in the same families?

EDIBLES AND EVILS

If you opened your refrigerator or kitchen cabinets, what foods would you see? Cans of corn or beans? A head of lettuce? A jar of dried oregano? Here is a list of the basic plant family food groups, and their weedy cousins:

- Beans and peas - clover, kudzu, locoweed, vetch
- Beets and spinach - lambsquarters, pigweed
- Cabbages and cauliflowers - hairy bittercress, wild mustard
- Carrots and celery - hogweed, Queen Anne's lace
- Grains and cereals - Bermudagrass, crabgrass, foxtails
- Melons and squash - buffalo gourd, bur cucumber
- Mint and other herbs - bugleweed, ground ivy
- Onions and garlic - rain lilies, wild onions
- Sunflowers and salad greens - cornflowers, dandelions, sneezeweed
- Tomatoes and potatoes - jimsonweed, nettle, thorn apple

Berry bushes, grape vines, and fruit and nut trees need to be treated differently, but we'll get to them.

Before you start planting seeds and seedlings, contact your local County Extension Office or Department of Agriculture for recommendations. They have plant-specific growing, pest, and disease information for your region.

There's no sense reinventing the wheel, right?

Now, let's look at the different family groups and all the delicious crops you just might be able to grow at home!

39

Chapter Five

BEAN FAMILY

The bean family includes peas, peanuts, cowpeas, soybeans, fava beans, alfalfa, and lentils. All of these plants have seeds called pulses. Also known as legumes, these plants make easy-to-store edible crops, and they can help improve your soil.

Dried pulses and fresh legumes

Legumes have a pact with some talented soil bacteria. These bacteria are found on and in legume roots. These bacteria can "fix" nitrogen from the air into a form plants can use. Plants use a lot of nitrogen. This nitrogen is available to any nearby plants until the host begins flowering and producing pods. When fava beans and cowpeas start producing baby beans and peas of their own, they keep that nitrogen for themselves.

Some people inoculate their bean seeds with these bacteria before planting. This means you dust, roll in, or briefly soak seeds in an inoculant just before planting. This helps the seeds get as much nitrogen out of the soil as possible, for a better start. I've never used inoculants, but many gardeners and most farmers swear by them, especially in areas where beans have not been grown for a long time.

Members of the bean family are popular companion plants. More accurately known as intercropping, this just means plants that work well together are planted together. The Three Sisters method of growing beans, squash and corn together is a type of intercropping. The squash shades the ground and reduces weeds, the beans feed the soil and climb the corn, and the corn soars skyward. Everybody wins.

Speaking of weeds, burr clover and vetch are the most common bean family weeds in many areas. Locoweed and kudzu are other bean family weeds. If you see these plants popping up in your yard, odds are pretty good that edible members of the bean family will grow well.

Most members of the bean family are summer crops, with chickpeas and fava beans preferring cooler temperatures. All of them can be grown in full or partial sun. These plants do not transplant as well as many others, so it is best to plant seeds exactly where you want them, once the soil has warmed.

Bean Family Problems

If you grow members of the bean family regularly, it is a good idea to rotate those crops with sunflowers, tomatoes, or wheat, to interrupt the life cycle of some fungal diseases, such as bean rust.

Most bean family diseases can be prevented by employing good cultural practices. For instance, to prevent something called stem blight, common beans should not be planted near soybeans.

Bean Family Diseases

alfalfa mosaic	leafroll virus
broad bean mottle	pea streak
broad bean stain	Pythium wilt
crown rot	Rhizoctonia limb rot
curly top	tomato spotted wilt
diplodia collar rot	web blotch

The real battle, when growing any type of bean, is the army of pests that may come after your crop. Along with disease-carrying ants and other common garden pests, this family is commonly damaged by beetles, borers and other bugs.

Bean Family Pests

bagrada bugs	Lycaenid pod borers
bean beetles	lygus bugs
bean weevils	root knot nematodes
corn earworms	salt marsh caterpillars
cucumber beetles	seed corn maggots
darkling beetles	stink bugs
dried fruit beetles	wireworms

Some caterpillars may also gnaw on your beans, as well. It's amazing we get any beans at all, with a list like that! The truth is, these plants are very productive and the problems are all manageable. The most common pests are herbivores such as birds, deer, gophers, rabbits, rats, squirrels, and voles.

Bindweed can also choke out your bean plants. (Did you

know that sweet potatoes are related to bindweed? I didn't either.)

Beans

Zones 2—11
Sun exposure: full sun
Ideal soil temperature: above 65°F

Beans are crazy easy-to-grow, they germinate quickly, add nitrogen to the soil, and they are just plain fun to watch. (And you can reduce the gaseous problem by changing the water when cooking or soaking dried beans.)

Did you know that when you eat green beans, you are eating the immature bean pods of any number of types of beans? Much like bell peppers, they all start out green and then change color as they mature.

Dried beans

TYPES OF BEANS

All beans are self-pollinating annuals. There are more than 40,000 different type of beans found in the world. Some of the more popular bean varieties are:

- Adzuki (*Vigna angularis*)
- Blackeyed pea (*Vigna unguiculata*) or cowpea, and red noodle beans
- Common beans (*Phaseolus vulgaris*) including black beans, pinto beans, kidney beans, and (my favorite) purple beans; also lima beans and runner beans
- Fava beans (*Vicia faba*) or broad beans, Windsor beans, field beans, bell beans, tick beans
- Mung beans (*Vigna radiata*)

Whichever bean species you prefer, it will help to know that there are two basic growth types: bush beans and pole beans. Pole beans are climbers and can be trained up trellising, fences, lattice, sunflowers, trees, pretty much anything they can wrap their little tendrils around. Pole beans grow more slowly, taking 85-90 days to reach maturity, and they are indeterminate, which means they will continue producing pods throughout the growing season. Pole beans are used in the traditional Three Sisters Method, with corn and squash. Trellising pole beans on something that goes over your head looks really nice, with ripe beans hanging down. It's makes picking easy, too!

Red noodle beans grow well on a trellis

Bush varieties stay upright without support and grow to 18"-36" tall and about 12" wide, all within 60-80 days. Bush beans tend to be determinate, which means they will generally produce all of their pods within a two-week time frame. Pole beans take up less space and produce more pods than bush beans, but bush varieties are best if you are planning on doing any canning.

HOW TO GROW BEANS

Beans are generally planted directly in the soil in spring and early summer, once temperatures are above 60°F. Germination and growth are optimized at 75°F-85°F. If planted too soon or too late in the season, the seeds will simply rot in the ground. Lima beans and fava beans are the only exceptions, preferring cooler temperatures.

You can start bean seeds in small pots, but they have delicate roots and do not transplant well. You can also grow them in containers. Just keep in mind that bean root systems need pots that are at least 16"-24" deep to thrive.

Bean seeds are large and easy to work with. They should be planted 1"-2" deep, depending on the size of the seed. Bush beans can be planted 6" apart and will help support each other as they grow. Pole beans need something to climb and should be planted 10" apart.

Water your bean seeds enough to keep the soil moist (but not soggy) until germination occurs. This should take 4-14 days. After that, water deeply every few days, allowing the soil to dry out between waterings. Do not overwater. For a continuous harvest of beans, start new seeds every week or two throughout the growing season. This is called succession planting.

Beans are not very competitive plants, so you can help them thrive by regularly weeding the area until they are well established. Hand-weed around bean plants by cutting weeds off at soil level. This avoids disturbing bean roots while eliminating competition for water, nutrients, and sunlight. This practice also leaves valuable soil microorganisms in place, where they can benefit the bean plants.

HARVESTING BEANS

Beans are one of those edible plants that produce more food if ripe beans are harvested regularly. In other words: the more you pick, the more you get. Beans should be harvested as soon as the pods have plumped up. Leaving them on the plant for too long makes them tough.

Once picked, you can eat them fresh, steam them, add them to stir-fry, or you can freeze or can them for later eating. Beans are sensitive to ethylene gas, so they should be stored away from apples, bananas, and other "gaseous" produce. Ethylene gas is what makes fruits and vegetables ripen.

Yardlong beans are handled a little differently. They are generally eaten before they reach full size. This means checking every day during peak production. They taste their best when about the diameter of a pencil. If you leave them on the vine longer than that, production will slow and the beans will become tough. You can, however, allow them to get close to full maturity and then harvest the beans for food and next year's crop. Just be careful when harvesting. Do not damage the buds from which the beans grow. These buds can produce multiple beans throughout the growing season.

TOXIC LIMA BEANS

Lima beans have the ability to poison their attackers and groups of lima bean plants work together to counteract threats caused by caterpillars. The lowly lima bean, hated by many, loved by some, puts out chemicals that attract parasitic wasps whenever caterpillars start chewing on their leaves. The wasps lay their eggs on the caterpillars, these eggs hatch, and the larvae devour their host. Lima beans also contain certain chemicals, stored in different parts of the plant, that become activated when the seeds are chewed, creating potentially fatal cyanide poisoning. Before the Lima Haters shout a resounding, "We told you so!", it is important to note that cooking lima beans for at least 10 minutes eliminates those chemicals. So, in the case of lima beans, simply soaking isn't good enough. You need to put them to the fire before eating.

Don't let childhood nightmares of lima beans keep you from trying beans in your garden or landscape. Plant some beans today!

Chickpeas

Zone 3—9
Sun exposure: full sun, partial sun, or partial shade
Ideal soil temperature: 60°F to 85°F

Chickpeas, grams, or garbanzo beans, these legumes have been cultivated for 7,500 years. High in protein and easy-to-grow, chickpeas also make an excellent green manure.

Speaking of green manure, chickpeas produce the most seeds when they are provided with plenty of sunlight and very little nitrogen. Being a legume, chickpeas are able to convert atmospheric nitrogen into a form usable as plant food. If they have access to too much nitrogen in the soil, you will get plenty of vegetative growth and very few seeds.

Garbanzo beans and 'Desi' chickpeas
(Sanjay Acharya) CC BY-SA 3.0

THE CHICKPEA PLANT

Chickpea plants (*Cicer arietinum*) grow 8"-20" tall and are bushy. They have feathery leaves and delicate white flowers with pink, violet, or blue veins. Like other legumes, the seeds are called pulses. Often (incorrectly) called a pod, pulses are simple fruits that develop from a single carpel, and that usually open along a seam (dehisces). Each pulse contains one or two seeds. Chickpeas have taproots that can reach 15"-40" down into the soil. This makes them a good choice for reducing compacted soil and improving soil structure. (Translation: this fall, pick the worst spot in your landscape and plant chickpeas. Fava beans are another good choice.)

Black chickpeas
(Thamizhpparithi Maari) CC BY-SA 4.0

CHICKPEA VARIETIES

There are four major chickpea varieties, and more than 90 genotypes. The familiar garbanzo bean (kabuli chana) is light-colored, large, and smooth-coated. *Cicer reticulatum* only grows in Turkey. There are two black chickpeas: Desi chana and ceci neri. Ceci neri are a rare large, black chickpea grown only in southeastern Italy. Desi chana is the closest relative to ancient chickpeas. It is small, dark, and rough-coated, and can be black, green, or speckled.

HOW TO GROW CHICKPEAS

In warmer regions, chickpeas are a winter crop that is usually started around the first frost date. To speed the process, you can start chickpea seeds indoors, in pots, several weeks ahead of time, as long as you can provide them with enough sunlight and protection from summer heat. Transplant seedlings into the garden when they are 4"-5" tall. Chickpeas prefer full sun. They can be grown in partial shade, but you won't get nearly the same production.

Chickpea seeds are planted deeply, from 1½" to 2" deep. Contrary to popular myth, do not soak chickpea seeds before planting, or water heavily after planting, as this makes them susceptible to cracking.

Seeds should be planted 3"-6" apart and thinned to 6" between plants. If you are growing chickpeas in rows, space rows 18"-24" apart. Your chickpeas will be ready to harvest in approximately 100 days. Chickpeas do not handle competition from weeds very well, so you need to stay on top of them. Also, high boron levels can stunt chickpea growth, so be sure to get your soil tested.

There are a few pests and diseases you'll need to watch for. Bacterial blight, black rot, charcoal root rot, Fusarium wilt, and Verticillium wilt are diseases unique to these members of the bean family.

Did you know that roasted chickpeas can be ground up and used as a coffee substitute, or that chickpea water (aquafaba) can be used as an egg substitute to make merengue? I didn't either.

Fruiting and flowering chickpea plant (Nundhaa) CC BY-SA 4.0

Cowpeas

Zones 3—11
Sun exposure: full sun
Ideal soil temperature: above 65°F

Cowpeas (*Vigna unguiculata*) are their own branch of the bean family tree.

Cowpeas are drought tolerant, they germinate rapidly, and they don't seem to be bothered by heavy soil. In fact, these garden workhorses can be used to break up compacted soil with little to no effort on your part! If you have areas of compacted or bare soil, it is simple enough to poke (or drill) holes in the soil and drop in a cowpea. Cowpeas are not particular. The hole can be 1"- 4" deep. Plants should be spaced 2"-3" apart and protected from birds until they sprout, which can happen in as little as four days!

Often grown as an edible cover crop, cowpeas can reduce erosion and add nitrogen to the soil. The two most well-known members of the cowpea clan are blackeyed peas and yardlong, or noodle beans.

Blackeyed Peas

Delicious in Hoppin' John, blackeyed peas are said to bring good luck when eaten on New Year's Day, but don't wait that long to enjoy this unique crop. Unlike many other bean pods, cowpea pods point skyward for easy picking. Put them to work in the garden for better growing all year long.

Blackeyed peas

If you are feeling particularly creative or ambitious, you can plant cowpeas into patterns around trees, walkways, or other landscape features. As the plants come up, they will add a new texture to the garden, along with improving the soil structure and providing a delicious crop!

Red Noodle Beans

The red noodle bean plant looks spectacular, grows rapidly, and provides a bountiful harvest. My dear friend Carol gave me a packet of red noodle bean seeds a while back. As they were a type of pole bean, I planted them around things they could climb and watered them regularly. At first, nothing seemed to hap-

Red noodle beans

pen, as is normal in the world of gardening. Then I went away for a few weeks. When I returned, I was delighted to find my red noodle beans had completely lived up to their reputation.

POLE BEAN STUNNER

These climbing beans start out looking much like other pole beans. Heart-shaped leaflets appear in groups of three as tendrils take hold wherever they can, pulling the vine upward. Lovely small white, pink, or lavender flowers appear along the way, but are easily overlooked.

The real surprise comes when the pods appear. Pairs of striking scarlet pods can reach over a foot-and-a-half in length. Even if you never ate them, they would still be a stunning addition to your landscape, but you really should eat them. Both the beans and the pods are edible, but they do not take well to steaming.

HOW TO GROW RED NOODLE BEANS

Red noodle bean seeds should be planted 1" deep and 4" apart. Like other legumes, red noodle beans have delicate root systems that do not recover well from transplanting. These plants need heat to grow, so be sure to install them in a sunny location after the soil has warmed from its winter nap. In fact, where other legumes succumb to scorching summers and drought, red noodle beans thrive.

Vines need a sturdy support as they can reach 8' in length or more. Trellises, cat-

Red noodle beans growing in a raised bed

tle panels, fences, tuteurs, old ladders, and pergolas can all be used as supports. Plants will need a thorough watering every 7 to 10 days to develop deep roots. Because red noodle beans are legumes, they do not need nitrogen fertilizer. In fact, they generally don't need fertilizer at all, assuming your soil is healthy.

Being native to tropical rainy areas, red noodle beans need a fair bit of irrigation, just be sure to allow the soil to dry out between waterings to avoid many of the diseases common to legumes. Yardlong beans are not as susceptible to bean weevils as other bean species.

HARVESTING RED NOODLE BEANS

Plants start producing pods within 80 days. By harvesting pods as they appear, you will stimulate the vines to continue producing. Pods can be harvested when pencil thin to be used whole in stir-fry, or you can allow them to reach full size to harvest what will dry into small, red beans. Keep in mind that allowing the beans to dry on the vine will slow or halt pod production. When harvesting, be sure to leave the buds above the pods in place. These buds can produce multiple sets of pods over time.

You can also plant red noodle beans in succession to make full use of your local growing season. Give red noodle beans a try! You are going to love how they look (and taste)!

Fava beans

Zones 2—9
Sun exposure: full sun
Ideal soil temperature: 40°F to 75°F

Unlike common beans, which are from the Americas, fava beans are Old World beans. They grow a little differently than common beans. For one thing, they prefer cooler temperatures. For another, they have a double hull. After harvesting your favas, you will need to remove both the outer and inner hulls. This is a labor-intensive practice, but is easy enough to do while watching a favorite movie or chatting with a friend.

Fava beans have double seed coverings (Rasbak) CC BY-SA 3.0

FAVA BEANS AS COVER CROP

Fava bean roots are tough. If you have compacted soil, fava beans can go a long way toward reducing that compaction. If your soil is like mine was, you may need to use a power drill to plant the seeds. Add some water and your favas will do the rest of the work for you. But not everyone should eat fava beans.

FAVA BEAN SENSITIVITY

Some people lack a certain enzyme, making them genetically predisposed to a sensitivity to fresh fava beans. These individuals are generally men from southern Mediterranean and northern African regions. This condition is called favism. Symptoms include jaundice, back and abdominal pain, and dark urine. Fava beans also contain high levels of tyramine, so individuals taking monoamine oxidase inhibitors should avoid eating them. They also contain oxalic acid, so fava beans should be avoided by those prone to urinary tract stones.

Peanuts

Zones 2—11
Sun exposure: full sun
Ideal soil temperature: above 65°F

I started my journey growing peanuts when I saw something peeking through the soil of a container that I hadn't planted. It was unmistakably a peanut.

The only thing I could figure was that one of my local scrub jays had "planted" it for later consumption. At the time, I had no bandwidth for growing peanuts. So, I dug it out to take a closer look at the root system.

An unexpected peanut

Immature peanut plant

Nuts that are not nuts

Peanuts (*Arachis hypogaea*) are also known as goobers and groundnuts. Their botanic name tells us that peanuts produce their seeds "under the earth." This is called geocarpy. Geocarpy is rare in the plant world.

Once a peanut flower is pollinated, it changes into a specialized stem, called a peg. Pegs are budding ovaries that bend downward and push their way into the soil. Seeds are produced along these pegs. And they are not nuts at all.

PEANUT VARIETIES

Some 8,000 years ago, people living in Argentina or Bolivia decided to cross-pollinate two wild plants to see what would happen. Peanuts are what happened.

From those two wild ancestors, we now have two types of peanuts: runner and bush. Bush plants grow 18"-22" tall, while runners can spread out 28"-31". Thanks to more human intervention, there are now several regional domestic peanuts.

Peanut Particulars

Runner peanuts are grown in Georgia; with higher yield, better flavor, and a better roaster than Spanish.

Spanish peanuts are grown mostly in Texas, Oklahoma, and New Mexico; they have the highest oil content.

Tennessee peanuts are similar to Valencias, but stems are green and kernel production is lower. There are Tennessee Reds, with red kernels, and Tennessee Whites, with white kernels.

Valencia peanuts are grown in west Texas and New Mexico; they are taller than other varieties (49"); and usually boiled.

Virginia peanuts are grown in Virginia, Texas, and much of the southeastern seaboard states; the seeds are large.

Until the 1930s, peanuts were used predominantly as a livestock feed. That was when the USDA actively promoted peanuts as a commercial crop for human consumption.

How to Grow Peanuts

While it's true that peanuts prefer the sandy loam of the south-eastern U.S., peanuts can be grown in raised beds and large containers that are filled with a lightweight potting soil. Plant shelled peanuts one inch deep. For the next four or five months, underground and out of sight, your peanut plants will be busy storing up starches and sugars for next spring's crop. (Or your autumn harvest!) Before that time, however, there are certain pests and diseases that you must watch for, along with the usual problems.

Mature peanuts (Pollinator) CC BY-SA 3.0

Harvesting Peanuts

In commercial peanut fields, as peanut plants begin to yellow, machinery is used to dig plants out of the ground, give them a good shake, flip them over and leave them on the ground for a few days to dry.

In the home garden, you will harvest your peanuts the same

way. Simply pull them out of the ground, give them a good shake to get rid of any clinging soil, and then lay them upside-down on a towel in your garage for a few days. This way, you can protect your crop against squirrels and other peanut lovers.

Next, peanuts are threshed, or removed from their stems. You may be surprised to learn just how important the drying aspect of peanut harvesting is: peanuts stored with too much moisture can become infected with a fungus (*Aspergillus flavus*) that produces toxins that can be carcinogenic. Be sure to dry your peanuts thoroughly!

Peanuts, like other legumes, are an excellent crop rotation choice. Not only are they able to fix atmospheric nitrogen, they also help improve soil structure and soil health. So, plant a peanut and see what happens!

Peas

Zones 2—11
Sun exposure: full sun, partial sun, or partial shade
Ideal soil temperature: 70°F to 80°F

Peas have received a bad reputation from those forced to eat the canned spheres of mush that claim to be peas. As any gardener knows, plucking a fresh pea from the vine and eating it whole offers a crisp, sweet flavor that shares nothing with its canned (or even frozen) siblings.

PEA PLANTS

Peas (*Pisum sativum*) are legumes, which means they have a tidy little business arrangement with certain soil bacteria, called rhizobia, which allow them to use atmospheric nitrogen. Pea seeds develop in pods, making them a pod fruit. Peas are either green or yellow and pods can be green, brown, or purple.

Peas are annual plants that can be low-growing bush varieties, but vining cultivars are the most commonly grown. Pea plants are self-pollinating, but the more plants you have, the better the pollination rates will be and the bigger your harvests will be.

PEA VARIETIES

Modern peas are generally described as either edible pod or shelling varieties, but the story behind pea evolution may surprise you. Wild peas have been around for thousands of years. They were being cultivated back in the 3rd century BC. These early cultivated peas were shelling peas, or field peas. Field peas have a tough, dehiscent pod that is not eaten. Dehiscent means the pods unzip themselves when the peas are ripe and dry. Of course, dried peas are pretty tough eating, unless you cook them. As a rule, shelling peas are grown to be dried for later use in pea soup and pease porridge. (Pease porridge is a thicker version of pea soup, more of a pudding, often made with a ham hock or bacon.) These were dietary staples in medieval times.

Sometime around the 15th century, somebody figured out that immature pea pods could be eaten whole. These "garden peas" or "sugar peas" were a decadent luxury back then. Over time, cultivars were developed that retained that tenderness. These sugar peas, or "English peas," gained in popularity, especially after canning was developed.

Edible pod peas are indehiscent, which means the pods do not open themselves. Rounded edible pod varieties ultimately became known

Pea plant (Rasbak) CC BY-SA 3.0

as sugar peas while the flat-podded varieties were named snow peas (*Pisum sativum* var. *saccharatum*).

In 1952, sugar peas were crossed with a mutant shelling pea in an effort to counteract some pod distortions that were occurring at the time. The offspring of that cross turned out to be a delicious new class of snow pea, and it was named snap pea (*Pisum sativum* var. *macrocarpon*). Snap peas, also known as sugar snap peas, are now the pea workhorse of modern gardens.

How to grow peas

Peas are easy to work with. They prefer cooler weather, making them excellent winter crops. While peas grow best in full sun, they can also work well for shade gardening and container gardening. Many birds love pea seeds, so you may have to protect your crop with netting until the seeds germinate.

Seeds should be planted 5 inches apart and one inch deep in rich, loose, moist soil. As they grow, vining pea plants will use tendrils to grasp and climb, so you will want to provide stock panels, tuteurs, or trellising for them to climb. As tempting as it may be to let your peas climb up netting, don't do it. You'll have a mess on your hands at the end of the growing season. Take my word for it. If peas are being grown in a container, a tomato cage works well.

Purple-podded peas

Water regularly, allowing the soil to dry out between waterings, and be sure to harvest pods as soon as they are ready. This will keep the plant producing. Peas left on the vine will become too tough and starchy to eat, but they can be saved for planting or cooking. Succession planting can provide many months of harvestable peas.

Viral diseases, such as pea enation mosaic and pea streak, both transmitted by aphids, can also appear on your pea plants. These diseases cause distorted pods and leaves. To avoid this, just space plants properly and allow the soil to dry out between waterings.

Snow peas

Those deliciously crisp snow peas in your stir-fry can also be grown at home.

The story behind pea evolution is fascinating. Even more intriguing is why more people don't grow their own snow peas at home.

Snow peas are flat-podded peas that are eaten whole while unripe. Like sugar peas, snow peas are indehiscent, which means the ripe pods do not open on their own. Shelling peas, which are grown to be dried and used in cooking, have a much tougher pod that is dehiscent.

Snow pea plant (JS-JS) CC BY-SA 3.0

Like fat-podded sugar peas and shelling peas, snow peas are a cool season crop. In fact, that's how snow peas got their name, being grown in winter. Seeds should be planted one to two inches deep and five inches apart in loose, nutrient-rich soil. Snow peas use tendrils to climb supports, such as stock panels and trellising.

Harvest pods as they form to make the vines keep producing. Once plants sense that they have completed their reproductive cycle, pod production stops.

Snow peas are easy to grow. You can add them to your stir-fry garden, salad garden, or just grow them! Did you know that the immature leaves and stems are also edible? Now you know.

Forget the mushy peas of your childhood. Grow your own peas for a delicious treat!

Soybeans

Zones 2—11
Sun exposure: full sun or partial sun
Ideal soil temperature: 60°F to 80°F

People started growing and eating soybeans three thousand years before the invention of written language. Originally from East Asia, this high protein legume is now found practically everywhere. Soy milk, tofu, and soy sauce are just a few products made from soybeans, but what about the plants themselves? Is there a place for soybeans in your summer garden?

THE SOYBEAN PLANT

Mature soybean plants can reach two to four feet tall, and they have trifoliate leaves. This means that each leaf is made up of three leaflets. Like other legumes, soybean roots have a symbiotic relationship with certain soil bacteria (Rhizobium) that help them use atmospheric nitrogen. They are deep rooted plants, going down three to five feet.

Soybeans are photoperiodic plants. This means shortening days is what triggers them to start producing flowers. Soybean plants have small, self-fertile flowers that can be purple, pink, or white. Once flower production begins, many soybean plants drop their leaves. Soybean fruits are three inches long. Hairy pods that contain two to four seeds, called pulses. Soybean pulses can be brown, black, green, yellow, or multicolored. By 2010, 93% of soybeans grown commercially in the U.S. were genetically modified. In that same year, scientists mapped the soybean genome, the first bean to be sequenced.

Soybean fruit (H. Zell) CC BY-SA 3.0

TYPES OF SOYBEANS

There are two basic categories of soybeans: vegetable and field. Field soybeans are grown for oil production. Vegetable varieties are higher in protein, easier to cook, and taste better than field soybeans. Soybeans contain 38%-45% protein and up to 19% oil.

HOW TO GROW SOYBEANS

Soybeans (*Glycine max*) are an annual bean plant that loves hot, summer weather. Pulses should be planted 1" deep and spaced with mature sizes in mind. To provide an ongoing harvest, you may want to use succession planting, adding new plants every week or two during the growing season. Soybeans are ready to harvest within 80-120 days after planting. Pick pods while they are still green. Once they brown, the pulses lose flavor. Of course, you can always use mature pulses to plant the next season's crop! Because of their nitrogen-fixing ability, soybeans make an excellent player in crop rotation plans.

SOYBEAN PESTS AND DISEASES

Spider mites are the most destructive pest of soybeans, followed by corn earworm moths, Mexican bean beetles, bean leaf beetles, and cyst nematodes. Fungal diseases, such as stem blight, rust, and white mold can infect soybean plants, along with bean yellow mosaic and other viral diseases. But don't let that stop you!

If you have the space, give soybeans a try in your yard.

Chapter Six

BEET AND SPINACH FAMILY

Until recently, we all thought beets, chard, and spinach were in one family, while amaranth and quinoa were in another family. Now we know it's the same family (Amaranthaceae). These plants all produce flowers with no petals, deep roots, and big seed heads—probably not what you'd expect from a beet.

Lambsquarters and pigweed are the most common beet family weeds. If you see these plants popping up in your yard, edible members of the beet family should grow just as well.

These plants are not picky about soil, though they seem to prefer slightly alkaline conditions. Members of the beet family grow best in partial sun and partial shade.

BEET FAMILY PESTS AND DISEASES

Birds love seeds, so they can be a major pest of the beet family.

Along with all the normal garden variety diseases, beet family members may come down with brown stalk or curly top. If you water at ground level and space plants out enough, these diseases shouldn't be a problem.

Beets

Zones 2—11
Sun exposure: full sun, partial sun, or partial shade
Ideal soil temperature: 75°F to 85°F

There is far more to beets than the canned, pickled variety. These easy-to-grow, sweet tasting vegetables love mild winters, making them an excellent autumn crop.

Beets (*Beta vulgaris*) are perennials grown as annuals. Beets prefer loose, slightly alkaline soil, but they are pretty tolerant. Mixing aged compost into poor soil creates the perfect growing medium, just be sure to remove any rocks that might interfere with your beet roots as they grow.

Aside from the usual pests and diseases of this family, beets are also susceptible to root rots, and several viral diseases that are transmitted by aphids and whiteflies, as well as damage caused by wireworms.

Beets ready for baking (Rod Waddington)
CC BY-SA 2.0

BEET VARIETIES

You are not limited to the deep purple of canned beets. There are yellow, white, and even beets with red and white stripes! These other colors tend to have a mild, nutty flavor, and they don't stain everything they touch. Every part of the beet plant is edible. In fact, beet leaves are tasty and nutritious. Young leaves can be eaten raw and older leaves can be cooked the way you cook spinach.

HOW TO GROW BEETS

Beets grow well in full sun or partial shade and they absolutely love raised beds. Seeds should be planted ½" deep and thinned to 12" apart. It is a good idea to top dress around beet plants to keep things moist and add nutrients. Be sure to water regularly, allowing the top inch of soil to dry out between waterings. Once you discover how delicious fresh beets really are, you will probably want to start planting them in succession, for a regular supply.

Beets (Brianna Walther) CC BY-SA 3.0

Your beets can be harvested at any time, but most people wait until their beets' "shoulders" have pushed their way above ground. Before you pull up all of your beets, consider this: beets make a lovely landscape plant.

Rather than harvesting all of your beets, leave a strategic few in the ground. These plants will develop short, gnarled trunks that put out tall, feathery, flowering stems that can reach four to five feet in height.

Old beets plants produce abundant leaves for several years

A seven-year-old beet root looks more like a tree trunk

Beet Bonus

If a delicious, nutritious crop isn't reason enough to grow beets, cat owners have yet another reason: Research has shown that adding beet pulp to your cat's food will help them poop out more hairballs, rather than hacking them up.

These stems will be covered with seed heads that you can collect or let scatter naturally. Birds and other seed eaters will get most of your rouge beet seeds, but a lucky few, will, in time, germinate and produce new beets. The greens of your seed-producing beets will continue to be edible for, well, I'm not sure how long.

Quinoa

Zones 4—10
Sun exposure: full sun
Ideal soil temperature: 60°F to 90°F

Did you know that you can grow your own quinoa?

Quinoa (*Chenopodium quinoa*) is an ancient grain grown for its high protein seeds. Unlike most cereal grains, quinoa is not a grass plant. Instead, it is called a pseudocereal. People started farming quinoa 4,000 years ago in the Peruvian Andes, but we've been eating it for nearly 7,000 years. Quinoa is unique because it is a complete protein, and it is gluten-free.

Quinoa plants are self-pollinating. They have green 4- and 5-petaled flow-

Quinoa field in Bolivia
(Michael Hermann) CC BY-SA 3.0

ers and deep taproots that make them drought-resistant. Lobed leaves are broad, with tiny hairs (trichomes). Plants can grow from 18" to taller than a person. The main stem can be green, purple, or red, depending on the variety. Quinoa seeds can be black, tan, white, pink, red, or purple, depending on the cultivar. All quinoa seeds are coated with bitter saponins. This bitterness helps protect developing seeds from birds and other seed eaters. You need to rinse that coating off before you eat your quinoa. (In parts of Africa, those saponins are collected and used as laundry detergent!)

How to grow quinoa

Quinoa plants are rugged. They can be grown from sea level all the way up to the highest mountaintops (13,000 ft.). Just give them plenty of sunlight. You will want to grow a variety that is suited to your microclimate and elevation. Quinoa grows best in loose, sandy soil. Do not try growing quinoa in containers— it needs more root space than a container can provide. Quinoa prefers a soil pH of 6.0 to 8.5. Seeds should be planted ¼" deep and watered very gently to avoid washing them away before they get a chance to grow.

Quinoa plants prefer temperatures from 25°F to 95°F. They take 90-120 days to mature. Freezing temperatures will sterilize quinoa pollen. This means that a light frost during flowering can reduce your crop. These plants grow very slowly during their first two or three weeks, so snipping off weeds at ground level is the best way to reduce competition without disturbing the soil. Depending on the variety, plants only need 10"-39" of water during the growing season. They should not be watered once they start producing seeds.

Quinoa problems

While quinoa seeds protect themselves with saponins, many birds will still feast on your crop. You can use netting to reduce losses. The recently discovered quinoa plant bug (*Melanotrichus sp.*) may also cause problems. *Bacillus thuringiensis* can be used to control caterpillars. According to a report from Purdue University, there are no pesticides cleared for use on quinoa. Quinoa is prone to several fungal diseases, including seed rot, leaf spot, and brown stalk rot, which is why good drainage is so important.

HARVESTING QUINOA

You will know it is time to harvest your quinoa when the leaves turn color and start to drop off. The difficult part about harvesting quinoa is separating the seed from the rest of the plant. Similar to harvesting stone pine nuts, this is a labor-intensive process. Start by allowing the seed head to dry completely. Exposed to moisture, those seeds will begin to germinate within 24 hours. You will know the seeds are completely dry when you cannot leave a dent in one with your fingernail. Once they are completely dry, you can gently rub the seed heads against a colander to knock the seeds loose.

Even if you don't harvest your quinoa, adding this plant to your garden or foodscape can increase biodiversity, and, hey, it's a strikingly beautiful edible plant.

Spinach

Zones 2—11
Sun exposure: full sun, partial sun, or partial shade
Ideal soil temperature: 35°F to 70°F

Spinach isn't just for cartoon sailors! This delicious member of the Amaranth family can hold its own in your garden, on a windowsill, or

Savoy Spinach

growing on a balcony. Cousin to beets, quinoa, and chard, spinach lives up to its reputation as a nutritional powerhouse, but not for the reason you think.

As children, many of us cringed to see spinach on our plates. Part of that was because it was cooked into a stringy, green ooze. Also, kids' taste buds are more sensitive to bitterness than grown-ups'. Now that we are older and wiser, we can enjoy eggs Florentine, a spinach omelet, or a fresh, crisp spinach salad. And freshness is the key.

While working as a USMC Family Childcare Provider, I overheard a conversation that no one expects to hear. One toddler was scolding another toddler for eating too many baby spinach leaves. These were spinach seedlings they had planted a few weeks earlier. The toddler kept telling her friend that he was hurting the baby plants, that they had to wait until the plants were more grown up.

SPINACH SEEDS AND LEAVES

Most of the spinach sold in American grocery stores has smooth leaves. These leaves may be light to dark green, and oblong or triangular. There are also varieties with crinkled leaves. Crinkled spinach is called "savoy," after a cabbage with similar tendencies. Savoy spinach has thicker, more rounded leaves. There are also crosses between the two, called semi-savoy.

Spinach seeds are rather large, compared to other greens. Spinach seeds can be prickly or smooth. You might expect the smooth seeds to produce smooth leaves and vice versa, but it's just the opposite. Smooth seeds grow into crinkled spinach plants, while prickly seeds give us smooth spinach.

SPINACH LIFECYCLE

Spinach (*Spinacia oleracea*) is an annual that tends to bolt, or go to seed, as soon as temperatures rise. Bolting makes the leaves lose their flavor, but it can also provide you with seeds for your next spinach crop. You can collect your own seeds as long as you do not plant hybrids. (Hybrids generally do not produce plants that look or taste like the parent.) You can also let them fall where they will, as I do. They always seem to find the spots that suit them best.

Most varieties of spinach are dioecious, which means there are male plants and female plants. The "Bloomsdale" variety is monoecious, which means each plant is both male and female and can self-pollinate. Spinach grows relatively fast. You can have harvestable spinach within three weeks, so you may want to stagger your plantings for a continuous crop.

You can allow your spinach plants to go to seed naturally, which can give you a perpetual bed of spinach for most of the year, plus the flowers provide nectar and pollen for many beneficial insects.

Super Spinach

Cartoonists weren't exaggerating when they said spinach pumped up our beloved sailor man, but iron isn't the reason. Spinach also has high levels of carotenoids, which help prevent cataracts. One cup of fresh spinach gives us:

- Folic acid - 15% RDA
- Iron - 5% RDA
- Manganese - 13% RDA
- Vitamin A - 56% RDA
- Vitamin C - 14% RDA
- Vitamin K - 181% RDA

And all for less than 7 calories.

HOW TO GROW SPINACH

Spinach can be added to flowerbeds, next to walkways, at the base of peas and other climbing plants, and anywhere else these fast-growing greens will look nice. Spinach prefers sunny locations during cooler weather and some shade protection during warmer months. You can also grow it indoors, in containers, year-round if you have a sunny window or grow lights. Containers should be at least 8" tall.

Seeds should be planted ½" deep and kept moist until germination occurs. Seedlings should be transplanted at a time when they are most likely to survive, which means when temperatures are not scorching. Transplants should be spaced 8" to 10" apart. The same is true for seeds sown directly in the ground. Spinach favors light, sandy soil and it is a heavy feeder. You can add nutrients by side-dressing, which means placing aged compost around and next to plants once they are in place. As you water, the nutrients will leach into the root zone and be absorbed by the plants. Spinach prefers a pH of 6.5 to 7.5. Spinach plants have shallow roots, so be sure to water regularly, especially as temperatures begin to rise.

Some varieties of spinach perform better when grown in the fall, while others prefer spring. If you keep seeds of several varieties handy, you can maintain a constant supply of fresh spinach throughout most of the year. Be sure to read the packet before you start planting.

SPINACH PROBLEMS

Spinach is susceptible to many Pythium fungal diseases, along with the usual garden problems. Bulb mites, darkling beetles, seedcorn maggots, Rhizoctonia parasites, wireworms, rabbits, and uncaged chickens can also wreak havoc on your spinach plants. Personally, I conduct a weekly leaf inspection of my spinach and beet plants. A quick peek under each leaf makes it easy to wipe off whitefly eggs before they can hatch. These eggs look like clusters of tiny white rectangles.

SPINACH SUBSTITUTES

Since spinach only grows successfully in hot regions during the cooler months, you can grow other plants in the summer that provide similar taste and nutrition. These plants are New Zealand spinach (*Tetragonia tetragonioides*), Malabar spinach (*Basella alba*), and Lambs quarters (*Chenopodium giganetum*).

SPINACH HISTORY AND TRIVIA

Spinach was first grown in Persia, around 500 B.C. Known as the "Persian vegetable", it was brought to China in the 7th century. Two hundred years later, spinach seeds made their way to Italy. Florence's Catherine de' Medici loved spinach so much that foods served on a bed of spinach became known as "Florentine." Another five hundred years passed and spinach found a new home in western Europe, appreciated for appearing in early spring, when food was scarce, and by not breaking any religious food rules. Spinach was even included in the first known English cookbook in 1390!

Swiss Chard

Zones 2—11
Sun exposure: full sun, partial sun, or partial shade
Ideal soil temperature: 55°F to 75°F

Swiss chard (*Beta vulgaris vulgaris*) is a beet that doesn't grow a fat round root. Both plants, beets and chard, evolved (with some help from humanity) from the sea beet (*Beta vulgaris maritima*). Swiss chard is also called chard, spinach beet, silver beet, mangold, seakale beet, and bright lights. The bright lights name is a reference to the brightly colored leafstalks (petioles), that can be red, yellow, orange, purple, pink, or white. They look as amazing in your salad bowl as they do in your garden!

One of the nicest things about growing chard is that outer leaves can be removed frequently and the plant just keeps making more leaves! Chard is an easy-to-grow, highly nutritious food. Chard is so nutritious that just under half a cup of fresh chard gives you 122% of the RDA of vitamin A, 1038% of vitamin K, and 50% of vitamin C, and only 19 calories. Research has also shown that Swiss chard provides tons of antioxidants and even type 2 diabetes protection.

Like parsley, chard is a biennial plant. This means it creates leaves and roots its first year and seeds the second year. Chard can handle a light frost. Too much cold will trick it into thinking it has experienced a winter and the plant will start producing seeds instead of leaves.

Swiss chard

HOW TO GROW CHARD

Chard can be grown as a summer or winter crop. In areas with hot summers, Swiss chard will perform better as part of your shade gardening plan. Chard seeds should be planted ½"-1" deep when temperatures are between 40°F to 95°F. Mature plants can be spaced 6"-12" apart, with rows 15" wide. Keep in mind that the plants will grow 12"-36" tall, with a spread of 6"-24" wide. Mulching around each plant with aged compost will help stabilize soil temperature and add nutrients to the soil.

To keep yourself in year-round chard, these plants can also be grown indoors in containers. Because chard has a taproot, a 5-gallon planter is recommended.

SWISS CHARD PROBLEMS

Swiss chard is a durable plant that has few pest or disease problems, besides the most common ones. You may find that an overabundance of harvestable chard is your bigger problem, but you can always cook and freeze or give away the extras.

Leafminer damage on
Swiss chard leaf

HOW TO HARVEST SWISS CHARD

Chard is a very satisfying plant to grow. Germination occurs in only five to seven days and you can begin harvesting very early in the plant's life using either of two approaches: leaf-by-leaf or cut-and-come-again. The leaf-by-leaf method simply means outer leaves are removed as needed. The cut-and-come-again method means you cut the plant down to just an inch or two above the soil line, avoiding the growing point in the middle. New leaves will emerge from this point.

Chapter Seven

CABBAGE FAMILY

Cole crops, or cruciferous vegetables, such as broccoli, cauliflower, Brussels sprouts, and the lowly cabbage were placed in the same family partly because they all have four-petaled flowers that look like a cross (Cruciferae is Latin for "cross bearing"). Luckily for us, there is no cross to bear when it comes to growing members of the cabbage family.

These plants produce long, narrow seed pods, called siliqua, that open when ripe. I use the word ripe because these are actually a type of fruit. While you probably wouldn't want them sliced up on your breakfast cereal, immature siliqua can be added to stir-fry.

Recent science renamed this group the Brassicas. Whichever name you use, these plants are identified by their flowers. Most of these plants have a distinct sulfur-like odor. They are usually cool weather crops that prefer neutral or slightly alkaline soil that grow best in partial sun or partial shade.

Arugula flower (Alvesgaspar)
CC BY-SA 3.0

Hairy bittercress and wild mustard are two common cabbage family weeds. If you see these plants popping up in your yard, odds are pretty good that edible members of the cabbage family will grow equally well.

CABBAGE FAMILY PESTS AND DISEASES

Imported cabbageworms will probably cause the most damage to your cole crops. Incorrectly called cabbage moths, these erratically flying white butterflies have black wing spots. They lay tiny, cream-colored eggs on the underside of leaves. These eggs hatch into little green caterpillars that can eat your plants to death.

Wiping off, or extermigating, eggs as soon as you see them goes a long way toward protecting your crops. Row covers can, too. Since the butterflies fly, they can always come back to lay more eggs. (I trained my dogs to chase them away. Once in a while, they actually catch one!) Braconid wasps will help fight off some of these pests, so avoid using broad spectrum pesticides.

Other pests specific to the cabbage family include bagrada bugs, cabbage root maggots, darkling beetles, diamondback moth larvae, harlequin bugs, leaf rollers, millipedes, and wireworms. And all the usual troublemakers. Of course, your pests may vary. *Bacillus thuringiensis* (*Bt*) sprays can help protect against many of these pests.

Clubroot can become a problem if crops are not rotated. Black leg, curly top, Fusarium yellows, and ringspot are other diseases that may appear in your cabbage patch. Good sanitation and ground level watering are your best methods of prevention.

Don't let all those threats deter you from trying your hand at growing plants in the cabbage family. If you buy cabbage in the store, chances are 30:1 that it was grown in China. This is too bad, because cabbage and its cousins are easy to grow, taste sweeter when fresh, and they look nice in a landscape, and all that shipping traffic is bad for the environment. Grab a pack of seeds, or a couple of seedlings from your local garden store, and give the cabbage family a try.

Arugula

Zones 2—11
Sun exposure: full sun, partial sun, partial shade
Ideal soil temperature: above 50 °F

Containerized arugula grows well on a patio protected by a pergola

Arugula was banned from monastery gardens in Roman times. They thought it was an aphrodisiac. I'm pretty sure they were wrong. Arugula is a tangy salad green with lots of vitamins A, C, and K, and potassium. All that nutrition probably gave monks the energy and good health they needed for all sorts of physical activity. In any case, arugula is now recognized as a delicious, healthy, gourmet salad green.

Also known as rocket or Mediterranean salad, arugula (*Eruca vesicaria* ssp. *sativa*) makes an easy addition to the garden. It grows fast. You can start eating your arugula in only 40-50 days after planting seeds.

ARUGULA PLANTS

Arugula plants look like a deeply lobed, open head of lettuce. Some arugula plants will only reach eight inches while others can be more than three feet tall. Arugula is a cool season plant. When things start warming up, arugula plants bolt, or go to seed. They send up a flowering stalk (pedicle) with lovely, edible flowers. You can slow this process by growing arugula in the shade. Being a shallow-rooted plant, arugula can also be grown in containers.

HOW TO GROW ARUGULA

Arugula roots enjoy muddy, mucky soils and cooler temperatures. If you have clay soil, which can hold a lot of water, autumn and early spring are the perfect times to plant this healthy salad green. Plant seeds ½" deep, and water them well. When seedlings are 1" tall, thin them to 6"-9" apart. You can do this by tickling their roots apart and transplanting, or snipping off any extras at ground level. This reduces stress to delicate new roots. To keep leaves tender and tasty, be sure to keep the soil evenly moist. Periods of dryness will increase bitterness and trigger bolting.

ARUGULA'S CONTINUOUS CROP

By regularly snipping off outer leaves for kitchen use, your arugula plants will keep growing new, tender leaves. Because arugula becomes peppery and bitter as it matures, you may want to start new seeds in succession, for a continuous crop. If allowed to go through their life cycle unmolested, arugula plants will readily self-seed an area, providing many years of salad greens with little to no effort on your part. Local pollinators, and pollen and nectar eaters, will appreciate the banquet, as well.

As with many other older plant species, arugula tends to be relatively pest and disease free.

Broccoli

Zones 2—11
Sun exposure: full sun, partial sun
Ideal soil temperature: 70°F to 85°F

Broccoli (*Brassica oleracea*) has been dreaded by children for decades. This is often due to overcooking and freezing.

"Eat your trees!" mothers have cajoled for generations. The truth is, broccoli contains bitter compounds, and some people are more sensitive to them than others. There is no sense fighting over genetics. What you can do, for those family members on the broccoli fence, is to offer fresh, tender broccoli shoots, steam broccoli lightly, and there is always the cheddar cheese trick. (Cheese makes everything taste better, right?)

Broccoli is a flowerhead. Native to the northern Mediterranean region, modern broccoli is the result of centuries of careful breeding that started in the 6th century BC.

HOW TO GROW BROCCOLI

Broccoli is a slow grower. It can take three months or more, from seed to harvest. In warmer regions, broccoli can be started from seed twice a year. For a summer harvest, plant in February, March, and April. For a late winter, early spring harvest, you can plant broccoli in August and September. Some years, you can

Broccoli (artverau)

plant as late as October. Broccoli loves cold temperatures and will bolt in hot weather. Also, heat stress can cause bitterness. Broccoli prefers full sun, but your spring crop can be grown in partial shade, to avoid heat stress. Still, it will benefit from strong morning sun.

Broccoli prefers slightly acidic soil, so your plants will thank you if you perform a little acidification before planting. Seeds should be planted ½" deep. It is best to start plants in small containers and then transplant when they have three or four true leaves. Plants can be placed in the ground slightly deeper than the soil level when transplanting. These plants get large, so be sure to provide plenty of growing room. They usually need a 2-foot square space, or more, per plant. Broccoli roots are shallow, so avoid digging around plants. To reduce weeds, mulch heavily. Broccoli needs a lot of water, so irrigate consistently, without getting the heads wet.

BROCCOLI VARIETIES

There are three basic types of broccoli. The common grocery store variety is Calabrese broccoli, which sprouts with many small heads on thin stalks. Purple broccoli looks more like its cousin, cauliflower, with an occasional purple tint to flower buds. Romanesco broccoli has spiky heads.

Not exactly a true broccoli, broccolini is a cross between standard broccoli and Chinese kale, or gai lan.

BROCCOLI PROBLEMS

Environmental conditions can interfere with a successful broccoli crop. Early stress can cause plants to flower too soon, creating tiny heads. This is called buttoning. Too much heat can cause brown bud—it's not pretty. Heat (and insufficient boron) can also cause hollow stem. Too much nitrogen in the soil can cause broccoli plants to produce lots of (edible) leaves, but no flowers. Be sure to get your soil tested.

HARVESTING BROCCOLI

As flowerheads develop, use a sharp knife to cut the stem an inch or two below the head. Delicious fresh, broccoli can be stored in the refrigerator for a short time, or frozen for longer storage. Broccoli is especially susceptible to the ripening effects of ethylene gas, so keep your broccoli away from foods such as ap-

Romanesco broccoli

ples and bananas.

After you have harvested your broccoli, cut plants off at ground level and chop up the remainder, spreading it out over any areas in the garden prone to Verticillium wilt. There are chemicals in broccoli that harm the fungi.

Young broccoli sprouts, cauliflower, and mustard greens all contain a chemical called glucoraphanin, which is converted into substances that fight infection, arthritis, and cancer. They can also "retune" metabolism.

So, eat your trees! And start planting!

Brussels Sprouts

Zones 2—11
Sun exposure: full sun, partial sun
Ideal soil temperature: 70°F to 85°F

Brussels sprouts: prehistoric weapons, baby cabbages, or healthy garden addition? Many years ago, my mother showed up for a Thanksgiving dinner armed with what looked like a medieval weapon. Having never seen the unopened flower buds still attached to the stalk, it confused me at first. If you have never seen Brussels sprouts growing on a stalk, you are in for a surprise!

Brussels sprouts

Brussels sprouts (*Brassica oleracea*) were first grown as far back as the 5th century throughout the Mediterranean. The Romans liked them, so the sprouts moved around quite a bit. They were widely grown in Belgium, back in the 16th century, hence the name Brussels. These plants prefer cooler, coastal weather, so they are a winter crop in California. Lucky for us, a touch of frost actually makes Brussels sprouts sweeter! In fact, California grows Brussels sprouts on several thousand acres each year.

How to Grow Brussels Sprouts

Brussels sprouts seeds can be planted in warm regions in July and August, and transplants can be put in place as late as September. Brussels sprouts and other cole crops love growing in raised beds, with their nice loose soil with plenty of nutrients. (It makes weeding a lot easier, too!) These plants do not perform well in poor soil. Each plant will need an area 24" square, so thin accordingly. Seeds should be planted ½" deep and watered well. Keep the soil moist until germination occurs. A nice light mulch can help keep that moisture in place. If you are placing transplants, be sure to dig the planting hole large enough to accommodate the root ball plus the stem, up to the first set of true leaves. Mud them in by watering thoroughly, to eliminate any air pockets, and water every day for the first week. After that, allow the soil to dry out between waterings to prevent fungal diseases.

Caring for Brussels Sprouts

As your plants grow and start to produce buds, break the lower leaves off, over a period of a few weeks, starting from the bottom of the plant. Brussels sprouts are susceptible to sunburn damage and will bolt if temperatures get too high. You can help prevent these problems by covering them with a 50% shade cloth or a double layer of row covers. You can also plant them in a location that is protected from direct sun in the hottest part of the afternoon. This isn't much of a problem as we get into winter.

Brussels sprouts should be on a two- to four-year crop rotation to break the disease triangle. Research shows that intercropping Brussels sprouts with fava beans reduces pest damage significantly.

HARVESTING BRUSSELS SPROUTS

Your crop is ready for harvest when the sprouts are 1"-2" in diameter, which usually takes 80 to 120 days, depending on all the usual variables. Buds tend to ripen from the bottom of the plant to the top. Commercial growers pinch off the tops of their plants when the buds are ¾" in diameter to create a uniform crop. You can expect to harvest 2 pounds of produce from a single stalk. One of the most common reasons people dislike Brussels sprouts is because of overcooking. Overcooking Brussels sprouts makes them gray, mushy, and bitter. Fresh Brussels sprouts are sweet and tender. Roasting and sautéing quickly on a high heat bring out a Brussels sprouts' sweet side. Try adding just one Brussels sprout plant to your garden this fall and share the rest of your seeds with family and friends.

Cabbage

Zones 2—11
Sun exposure: full sun, partial sun
Ideal soil temperature: 70°F to 85°F

Cole slaw and corned beef simply wouldn't be the same without cabbage. These densely headed members of the Brassica family are biennials grown as annuals. If you grow cabbage for seed, you will want to make sure there is some distance between your cabbage plants and other members of the Brassica

A light frost makes cabbages taste sweeter

family because cross-pollination can occur. Seriously. In fact, that's how rutabagas came to be—cabbages crossed with turnips. Hmm, how about tiny cauliflowers that grow on a stalk, like

Brussels sprouts—we could be on to something!

How cabbage grows

In the wild, as temperatures reach 80°F, two-year-old cabbage heads send up a flowering stalk, the same way lettuce and spinach do, in a process called bolting. Tiny helicoptered seeds catch rides on every breeze, spinning their way to new homes. Over the next year, a taproot will go down and a head will form, preparing the repeat the cycle.

How to grow cabbage

Cabbage seeds should be planted ½" deep, with plenty of space around each plant. Cabbage plants can reach two feet in diameter. The more space they are given, the faster they will mature and the less likely they are to being attacked by pests or disease. Cabbage plants prefer sunny locations with good drainage, but they can tolerate partial shade.

Cabbage grows best when given occasional deep waterings, rather than frequent shallow irrigation. Also, you can prevent many diseases by employing good cultural practices. Cabbage is a heavy feeder, so you may want to work some aged compost into the soil before planting. In spite of having a taproot, cabbages can be grown in containers that are at least eight inches deep. Rather than have all your cabbages reach harvestable size on the same day, it's a good idea to plant seeds in succession.

Peasants and Senators have been growing cabbage for nearly 3,000 years. You can do it, too!

Cauliflower

Zones 2—11
Sun exposure: full sun, partial sun
Ideal soil temperature: 70°F to 85°F

As a child, I hated cauliflower. It probably had a lot to do with the day an encyclopedia salesman arrived just at dinner time. My single parent mother was bad at telling people no, so our already overcooked cauliflower sat on our plates, congealing, for nearly an hour. We didn't have a microwave, so we ate it at room temperature. Mom's bad mood didn't help.

Clockwise from top left: Traditional white cauliflower, Orange 'Cheddar' cauliflower, Purple cauliflower, Romanesco cauliflower

Since those days, I have come a long way in my view of cauliflower. Apparently, so has the rest of the world. The peppery flavor of this low calorie cole crop now graces grilled cauliflower burgers, cauliflower pizza crusts, and pureed or riced cauliflower instead of mashed potatoes. And the list of popular dishes keeps growing.

CAULIFLOWER PLANTS

When we eat cauliflower, we normally assume we are eating a flower, but we're not. Broccoli heads are unopened flower clusters. Cauliflower heads are undeveloped flower clusters, botanically known as "inflorescence meristem" tissue that forms a "curd". You know, the stuff Little Miss Muffet ate, sitting on her tuffet. Okay, she was eating a dairy product, but the appearance is similar.

HOW TO GROW CAULIFLOWER

Slow and steady is the name of the game when growing cauliflower. These plants need nutrient-rich soil, regular irrigation, and time to develop into substantial plants before head formation begins. In warmer regions, cauliflower seeds can be started in late winter, for an early summer crop, and again, in autumn, for a winter crop. Cauliflower cannot survive scorching summer heat. Seeds should be planted ½" deep in small containers and then transplanted when they look sturdy. Each plant will need an area 1½ to 2 feet square to reach full size. Cauliflower (*Brassica oleracea*) uses a lot of water, so frequent irrigation is critical. As heads mature, protect them from sun damage by folding leaves over the flower.

CAULIFLOWER PROBLEMS

Along with the common pests and diseases faced by garden plants, cauliflower plants are subject to a condition called buttoning. Buttoning occurs when several days of excessive cold hit, causing plants to rush to create heads that end up being a lot smaller than normal. Cute as a button doesn't really fly in the world of cauliflower. (Individual minis might look amazing on the Thanksgiving dinner table.) Too much salt in the soil, too many weeds, and not enough water or nitrogen can also cause buttoning.

Basically, if the plant thinks it's on the verge of death, it will panic and produce tiny heads, rather than no heads at all.

Leave your cauliflower heads to mature fully before harvesting. When they are done growing, they will be fully open. Cut the plant off at soil level and leave the below-ground portion to feed the soil, worms, and soil microbes.

Chinese Cabbages

Zones 2—11
Sun exposure: full sun, partial sun
Ideal soil temperature: 70°F to 85°F

Chinese cabbages (*Brassica rapa*) are variations on the lowly turnip. The two subspecies we most commonly see are forms of Napa cabbage (var. *pekinesis*) and bok choy (var. *chinensis*). These healthful foods have been grown in China since before the 15th century.

<u>Napa cabbage</u>

Also known as Korean small cabbage or celery cabbage, Napa cabbage has a milder flavor than more domestic varieties, but it packs a nu-tritional punch that's difficult to beat. According to a study conducted by the Centers for Disease Control in 2014, Chinese cabbage ranks sec-

Napa cabbages
(Jay and Melissa Malouin) CC BY-SA 2.0

ond only to watercress as a nutrient dense food. Napa cabbages come in both head and loose-leaf varieties. Napa cabbages can be planted twice a year in warmer regions: first, in early spring; and again, at the onset of autumn.

<u>Bok Choy</u>

Unlike Napa cabbages, bok choy does not form heads. Bright white stalks give way to dark green blades, growing in a cluster, much like celery. Nutritionally speaking, bok choy is 95% water, but a single serving (100 g) provides more than 20% of the Daily Value of vitamins A, C, and K, and all for only 13 calories! Research has shown that eating bok choy, which contains chemicals called glucosinolates, may reduce cancer risk.

HOW TO GROW CHINESE CABBAGES

These biennial plants are generally grown as annuals. If you allow your plants to go to seed, you can create a seasonally perpetual crop within your landscape. To begin, find a location with full or partial sun and well-drained soil. Adding aged compost to the planting bed ahead of time can provide a nutritional

Baby bok choy

boost to your plants and improve soil quality. Chinese cabbages can also be grown in containers. Use pots that are 8"-12" across and 18"-24" deep. Seeds should be planted ¼"-½" deep, and they should germinate in 7 to 10 days. Successful seedlings should be thinned to 12"-18" apart. These plants do not transplant well, so it is better to put them where you want them right from the beginning. Plants take only 45 to 50 days to reach maturity, so this is a pretty rewarding crop.

HARVESTING CHINESE CABBAGES

Chinese cabbages are good candidates for succession planting. If you start one new plant per person every two weeks through fall and winter, you will have an abundance to harvest. You can extend that harvest by only cutting away outer leaves on an as-you-need-them basis. These plants will continue to produce inner leaves through the growing season.

STORING CHINESE CABBAGES

Like other cabbages, these plants do not produce a lot of ethylene gas. Cabbages are, however, very sensitive to the ethylene gas produced by other plants, so it is a good idea to keep harvested leaves or heads in a plastic bag in the refrigerator. Or, you can always try your hand at fermenting some cabbage for your very own kimchi!

Chinese cabbages grow quickly, require little care, and they take well to salads, soups, and stir-fry.

Collards

Zones 2—10
Sun exposure: full sun, partial sun
Ideal soil temperature: 55°F to 70°F

No New Year's Day celebration would be complete at my house without a big pot of Hoppin' John and collard, mustard, or turnip greens. Traditional folklore claims this meal ensures prosperity in the coming year. It's packed with good nutrition, but we just love how it tastes!

Collards

Collards (*Brassica oleracea* var. *acephala*) are cabbages that never form heads. So is kale. Both plants are two of humanity's oldest and healthiest vegetable crops. Collards and kale contain more vitamins and minerals than most other vegetables. Eating collards regularly has been found to reduce the chance of some types of cancer. A study published in Nutrition Research (June 2008) reported that eating steamed collard greens was 13% more effective at blocking "bad" cholesterol than the prescription drug Cholestyramine. Being dark leafy vegetables, collards contain a lot of vitamins A, K, and C, manganese, dietary fiber, and calcium. Frequently listed as one of the world's healthiest foods, why aren't collards growing in everyone's garden?

COLLARDS TASTE FUNNY TO SOME PEOPLE

Collard greens contain so much calcium that they taste bitter to some people. You can soften some of that bitterness by blanching or braising in salted water, cooking with smoked or salted meats, such as ham hocks, or with butternut squash, or dried fruit. Using recipes that include vinegar or citrus juice will also remove some of the bitterness. Unlike spinach, which can only tolerate gentle cooking, your collards may need to be cooked for 15-20 minutes. The liquid left behind after cooking collard greens is called pot liquor, or potlikker. Seasoned with salt, pepper, salted pork or smoked turkey, pot liquor makes an excellent broth, made even better when sopped up with a piece of freshly baked cornbread.

HOW TO GROW COLLARDS

Collards can tolerate temperatures as low as 5°F, but they will bolt in summer heat. Bolting does not affect leaf flavor (and it gives you seeds for next year), but they are generally a cool season crop. A light touch of frost actually sweetens the flavor. These plants can get large, with broad, waxy, dark green leaves. They prefer lots of sunlight and need plenty of organic matter in the soil. Collards grow best in soil with a pH of 6.0 to 6.5. Plant seeds ¼"-½" deep. Plants should be thinned to 18"-36" apart, depending on the variety. Side dress with aged compost or manure every 4-6 weeks, and mulch around plants. Collards have a shallow root system and they become more bitter when water-stressed.

PREVENTING PROBLEMS WITH COLLARDS

Research has shown that flea beetle and aphid populations can be reduced when collards are interplanted with beans. They found that the same was true for weeds, but I'd rather have beans than weeds! Apparently, the mixed plantings work better at attracting parasitic wasps, making crops harder to find, and by providing other food sources for the pests.

HARVESTING COLLARDS

Most collard varieties are ready to harvest in 55 to 75 days. Collards are one of those cut-as-you-go crops. Just keep picking outer leaves, as you want them, and the plants will continue producing for several months. It is a good idea to allow plants to reach a height of at least 10" before harvesting leaves. If you find that you have more collard greens than you can eat, you can always cook and freeze them. Your friends and neighbors may appreciate some, as well.

Collards are large, attractive plants. They do not need to be sequestered into traditional garden rows. Find a nice, sunny spot in your landscape and make it home to your very own collard plant.

Horseradish

Zones 3—9
Sun exposure: full sun, partial sun, partial shade
Ideal soil temperature: above 45°F

The fiery bite of horseradish adds its signature flavor to many dishes, and it also makes a nice patio plant. Supposedly, the Oracle at Delphi told Apollo that horseradish was worth its weight in gold. It's been around for a really long time.

HOW HORSERADISH GROWS

The horseradish you buy in the grocery store is usually peeled, pureed, and pickled. Grown for its root, horseradish (*Armoracia rusticana*) can grow over 4 feet tall, but most plants average just a couple of feet all the way around. Horseradish needs a long growing season to get started.

Horseradish roots (Anna reg) CC BY-SA 3.0

It also needs a chilly winter to induce dormancy. Horseradish plants spread underground and can become invasive, which is one reason they make good container plants. As they age, roots become woody and unusable as food, but they can still be used to start new plants. The first leaves usually look distinctly different from the normal large-lobed, tapered, or heart-shaped leaves, so don't pull them out by accident.

HORSERADISH AS FOOD

Roast beef, Bloody Marys, and salmon are always made better with horseradish. You can buy "prepared" horseradish, which contains grated root and vinegar, or you can buy "horseradish sauce", which adds mayonnaise. Growing your own horseradish allows you to create a unique recipe of your own. But, when you first dig up your horseradish root, you may feel as though you did something wrong. The root itself has no smell.

Horseradish makes a nice patio plant

It isn't until the root is chopped up that certain enzymes are released. These enzymes break down plant tissues, producing mustard oil. It is the mustard

93

oil that lights up your sinuses when you take a bite. Chopped or grated horseradish turns brown and bitter when left untreated, which is why vinegar is always added as a preservative. The longer chopped horseradish sits before the addition of vinegar, the hotter it gets. Whether you grow your own horseradish or buy it already prepared, you really should try my recipe for remoulade in the Resources section. Your tastebuds will thank you! Horseradish leaves are edible, as well. Use them sparingly in a salad for the same fiery bite you get from the root.

Did you know, when you buy wasabi, what you are probably really getting is horseradish? Wasabi plants are becoming scarce and horseradish is easy to grow. Manufacturers use the fact that these plants are closely related to mislead their customers. (Shame on them!)

How to Grow Horseradish

Horseradish plants are normally started from crowns in the spring. Attached to the crowns are slender roots called "stecklings". Spread the stecklings out just under the soil level in a large (24"-36" deep) container, or in the ground. Cover the stecklings with soil, up to the crown, and water well. Horseradish grows best in partial shade and plants need to be watered regularly in summer. In winter, your horseradish plant will die back to soil level. This is when you dig up the root and divide it. Keep the largest root for yourself and return the remaining roots back to the container or garden spot. Then cover the area with some straw or mulch and wait for spring.

You can add a horseradish plant to your patio, balcony, or garden for lovely spring and summer greenery, and year-round flavor.

Kale

Zones 2—11
Sun exposure: full sun, partial sun
Ideal soil temperature: 55°F to 70°F

Kale is a cabbage that never forms a head.

Edible kale, or leaf cabbage, is the wild and crazy cousin of the cabbage family and close sibling to collards. Kale was once the most commonly eaten green vegetable in Europe. (Probably because it is easy to grow and stores well.) Kale can grow in a wide range of environments. It can also get by in par-

Mature curly leaf kale
(Rasbak) CC BY-SA 3.0

tial shade, making it a good choice for shade gardens. In warmer regions, kale can be planted in early autumn, and again in late winter.

Each serving of kale contains many times the daily dose of vitamin K. We use vitamin K to coagulate blood, strengthen bones, and reduce calcification of the arteries. Kale also contains a lot of vitamins C, B6, folate, and manganese, along with many other important nutrients. If you enjoy eating kale, your body will thank you.

HOW KALE GROWS

Kale loves cold weather. Kale can tolerate occasional temperatures as low as 5°F below zero. If kale happens to be touched by frost, it tastes even sweeter! Kale is a biennial plant, which means it generally only grows leaves in its first year, and then produces flowers and seeds in its second year. A period of cold weather is what triggers seed production. This is called vernalization.

Kale comes in many different sizes, shapes, and textures. Plants can be compact or 6' tall, depending on the cultivar. Its green or purple leaves are used to classify different types of kale.

How to grow kale

Direct seeding is the way to grow kale in colder climates, but in areas with hot summers start seeds in small pots. Seeds should be planted ½" deep and the soil kept moist until germination occurs. As your seedlings are growing, use that time to prepare planting beds. Kale prefers loose, loamy soil, so mixing in some aged compost will improve the flavor of your kale. Two months before the first frost date, seedlings can be transplanted into their garden locations.

When transplanting kale, bury the plants up to the first set of leaves. This encourages a stronger root system. Side dress plants halfway through their growing season for the best harvest. Side dressing simply means placing aged compost around, but not touching, the base of each plant. Watering and critters will get the nutrients down into the soil, where the plants can use it, without the damage caused by digging.

Harvesting kale

Your kale plants can produce edible leaves for many months if you harvest leaves from the outside first. The plants will keep making new leaves from the center, creating an ongoing harvest.

Kale has a strong flavor, but it packs a powerful nutritional punch and is easy-to-grow. Give kale a try. You may find that the fresh, tender new leaves are just what your body has been craving!

Radish

Zones 2—11
Sun exposure: full sun, partial sun
Ideal soil temperature: 55°F to 75°F

Radishes are probably the easiest and fastest growing garden vegetable, but there is more to them than what you see in the grocery store.

People have been eating radishes for more than 2,000 years.

The radishes you see in the store were grown for their

Radishes

round taproots. Other varieties are grown for their leaves, and still others for the oil found in the seeds.

All parts of a radish plant are edible. If you let a tiny radish go to seed, you will be rewarded with a surprisingly big plant, covered with edible seed pods, called siliquae. Those pods get tough as they mature, so you'll want to use them early on.

Radishes can be red, white, pink, purple, yellow, or grayish-black (the black ones are especially pungent). Radish taproots can grow into either orb or cylindrical shapes.

How to grow radishes

Radishes (*Raphanus sativus*) germinate quickly, usually within a few days. Radishes prefer a soil pH of 6.5 to 7.0 and loose soil. Keeping the soil moist will speed germination and initial growth, but too much water can cause root rot. If you want smaller radishes, seeds should be planted ½" deep. For bigger radishes, plants seeds 1" deep. Plants should be thinned to 4"-8" apart, in rows 8"-12" wide. To maintain a constant supply of radishes, you can plant new seeds every few days.

Because radishes grow so quickly, there are very few pests or diseases to worry about.

RADISHES AS COMPANION PLANTS

Radishes are often planted along with corn, squash, and cucumber, which provide young plants with welcome shade. Radishes are said to repel cucumber beetles, squash bugs, and squash vine borers. Some sources claim that radishes repel tomato hornworms, ants, and aphids, but I could find no scientific research to verify these claims. If nothing else, planting radishes makes efficient use of the soil around these larger plants.

Radishes come in many shapes and colors
(Wikipedia) CC BY-SA 3.0

Rutabagas

Zones 2—11
Sun exposure: full sun, partial sun
Ideal soil temperature: 45°F to 85°F

Rutabagas look funny, their name sounds funny, and, let's face it, they have a rather odd family history.

Imagine deciding to cross a cabbage with a turnip. What would you get? A rutabaga! The name comes from the Swedish words for stumpy root.

Also known as swedes, yellow turnips, and Russian, Canadian, and Swedish turnips, rutabagas (*Brassica napobrassica*) were first noted growing wild in the early 1600s. Since before the Middle Ages, people have carved frightening faces on turnips and rutabagas and placed them on windowsills and doorsteps to ward off evil spirits. Yes, these are the early jack-o-lanterns of modern pumpkin fame!

Rutabagas are biennial plants, which means they take two years to go through their complete lifecycle. The first year is dedicated to leaves and roots and the second year is used for seed production. The root we eat is actually made up of the base of the leafy stem (think cabbage) and the hypocotyl. The hypocotyl is the part that grows between the true root and the first seedling leaves (cotyledons). You can tell the difference between a turnip and a rutabaga by the ribbed neck seen on rutabagas.

Rutabaga seedlings

RUTABAGAS AS FOOD

Rutabagas are grown for their roots and leaves. They contain a lot of vitamin C. The roots are a starchy equivalent to potatoes, used in soups, stews, and casseroles. In Scotland, potatoes and rutabagas are boiled and mashed separately to create "tatties and neeps". The tender new greens can also be eaten, just be sure to only remove a few leaves per plant. They can add a zesty bite to salads.

HOW TO GROW RUTABAGAS

Rutabagas grow and ripen best in cool weather. Rutabaga seeds should be planted ½" deep in rich soil. They transplant well, so starting them in small containers is a good way to give them a head start. Seedlings should be placed 12"-18" apart. Rutabagas grow a little larger than turnips and need a few extra weeks to reach maturity. They are normally ready to harvest within 80-

100 days. Rutabagas can grow pretty much anywhere, but their flavor and texture improve significantly when they are grown in soil treated with compost and watered regularly. Insufficient watering can cause a woody texture and splitting can occur with irregular watering. Soaker hoses are an excellent idea for rutabagas. Rutabagas prefer a pH of 5.5 to 7.0 and a rock-free environment. Like other cabbage family members, rutabagas should not be grown in the same spot for more than two years at a time.

The same rutabagas 8 weeks later

RUTABAGA HARVESTING AND STORAGE

One of the reasons rutabagas are an important food in times of hardship is that they store well. Rutabagas should be harvested when they are about the size of a grapefruit. When they are small, they are more tender and easier to damage. As they mature, they become sweeter. To harvest rutabagas, simply pull or dig them from the ground. You can leave them in the ground for longer periods of time by trimming the leaves and heavily mulching the area with straw. Harvested rutabagas can be stored for months by trimming all but the top inch or two of greenery and storing in a cool, moist place, as close to 32°F as possible, without freezing. Commercially, rutabagas are dipped in paraffin wax to prolong storage.

> Some people find rutabagas, as well as watercress, horseradish, and broccoli, extremely bitter-tasting. This is due to a specific gene that affects their bitter taste receptor. So, if someone says they really can't eat members of this group, believe them.

Turnips

Zones 2—11
Sun exposure: full sun
Ideal soil temperature: 45°F to 85°F

Turnips are a white, cool weather root crop.

Cousin to rutabaga, radishes, and other members of the cabbage family, turnips (*Brassica rapa*) are grown for the bulbous taproot that looks more like a white beet, and its nutrient rich leaves.

TASTE FOR TURNIPS

Many people believe that they do not like turnips, but this is often because the turnips they tried were too old. Old turnips taste bitter. This is because of a self-defense chemical produced by many members of the cabbage family. Also, some people have inherited a pair of genes that make them extra sensitive to the bitterness, so don't force anyone to try the fruits of these labors. It just might not be possible for them to enjoy the flavor. That being said, young, tender turnips do not contain as much of the bitterness, so harvest early and often! Also, consistent irrigation reduces the chance of your turnips becoming bitter.

TURNIP GREENS

Turnip leaves are a popular side dish in the southeast. Tender leaves are less bitter than older leaves. Bitterness can be reduced by pouring off the cooking water and replacing it with fresh water and reheating. Unlike rutabagas, which have a visible crown or neck between the taproot and the leaves, turnip leaves grow directly from the root.

HOW TO GROW TURNIPS

Like other root crops, turnips prefer loose soil, but they are resilient plants. They can handle conditions that thwart more gentle crops. In warm regions, turnips can be planted February through April, and again in September and October. Seeds should be planted ½" deep, directly into the garden. Seedlings should be thinned to 4"-6" apart, when grown for roots, and 2"-3" apart for greens. Depending on the variety planted, your turnip crop should be ready within 50 to 75 days. Tokyo turnips, which tend to be smaller, are harvestable after only 30 to 60 days!

Turnip roots (thebittenword.com) CC BY 2.0

THE LIFE OF A TURNIP

Turnips are biennial plants, which means it takes them two years to go from seed to seed. Most turnips grown in fields and gardens never get that chance. Planted in full sun or partial shade, first-year turnips put out roots and absorb as many nutrients as they can, storing them for the upcoming winter months. In the spring of a turnip's second year, it puts out tall yellow flowers with seeds in pods that look like tiny pea pods.

Turnips have been grown for more than 4,000 years. Pliny the Elder ranked turnips third only to cereals and beans as the most important crops. Turnips were also used in early experimentation with crop rotation.

Fun turnip trivia: the pink, purple, red, or greenish color of a turnip's shoulders is a result of being exposed to the sun.

Give turnips a try in your garden today.

Chapter Eight

CARROT FAMILY

The umbrella-shaped flower clusters of this family make them a favorite in the world of beneficial insects. Hoverflies and tiny parasitic wasps flock to these uniquely shaped flowers, taking a big bite out of pest problems. They look nice, too. And you can collect seeds for next year's crop while you're at it!

The carrot family includes coriander, celeriac, celery, fennel, and parsley. These crops grow slowly. And they can cross-pollinate, so you will want to put some distance between them if you plan on saving seeds. These are biennial plants, so they generally only flower during their second year.

Members of the carrot family grow best in loose soil under partial sun. If your soil is heavy clay, you can grow this group in raised beds or containers.

If you see hogweed or Queen Anne's lace coming up in your yard, members of the carrot family will feel right at home. (Poison hemlock is a member of this family, too, but be sure to stay away from that cousin!)

Carrots

CARROT FAMILY PROBLEMS

Along with the normal garden problems, members of the carrot family may be attacked by several other insect pests and plant diseases. These pests include carrot fly larvae, celery fly larvae, lygus bugs, root knot nematodes, root maggots, vegetable weevils, and wireworms. Diseases specific to members of the carrot family include Alternaria leaf blight, aster yellows, bacterial soft spot, cavity spot, crater rot, mosaic virus, Phytophthora tentaculata, and pink root.

Carrot and celery fly larvae are likely to attack roots. This creates places where fungal disease can get in. These pests are attracted to the smell of bruised plant tissue, so be gentle with your root crops. You can sprinkle diatomaceous earth (DE) on this family to deter many of those pests. Voles, rats, and rabbits can also take a bite out of your carrot family crops.

Carrots

Zones 2—11
Sun exposure: full sun, partial sun
Ideal soil temperature: 50°F to 85°F

Carrots are not just for bunnies! They are healthy, delicious, and more colorful than ever. You can grow them at home and surprise your family with carrots that are white, purple, red, and yellow, along with the familiar bright orange.

Carrots are biennial plants grown primarily for their taproots. Carrot tops and seeds are edible, too.

Purple carrots

How carrots grow

Carrot flowers change their gender as they develop. This means that a single umbel, or flower cluster, will contain both male and female umbellets at the same time, with the older female flowers on the outer edges, with male stamens closer to the center. After fertilization is complete, the umbel starts to curl upward, creating a bird nest shape. If allowed to grow through a winter and experience vernalization, your carrot plants will produce seeds for yet another crop. Selective harvesting can make your carrot patch a perennial food source.

True to their ancestral home of modern-day Iran and Afghanistan, carrots prefer growing in sandy soil. My heavy compacted clay is probably the worst soil for growing carrots. Plus, carrots are not exactly the most expensive produce in the grocery store. So, why bother? For the same reason we are compelled to grow our own tomatoes, peas, berries, potatoes, and more ~ they taste better, we have more control over what goes into our food, and we reduce our carbon footprint. And pulling a purple carrot out of your garden is a pretty satisfying experience.

Carrots come in a variety of colors

Carrot body and color types

Carrot varieties are grouped by shape and color. Our common orange carrots are Western, while the more colorful yellow, purple, and crimson varieties are Eastern. Both Eastern and Western color types are then divided up by shape. The shorter, stubbier, blocky shapes perform best in containers while the longer, slender growth carrots need more depth to grow well.

Carrot Classes

Chantenay - wide, stubby growth; heavy foliage, 'Carson Hybrid' and 'Red Cored Chantenay'

Danvers - heavy foliage, longer than Chantenay types and shorter than 'Imperator', able to tolerate heavier soils, store well, 'Danvers 126'

Imperator - long, slender growth, high sugar content, most popular commercially grown carrot, 'Imperator 58' and 'Sugarsnax Hybrid'

Nantes - sparse foliage; stubby, most adaptable variety, high sugar content, do not store well, 'Nelson Hybrid', 'Sweetness Hybrid' and 'Scarlet Nantes'

HOW TO GROW CARROTS

Carrots take 90-120 days to mature, depending on the variety. Carrots grow best in full sun and cooler temperatures, but they can be grown in partial shade. Carrots prefer alkaline soil, with a pH of 6.3-6.8. Carrots do not compete well with rocks and stones.

Carrot seeds are really tiny and can be difficult to space properly. One way to get around this is to stir together some carrot seeds, radish seeds, and some light soil or sand. Sprinkle this mixture over the planting area. The radishes will grow faster than the carrots, creating automatic succession planting. It will also create space for the carrots. Once they emerge, carrot seedlings should first be thinned to 1" apart. As you begin to see which plants are thriving, thin again to 4" spacing by cutting off the rejects at soil level. This avoids disturbing the roots of remaining plants. Be sure to compost or dispose of these cuttings, rather than leaving them on the soil. This way, you are not attracting carrot pests.

The Latin name for carrots is *Daucus carota sativus*. Daucus carota sounds an awful lot like "Doc" and "carrot" to me. Switch them around and I hear, "What's up, Doc?" Coincidence? Maybe. But, maybe not…

Give carrots a try in your yard or on your balcony.

Fennel

Zones 3—9, when grown as an annual
Zones 9—11, when grown as a perennial
Sun exposure: full sun
Ideal soil temperature: above 65°F

Once you plant this member of the carrot family, you will have a year-round food. It looks pretty in a landscape, too!

Large feathery fronds wave in the breeze. Yellow umbrella-shaped flowers attract hoverflies, ladybugs, lacewings, bees, and beneficial syrphid flies. The bulbous base looks like a closely packed celery. This perennial herb can grow quite large, up to five feet tall, depending on the variety.

Fennel bulb

Milder than anise, all parts of the fennel plant are edible. The large root bases, or bulbs, are often roasted, stewed, sautéed, or grilled. The small flowers (called "fennel pollen") have an intense flavor and are a tad expensive ($10-$15/oz.). Fresh green seeds or dried seeds are used as a breath freshener, "digestive", and in cooking a wide variety of dishes. Fennel is what gives Italian sausage and absinthe their unique flavors. Young leaves are added to salads, omelets, and many fish dishes and soups.

FENNEL AS MEDICINE

Fennel (*Foeniculum vulgare*) also has medicinal uses. Fennel seeds contain volatile oils that stimulate mucous production in the digestive tract, providing temporary relief from digestive upset, Crohn's disease, ulcerative colitis, Celiac disease, and irritable bowel syndrome. Fennel also reduces nausea and is said to ward off the effects of hangover (though I'm not sure about that one). In Medieval times, fennel was eaten as an appetite suppressant.

HOW TO GROW FENNEL

Fennel can be started in warmer regions in spring or fall. It prefers sunny locations and is often seen growing wild alongside freeways. Fennel grows so easily from seed that wild fennel has become invasive in many areas. Seedlings should be placed 8"-12" apart, depending on the variety. Young fennel plants need regular watering in summer, but you can wait to water mature plants until they start to wilt without any noticeable ill effects. As the bulbs grow, bank a little soil around them. This keeps them white and helps them to stay tender. When your fennel bulbs reach tennis ball size, use a sharp knife to cut away the roots, leaving them in the soil for beneficial soil microorganisms.

Along with the normal carrot family pests and diseases, fennel is also prone to cercospora leaf blight.

Fennel tends to bolt, or go to seed, when the roots are disturbed. This isn't necessarily a bad thing, as it will mean more new plants. If the roots are not overly disturbed, they will put out new bulbs. Voilà! Perpetual food either way!

Find a sunny spot in your yard or use a large container to add fennel to your edible landscape.

Lovage

Zones 3—9
Sun exposure: full sun, partial sun, partial shade
Ideal soil temperature: above 60°F

Lovage tastes like a cross between parsley and celery, but it can grow to over eight feet tall!

Lovage flowers (H. Zell) CC BY-SA 3.0

Lovage is a perennial herbaceous plant that requires very little care. Stronger tasting than either celery or parsley, a little goes a long way, but all parts of the lovage plant make an excellent addition to soups, salads, casseroles, and stews, and the minced leaves take pasta and potatoes to new heights. Lovage seeds and stems are also used in candy-making.

THE LOVAGE PLANT

Even though lovage looks and smells more like celery, it is actually a member of the carrot, or umbellifer family. While lovage plants can grow taller than a person, more often, they grow 36"-60" tall and 24"-36" wide. Small yellow flowers grow in umbrella-shaped umbels. Seeds are ½" long. Lovage is native to eastern Europe.

HOW TO GROW LOVAGE

You can start lovage seeds indoors, four to six weeks before the last frost date, or outside any time the soil has warmed to at least 60°F. Plant seeds ¼" deep and keep the soil moist until seedlings are several inches tall.

Lovage grows best in full sun to partial shade and it needs

soil with plenty of organic matter. You can help your lovage plant thrive by top dressing the planting area ahead of time with aged compost. As the growing season nears the end, you can allow flowers to produce seeds for future crops. In cold regions, the root is dug up and stored where it will be protected from freezing until the next spring.

Your lovage plants may be feasted upon by tarnished plant bugs and parsley worms, along with the normal contenders. The parsley worm has a bit of a bonus by being the larval form of the lovely swallowtail butterfly, so you may want to turn a blind eye to some damage. If you see signs of early blight, late blight, or leaf spot, however, take a closer look.

Lovage has very few pest or disease problems. Leafminers can cause cosmetic damage, but that's about it. Because of its rugged demeanor and its celery-like flavor, lovage is an excellent addition to many foodscapes.

Parsnips

Zones 2—9
Sun exposure: full sun, partial sun
Ideal soil temperature: 50°F to 85°F

Parsnips look like white carrots because they are related!

Cousin to carrots, parsley, celery, and other umbels, parsnips (*Pastinaca sativa*) are native to Eurasia and have been cultivated since ancient times. In fact, parsnips were used as a sweetener before sugar cane made its way to Europe.

Parsnips

Parsnips are a cool weather crop in Mediterranean climates. Parsnips leaves look almost like ferns, with pinnate (branched), toothed edges (margins). Parsnips are grown as annuals, but if you let a few of them go to seed, these biennials can start spreading edible roots in many areas of your foodscape. (Once they start that process, you won't want to eat them—they get quite woody.) Second year plants can grow five feet tall, but your first-year parsnip will be significantly shorter, at only 18"-24". Yellow, umbrella-shaped flowers grow into tiny "fruits" called schizocarps. (How's that for a fun garden word?)

How to grow parsnips

Parsnips, like other root crops, need loose soil. This makes them well suited to raised beds and container gardening. If you are planting parsnips in heavy clay soil, you will want to break up the soil down 18" and dig in 3"-4" of aged compost. If you don't, you will end up with forked and otherwise deformed roots prone to disease. Parsnip seeds should be planted ½" deep, with a heavy dose of patience. Parsnips seeds are slow to germinate and the plants take up to four months to reach harvestable size, but they are worth the wait! These sweet roots lend themselves to seasonings such as ginger and nutmeg, as well as more savory dishes such as soups and stews. Parsnips can be grown in full sun or partial shade. They prefer slightly acidic soil, so you may need to make some pH adjustments. Seedlings should be thinned to stand 3"-6" apart and be sure to eliminate all competition from weeds.

Parsnips pests and diseases

Parsnip canker is a real problem, showing itself as orange-brown or black areas on the crown and shoulders. Also, the root will crack. This condition is more likely to occur when seeds are planted in cold, wet ground that is too alkaline. It sounds, to me, that poor drainage is a parsnip's worst enemy.

Celery fly larvae may tunnel into parsnip leaves, much like leafminers. These pests can harm young plants, so remove infested leaves if you see them. On the upside, many moth and butterfly larval forms use the flowers and undeveloped seeds of second-year parsnips as a major food source. So, allowing a few parsnip plants to complete their lifecycle not only gives you free parsnip seeds and plants, it also adds biodiversity to your landscape and provides food for many beneficial insects!

HARVESTING PARSNIPS

Like many other root crops, parsnips taste sweeter after they've experienced a little frost. Since my California ground is not likely to freeze, we don't need to worry about getting our parsnip harvest out of the ground before it does. Other regions are not so lucky. Before you harvest your parsnips, however, be sure to wear gloves. Parsnips may be good sources of folic acid, potassium, fiber, and vitamins C and K, but they also have a powerful self-defense mechanism. Parsnip sap is toxic. If your skin is exposed to sunlight after handling parsnip leaves and stems, you are likely to get a rash.

Give these sweet root crops a try.

Chapter Nine

GRAIN AND GRASS FAMILIES

Ornamental grasses are often suggested as a low maintenance, drought tolerant addition to a landscape, but you can put those same characteristics to work in your yard with edible grains and grasses.

Most members of this group are true grasses (Poaceae), with buckwheat being the only exception. Bamboo, your lawn, and rice are also part of this clan. While we will not be discussing how to grow rice, there are plenty of good reasons for adding edible grains and grasses to your landscape. Besides the food factor, these plants are durable, tend to have deep roots, and look lovely in a landscape.

If you see Bermudagrass, crabgrass, or foxtails in your yard, edible grains should grow just as well—and you should get rid of those foxtails before your pet finds them!

These plants are rugged and can handle practically any soil as long as there is enough sunlight and occasional water.

GRASS PESTS AND DISEASES

Grains and grasses are prone to fungal diseases, such as leaf scald, leaf spot, net blotch, stripe rust, and stem rust. Along with the regular pests, this family battles crane flies, stinkbugs, and wireworms. Also, aphids may carry a viral disease called barley yellow dwarf.

So, how about making a little room for a patch of grain? As a food crop, I expect that it will be much like endive, nasturtiums, lentils, and tomatoes—it will continue to turn up long after I have stopped planting it.

Barley

Zones 8—12
Sun exposure: full sun
Ideal soil temperature: above 40°F

Barley was one of the first grains ever grown domestically. It was cultivated in Eurasia 10,000 years ago—before people had even figured out how to make pottery!

BARLEY HISTORY

Barley has been used as food, fodder, and currency. Barley is cited as a reason why many prehistoric cultures developed into cities capable of maintaining armies, because of its ability to be stored. Barley beer is believed to be the first alcoholic beverage, created by Neolithic people, who malted* the grains. Barley is still used today to make beer, whiskey, porridge, bread, soups, and stews. And the U.S. and the U.K. still base their shoe sizing on the size of a barley corn (seed).

Harvested barley

THE BARLEY PLANT

Barley (*Hordeum vulgare*) is a member of the grass family (Poaceae). It is a self-pollinating annual. Barley has a relatively short growing season, but it tolerates cool weather and drought, making it a good winter crop in warm regions.

Barley seeds grow on a brittle spike, made up of spikelets. When the seeds mature, the spikelets fall apart, allowing the seeds to spread. The long hairs that stick up are called awns. There are two main types of barley, based on the way the seeds are arranged along a central stalk (rachis) and their fertility: two-row barley and six-row barley. In six-row barley, all of the seeds are fertile, whereas only one in three of the two-row barley are fertile. Two-row barley has less protein and more starch than six-row barley, making a better choice for malting and fermentation.

2-row and 6-row barley
(Xianmin Chang)

Higher protein six-row barley is more commonly used for animal feed. There are spring and winter varieties of barley, depending on whether they need a period of cold to transition into their reproductive phase. In warmer regions, that generally means planting in either October or January. Barley's reproductive phase is characterized by true stems, called culms, carrying flowering heads, also known as a spikes or ears, that emerge from the sheath, or boot, surrounding the uppermost leaf (called the flag leaf). Barley grows 2-½ to 3 feet tall.

BARLEY HULLS

Barley seeds have tough coverings called hulls. Most varieties have hulls that are difficult to remove without losing or damaging some of the grain. These are also known as "covered" barley. The barley you see in the store is usually hulled or pearled barley. Hulled barley is a whole grain, but pearled barley is not. Pearling removes several outer layers of the grain along with the hull. There are also hulless, or "naked" barley varieties, but they aren't really hulless. Instead, the hull is simply easier to separate from the grain. Barley hulls are often used to make pillows.

WHY GROW BARLEY?

You may want to grow a small patch of barley simply as a testament to our agricultural history, to know that you can. You may want to try making your own beer or whiskey. You may want to grow more of your own ingredients for a hearty winter soup. Barley can also be grown as a cover crop or green manure to reduce erosion, improve soil structure, and suppress weeds. Barley is an excellent crop to install as your winter fava beans are ending their growing season. If you add a legume, such as peas or beans, and leave the plants in place, you can significantly improve nutrient cycling. Barley grown in winter has a deep, fibrous root system that can go six feet down! Also, because barley grows so quickly, it absorbs surface water that would otherwise be used by weeds. Barley plants also shade out weeds and they emit allelopathic chemicals that suppress weed growth. Barley can also be used as a nurse crop. Nurse crops provide protection for slow growing crops, such as beets.

HOW TO GROW BARLEY

Barley seeds are planted using a method called drilling. Drilling is exactly what it sounds like: you drill a hole in the ground and drop a seed in. Commercial growers have heavy equipment that drills and plants seeds automatically. You probably don't have one of those machines in your garage, so you will have to do it by hand. Barley seeds are planted two inches deep. When I first started growing things in my California concrete soil, I actually used a battery powered drill to plant seeds. After five years of composting, mulching, and top dressing, the drill is no longer needed. Now, I use a hand weeding tool to poke a hole in the ground.

Barley does not like waterlogged soils, so allow the soil to dry out between waterings. Of course, if it's a rainy winter, there isn't anything you can do about it other than continue to add organic material to the soil to improve drainage. Some people claim that barley acts as a natural pesticide, but research has not shown this to be true.

* WHAT IS MALTING?

Malting is a method used to make grains more appropriate for beer, whiskey, vinegar, shakes, and many other food products. Malting consists of soaking cereal grains in water to stimulate germination, but then drying the seeds with hot air before germination actually occurs. This triggers certain enzymes into action that convert starches into sugars, and break down certain proteins that are later used by yeast as food. Malted grains ferment quickly and become slightly alcoholic on their own. Rations of barley were given to workers in ancient times.

Corn

Zones 4—8
Sun exposure: full sun
Ideal soil temperature: above 60°F

Corn is the biggest U.S. grain crop and you can grow it, too! Fresh from the garden ears of sweet corn, heated, and then topped with butter, salt, and pepper, well, life just doesn't get much better than that! Now, we are not talking about the corn used to feed livestock. That brand is called grain corn. Sadly, I wasn't particularly happy with my Indian corn crop experience, either. It may have historical merit, but the kernels were tough and very starchy. Call me spoiled, but I prefer my corn with fat, sugar-filled kernels that burst on my tongue with every bite.

HISTORY OF CORN

For anyone who has had the opportunity to explore Mitchell, South Dakota, you know there's a lot to be said for corn. Corn (*Zea mays*), or maize, was domesticated by people in what is now Mexico nearly 10,000 years ago. Early corn plants only grew one-inch-long cobs, and only one cob per plant. Selective breeding brought us to cobs of several inches in length and plants capable of producing multiple cobs. Corn is one of the three most genetically modified crops, with GMO varieties composing nearly 90% of the U.S. corn harvest. In addition to being eaten from the ear, or as grits or meal, corn is also used as a sweetener (high fructose corn syrup), biofuel, and to make plastics, fabrics, adhesives, and liquor. There are six types of naturally occurring corn (and 142 GMO types as of 2015). Those six types are dent corn, pod corn, flour corn, flint corn, popcorn, and our beloved sweet corn.

Corn on the cob

HOW CORN GROWS

Being a member of the grass family (Poaceae or Gramineae), corn is cousin to bamboo, rice, and your lawn. Corn grows a hollow stem that is wrapped with leaf blades. Each corn plant produces both female and male flowers, but they are not self-pollinating. This is called monoecious. These flowers both start out bisexual (referred to as "perfect" in the world of botany), and then develop into one gender or the other.

Corn kernels are actually female inflorescences, or flower

clusters, that turn into fruit. These fruits are protected by tightly wrapped leaves that we call husks. At the top of each stem (or cob) is a male inflorescence (tassel) that releases pollen onto the wind. The silks we work so hard to remove are actually elongated stigmas from the female flower. There is an ovary at the end of each silk thread that must be pollinated for fertilization to occur, allowing a kernel to develop. Since pollen is carried on the wind, corn must be planted in blocks, rather than rows.

HOW TO GROW CORN

Corn needs lots of nutrients in the soil, so be sure to prepare the beds ahead of time with plenty of aged compost. Corn does not transplant very well, so wait a couple of weeks after your last frost date before planting. Seeds should be planted 1" deep and 4"-6" apart. Soil needs to be at least 60°F for germination to occur. Once your corn seedlings emerge, thin them to 8"-12" apart. Corn plants have very shallow roots, so proper irrigation is important. In the heat of sum-

Young corn plants

mer, your corn plants will need an average of five gallons of water per square yard each week. Since each microclimate is different, you will have to make your own adjustments. Just keep in mind that insufficient irrigation can reduce the number of silks that emerge and that means less developed kernels on your ears of corn. One way to give your corn seedlings an extra boost of nitrogen is to use the Three Sisters Method and plant corn with beans and squash. The beans "fix" atmospheric nitrogen, making it available to nearby plants, and the squash produce large leaves that shade the soil.

CORN PESTS AND DISEASES

We are not alone in our love of corn. An old saying tells us, "One for the blackbird, one for the crow, one for the soil, and one to grow." You may or may not be able to scare away the crows with scarecrows, but nothing can stop a determined raccoon. It is the smaller pests, however, that will probably cause you the most problems. These generalists include European corn borers, corn earworms, cucumber beetles, seed-corn maggots, and wireworms, along with the normal troublemakers. Corn is also subject to fungal and bacterial diseases, such as Fusarium root and ear rot, maize dwarf mosaic, Pythium stalk rot, seed rot, soft rot, and smut. Of course, corn smut really is delicious, so don't panic if it shows up.

Corn Smut

Juicy, sweet kernels of corn transform, overnight, into hideous, purple-gray tumors. And these tumorous galls are delicious!

If you are an American corn farmer, corn smut is not what you want to see in your field. A lot of money and effort have gone into eradicating corn smut in North America. Corn smut in your garden is something else entirely.

While this distant cousin of mushrooms reduces crop size and makes ears of corn unmarketable for July picnics, it is edible. Unlike other corn problems, corn smut is said to

Corn smut

taste like truffles, with a sweet, earthy, inky flavor. If it appears in your garden and you don't want it, your local chef would love to hear from you! To my way of thinking, if life gives you lemons, make lemonade. Or, if you are given corn smut, make quesa-dillas! Corn smut can be eaten raw, or added to omelets, soups, sauces, meat dishes, or even desserts! Corn smut is high in lysine. This means eating it with corn, or any other seed, provides a complete dietary protein.

CORN SMUT LIFECYCLE

Also known as devil's corn, common smut, boil smut, Mexican truffles, or huitlacoche [pronounced weet-la-COH-cheh], corn smut is a parasitic fungus that can occur on any aboveground portion of a corn plant as purplish blobs covered with papery greenish-white tissue.

Corn smut gets its purple color from pigments called anthocyanins. These are the same pigments found in blueberries, raspberries, and purple cauliflower. When you cook with corn smut, don't be surprised to see the purple color change to black, because it will. Purple pigments generally don't hold up well to heat.

The corn smut fungus (*Ustilago maydis*) infects plant ovaries, causing kernels to swell up into large purple galls that are filled with fungal threads, called hyphae, and spores. Corn smut spores are already in the soil and can be carried on the slightest breeze or splashed water from rain or irrigation. Dry conditions and temperatures between 78°F and 93°F are all that corn smut needs to get started. Adding nitrogen or applying manure increases the chance of corn smut developing on your corn plants. Plant injuries also increase infection rates.

Corn plants try to defend themselves against corn smut by blasting the invaders with reactive oxygen (hydrogen peroxide). Sadly, from the corn plant's perspective, this bubbling action simply spreads the smut spores. If smut appears on your corn, fear not! Instead, harvest the galls while they are young and have the texture of a foamy popcorn, kind of firm and spongy. These moist galls are ready for harvesting two or three weeks after infection appears. As the galls mature, they turn dry and are mostly filled with unappetizing dry, black fungal spores.

Love it or hate it, corn smut is here to stay, so you may as well learn to cook with it (or sell it).

Lemongrass

Zones 9—10
Sun exposure: full sun
Ideal soil temperature: 65°F to 85°F

Lemongrass (*Cymbopogon citratus*) is an easy-to-grow edible that makes a nice patio, porch, or indoor plant.

USES OF LEMONGRASS

The inner, white core of lemongrass is used in Thai food, marinades, spice rubs, curries, stir-fry, and many other delicious recipes. It can be used fresh or dried.

GROWING LEMONGRASS

You can buy lemongrass seedlings at most garden supply stores and online. If you have a friend growing lemongrass, ask for some! These plants need to be divided every once in a while.

Lemongrass plants prefer full sun and well-drained soil. They can grow as tall as an adult, but lemongrass grown in containers is usually only half that size. A 5-gallon container is ideal. Plants should be spaced at least two feet apart.

Lemongrass makes a nice patio plant

Lemongrass uses a lot of nitrogen, so feed monthly. Blood

meal, composted manure, fish emulsion, feather, cottonseed, soybean, or alfalfa meal are all good sources of nitrogen.

Whether you cook with it or not, lemongrass is a lovely plant with a faint lemony aroma.

Oats

Zone 7—10
Sun exposure: full sun
Ideal soil temperature: above 45°F

Oats in the garden or landscape? Why not?

Long, long ago, when people were first growing cereal grains in the Fertile Crescent, there was a weed on the side of the fields. These weeds may have benefited from the irrigation and fertilizers used on the primary crop, or they may have cross-pollinated with the crop—I don't know. But that pesky weed turned out to be oats, of oatmeal cookie fame.

Oats and wheat

Oats are members of the grain plant family (Poaceae). Like other cereal grains, the seeds we use to make oatmeal are actually a fruit, called a caryopsis. Unlike other grains, oats contain a legume-like protein, and eating oats regularly can help reduce cholesterol levels. Along with alfalfa, wheat, ryegrass, clover, and timothy, oat hay is grown as animal fodder. Even today, oats (*Avena sativa*) are grown more as livestock fodder than for human consumption. (My chickens LOVE oat seed heads and leaves.) But, there are plenty of other reasons to grow this versatile weed-come-cereal grain.

OATS IN THE LANDSCAPE

Oats make an attractive stand of tall stalks and waving seed heads. As an annual, oats can reseed an area. Unlike many other grain crops, oats are not as attractive to most small songbirds. Larger birds, such as mourning doves, may flock to your oat stands. I think that their pretty coo-ing often makes up for any lost grain. But why would you want to add oats to your landscape or garden? There are several good reasons.

> **Wild Oats**
> The oats you see growing along roadsides are prob-ably wild oats (*Avena fatua*). Many farmers don't like wild oats because of cross-pollination.

First, oat root systems are strong and tend to grow two to three feet deep, making them a good choice for counteracting compacted soil, improving soil structure, and preventing erosion. Research has also shown that oats help retain nitrogen in the soil. Oats make an excellent catch crop, protecting soil health between other crops and they can be grown as a green manure. Oats also act as a weed control when grown with other crops.

HOW TO GROW OATS

You can plant oats as soon as temperatures are consistently above 40°F. Seeds can be broadcast over an area and raked in or, in the case of severely compacted soil, a drill can be used to create holes ½"-1" deep. How much seed was a little tricky to calculate for the home garden. All I could find was information for farmers, which told me 2.75 to 3.25 bushels per acre. Huh. I own a bush-el basket but I have never had a bushel basket full of seeds. Ever. After extensive research, I have come to the conclusion that you should simply follow the directions on the seed packet.

Oats grow quickly. Also, oat plants are triggered to flower as nights get shorter, in a behavior called photoperiodism, so seeds become available rather quickly. Oats are heavy feeders, so side dressing young plants will give them the nutritional boost they need to thrive.

Oats are more tolerant of cooler temperatures and rain than other cereal grains, which makes them a good late winter and early spring crop, in regions with hot summers. Most oat plants will go dormant in the high heat of summer. The stems and stalks left behind by your oats are called stover. Stover can be added to the compost pile, used to create barriers, or left in place for climbing beans to use as a trellis.

PESTS AND DISEASES OF OATS

Bacterial blights can affect oats, along with stem and bulb nematodes, and barley root knot nematodes, dried fruit beetles, and crane fly larvae. Fungal diseases, such as leaf blotch, stem rust, and crown rust are common, but not serious threats for the home garden. Crop rotation can reduce these problems. In traditional crop rotation, a three-field system would grow legumes in one field, a grain, such as oats, in a second field, and allow the third field to rest. You can use a similar plan, whether you grow in rows, raised beds, or containers. This practice interrupts the disease triangle of many common plant pathogens.

HARVESTING OATS

You may never harvest your oats, but, then again, you may. If you harvest these tiny fruits while they are still green, you can eat them fresh from the stalk (they don't taste like much), or you can wait until they ripen and get hard. When I say hard, I mean it. These little suckers are like tiny oval rocks. Guess what? That's why oats are rolled. Rolling oats means they are crushed between two giant heavy rollers, to flatten them and make the fruit accessible. Honestly, unless you are growing acres of oats, it probably isn't worth trying to make your own oatmeal (even though you can).

Grain and Grass Families

Their attractive, soil improving, chicken feeding properties are reasons enough for adding these members of the cereal grain family to your annual crop rotation, garden, or landscape.

Chapter Ten

HERBS AND EDIBLE FLOWERS

If you grow nothing else, grow herbs.

Herbs require minimal care and they repay your efforts in spades. Not only do they add flavor to food, but many herbs can be used to make excellent teas, fragrant sachets, insect repellants, and for home decor.

Like other plants, herbs can be annual or perennial. Perennial plants keep coming back, while annuals tend to die off each year and must be replaced. Most herbs require a lot of sunlight. If you are growing indoors in containers, you may need to supplement light. Herbs are well-suited to container gardening, or they can be put in the ground. The same volatile oils that make herbs smell or taste so delicious (to us) often prevent pest problems.

Sage

Even though the vast majority of herbs are members of the mint family, we will be looking at them in alphabetical order, for convenience sake. For the most part, these plants are not picky, as long as they get enough sunlight.

Anise

Zones 4—9
Sun exposure: full sun, partial sun
Ideal soil temperature: above 60°F

Anise bush in a field (Fastily) CC BY-SA 3.0

There's no mistaking the licorice flavor of anise. Anise has been used as a digestive aid, culinary spice, and as the basis for liquor for more than 2,000 years. Anise is used to flavor black jelly beans and root beer. It is also used to make ouzo, sambuca, and absinthe. One trait common to each of those liquors is that they are clear, until water is added. Then they become cloudy. I don't know why.

Anise has also been incorporated into metal bearings used on trains as a warning of overheating, and as a fishing lure attractant. How's that for versatility?

ANISE OR STAR ANISE?

Before we begin, let me clarify that we are talking about anise (*Pimpinella anisum L. – anise burnet saxifrage*), and not star anise (*Illicium verum*). Anise and star anise are not related. They do, however, both contain anethole, an oil that gives them their strong flavors. In each case, people often mistake the fruits from these plants for seeds. Tiny anise and star anise fruits are schizocarps. Star anise has a distinctive star-shaped fruit, while anise fruit is oblong.

Anise plants are herbaceous annuals that start out as bright green mounds. Then, feathery leaves shoot skyward, much like fennel. Being umbellifers, these cousins to carrots, dill, and celery have flowers that are large, flat clusters of tiny flowers that pollinators and other beneficial insects love. Plants can reach 3' in height.

Anise fruits

Star anise (Sanjay Acharya) CC BY-SA 4.0

How to grow anise

Being native to the eastern Mediterranean and Southwest Asia, anise is a warm weather, full sun crop. It prefers loose soil with good drainage, and a soil pH of 6.0 to 6.7. These plants have a taproot, so they do not transplant well. They can be grown in containers, as long as the pot is at least 8" deep and wide. Seeds should be planted ¼" deep, at least two weeks after the last frost date. Thin plants to 12" apart. (Unless you really like anise, your family will probably only need one plant.) Regular irrigation is important, but an occasional top dressing is the only feeding these plants need.

Anise pests and diseases

Larva of the wormwood pug, a small brown moth, will feed on anise foliage, but that's about it. The oils that give anise its delicious flavor are the same components that most pests find offensive. Anise plants also have no major disease issues.

HARVESTING ANISE

Anise leaves can be harvested as needed. Seed heads should be snipped while green and hung upside down in a warm, dark, dry location until they are completely dry.

Basil

Zones 3—10
Sun exposure: full sun, partial sun
Ideal soil temperature: above 70°F

Basil is one of the most rewarding culinary herbs to grow. This member of the mint family isn't nearly as rugged as many of its cousins, but you'll be glad you planted basil when it's dinnertime!

Basil seeds are used in Thai cooking and the leaves are used to make many amazing dishes. Aromatic basil leaves, julienned with mozzarella and fresh tomatoes, make a delightful summer Caprese salad, and what would pesto be without basil?!!? You

Basil

may be surprised to learn that sweet basil seeds, also known as sabra, can be added to beverages, sherbets, and milkshakes.

BASIL VARIETIES

There are many varieties of basil. Sweet basil (*Ocimum basilicum*) is the most common, but you can also find these varieties:

- Purple or opal basils (*O. basilicum purpurea*) are big favorites of bees and it looks and tastes lovely in salads.

- Lemon or lime basil (*O. basilicum citriodorum*) pairs nicely with fish.
- Licorice-flavored Thai basil (*O. basilicum* 'Siam Queen') has serrated leaf edges.
- Cinnamon basil (*O. basilicum* 'Cinnamon') has a distinctly cinnamon flavor.
- Greek or globe basil (*O. basilicum* 'Spicy Globe') has very tiny leaves and makes a lovely little topiary tree.

HOW TO GROW BASIL

As a tender annual, temperatures must be at least 70°F for basil to grow. Start too soon and you'll just waste seeds. Basil loves hot weather, but may benefit from a little afternoon shade if your summers are really scorching. I have planted basil slightly east of a small apricot tree, in patio containers, and in a partially shaded tower. Our summers get very hot and basil performs well in each of these locations. If you are growing basil in a container, be sure to use one that is large enough to hang onto some moisture.

Start seeds indoors, six to eight weeks before warmer temperatures are expected to get a big head start on the growing season. You can also use succession planting to increase yield. Basil can be started from cuttings. Simply pinch off a stem and place it in a glass of water. This is an excellent way to make many plants out of a single plant!

Thai basil seedlings

Basil seeds should be planted ¼" deep. The soil should be kept moist, but not soggy. In five to seven days, seeds should germinate. It is easy to recognize basil seed leaves because they look like two capital D's, facing away from each other. Seedlings need 12"-18" between plants to reach full size and for good air flow. A 2"-3" layer of mulch placed around young plants will help retain moisture and reduce weeds.

Basil needs six to eight hours of sunlight a day and it prefers well-drained soil with a pH of 6.0 to 7.5. Depending on rainfall and temperatures, basil will need to be watered deeply every seven to ten days. Since basil is food, think twice about using any chemical pesticides.

By the way, ignore basil plants for sale in the grocery store. They look lush and full, but what they really are is overcrowded and root bound. If you try to separate the plants, it will damage the roots too much. Leave them the way they are and they will simply choke themselves to death. Even if they survive, air flow problems can lead to fungal disease. Buy a pack of seeds and share it with friends.

BASIL PESTS AND DISEASES

Being a tender annual, basil plants are susceptible to all the garden variety pests and diseases. Planting nasturtiums nearby is said to entice aphids away from basil. Apparently, aphids prefer nasturtiums, so you get more basil. Whether it works or not, the nasturtiums are lovely and tasty all on their own. Row covers can be used to protect basil from many of these pests.

Ensuring good air flow between plants and proper watering make a big difference in basil health. Too much water can cause root rot diseases. Allow plants to dry out between waterings. Stem rot, Fusarium wilt, bacterial leafspot, gray mold, and damping off disease can also infect basil. A relatively new disease, basil downy mildew, has been identified. Be on the lookout for purple or gray spore growth on the underside of leaves. Infected plants must be destroyed.

HARVESTING BASIL

Snip fresh leaves any time they are needed in the kitchen. If you need more than a few leaves, or if the plant is getting leggy, cut just above a pair of leaves to stimulate new branching.

Pinch basil above where a pair of leaves emerge

Pinching basil back stimulates bushier growth

Regular trimming will keep the plant productive. The basic rule of thumb is to pinch a stem just above a pair of leaves as soon as a stem has five or six leaves on it. If basil is allowed to go to flower and seed, the leaves may begin to taste slightly bitter. (The bees will love it, though!) Basil flowers are edible and they look lovely in a salad or candied and used to decorate baked goods.

STORING BASIL

Basil leaves can be dried or frozen. To dry basil, cut the stems and rinse off any dust, insects, or microorganisms. Then pat dry and hang the basil stems upside down until the leaves have dried out completely, just as you would with lavender and other herbs. Once the leaves are dry, they can be removed from the stems by rolling them between your hands over a sheet of wax paper. Store in a dark, dry location. (I use spice jars that used to hold something else and that have been thoroughly washed and dried.)

To freeze fresh basil leaves, rinse them off, pat dry and remove from the stem. Leaves can be frozen whole (not recommended) or pureed and then frozen in ice cube trays for easy portion control. My very favorite use for basil is pesto, which can transform everyday pasta, chicken, or pork into something truly delicious!

If you have a large container, you can create a lovely miniature herb garden by planting parsley, chives, oregano, and basil together. The spiky chives, trailing oregano, and bushy parsley and basil make a lovely arrangement that tastes even better than it looks!

Basil makes an excellent companion plant to asparagus, carrots, sweet peppers, and tomatoes. Apparently, asparagus beetles, carrot flies, and tomato hornworms don't share our love of basil. While there is no scientific proof, many gardeners believe flies, mosquitoes, and whiteflies are also repelled by basil. Whether it works or not, I can't plant enough of this delicious herb!

Caraway

Zones 4—10
Sun exposure: full sun, partial sun, partial shade
Ideal soil temperature: above 70°F

Caraway seeds taste similar to anise or licorice and caraway plants are easy to grow.

Frequently used in rye bread, goulash, Havarti cheese, and Irish soda bread, this cousin to carrots and dill has lovely umbrella-shaped flowers that attract many ben-

Caraway fruits

eficial insects, such as hoverflies and predatory wasps.

The caraway seed is actually a type of dried fruit, called an achene. Feathery leaves, strong stems, and small pink or white flowers make caraway (*Carum carvi*) both attractive and useful. Plants can reach 24"-30" in height, though they only reach 8" or so their first year.

As a member of the carrot family, caraway plants can look similar to poison hemlock, so make sure you know how to tell them apart.

How caraway grows

Caraway, like parsley and many other umbellifers, is a biennial plant. This means it uses its first year to develop a root system and become established. In its second year, flower production takes place and seeds are produced. Some varieties are grown as annuals, and one type of caraway is a perennial plant.

Caraway plants (Jerzy Opiola) CC BY-SA 4.0

Caraway plants prefer warm, sunny locations, good drainage, and nutrient-rich soil. Commonly grown in Europe and Western Asia, caraway plants prefer cool temperate zones and a soil pH of 6.5 to 7.0. While they prefer full sun, caraway plants can handle partial shade.

How to grow caraway

Caraway seeds should be planted ¼"-½" deep in spring or fall, directly in the soil. As is common with plants that feature a taproot, caraway does not transplant well. Plants should be thinned so they are 8"-12" apart. Caraway is a slow grower, so you may want to intercrop with something faster to reduce weeds and to act as a nurse crop for your caraway. Water plants well during their first year, but avoid getting the leaves wet. Soaker hoses are an excellent tool for irrigating caraway.

If grown as a biennial, cut plants back in the fall. They will regrow, bigger than ever, in spring. If grown as an annual, be sure to start a new crop in succession for a continuous harvest.

While caraway has very few pest or disease problems, it is a good idea to leave some distance between them and other members of the carrot family.

HARVESTING CARAWAY

Since all parts of the caraway plant are edible, you can use young leaves and stems in salads, soups, and stews. When seeds have turned brown, remove the flower head and hang it upside-down in a pillowcase until dry. Then you can simply rub the head between your hands to dislodge the caraway achenes. After seeds are produced and harvested, you can dig up the root and treat it the same way you would any other root vegetable.

Try adding some caraway to your foodscape this fall!

Chamomile

Zones 4—9
Sun exposure: full sun, partial sun, partial shade
Ideal soil temperature: above 60°F

The dainty white and yellow flowers of German chamomile have been grown and enjoyed for a really long time. According to the National Institutes of Health, "Chamomile is one of the oldest, most widely used and well documented medicinal plants in the world and has been recommended for a variety of healing applications." Research has shown chamomile's anti-inflammatory and soothing properties to be moderately to significantly effective against many digestive, respiratory, and sleep-related problems.

Chamomile makes a soothing tea or a nice ground cover,

but you can't have both. Not from the same plant, anyway.

There are many daisy-like plants we call chamomile, but only two true varieties: Roman and German. If you want chamomile tea, you need German chamomile. If you want a pretty groundcover, go Roman. These two plants have other differences, too.

Roman chamomile (*Anthemis nobilis*) goes by many other names. You may have heard it called English, Russian, or garden chamomile. This plant is a low-growing perennial. It makes a nice lawn replacement and is commonly grown from cuttings or by dividing.

Roman chamomile (H. Zell) CC BY-SA 3.0

German chamomile (*Matricaria recutita*), also known as "Water of Youth" or wild chamomile, is an annual that can grow up to two feet tall and wide. These plants are usually started from seeds.

These seeds require light to germinate, so they should not be covered with soil. They take one to two weeks to germinate. German plants should be cut back three to five inches every so often to prevent excessive size and legginess. Trimming will also promote flower production. If growing for tea, flowers should be removed on the first day they bloom for the

German chamomile (kallerna)
CC BY-SA 3.0

best flavor. Since many beetles enjoy these flowers as much as we do, it's a good idea to wash plants off before using them for tea.

You can dry chamomile flowers in an old pillowcase, the same way you can preserve lavender. Dried flowers should be stored in a dark, airtight container.

Just when you had every reason to add these flowers to your garden, you need to know they are not for everyone. All the chemicals that make it so helpful can also make it harmful. People who are sensitive to ragweed or chrysanthemums may be allergic to chamomile. Also, it should be avoided by pregnant and nursing women.

CHAMOMILE AND INSECTS

Chamomile is a sturdy, drought tolerant plant, but it can still become susceptible to common pests and diseases, especially if weakened by lack of water or other stresses. Many beneficial insects are attracted to these sunny little flowers. Hoverflies, parasitic wasps, tachinid flies, bees, and other pollinators will be more common in your garden if chamomile is part of the landscape.

So, put the kettle on and have yourself a piping hot cup of soothing chamomile tea.

Cilantro

Zones 2—11
Sun exposure: full sun, partial sun
Ideal soil temperature: above 65°F

What would salsa or stir-fry be without cilantro?

Cilantro (*Coriandrum sativum*), also known as coriander or Chinese parsley, is an herb frequently used in Mexican and Chinese cooking. It is also found in Indian, Russian, and many other regional dishes. Cilantro has been popular for so long that a pint of cilantro seeds was found in King Tut's tomb!

Some people call the leaves cilantro and the seeds coriander, but not always. Whatever you call it, all parts of the plant are edible and it self-seeds readily. Its deep taproot also helps break up compacted, clay soil and the umbel-shaped flowers (think umbrellas) are a big favorite of beneficial pollinators and parasitic wasps.

Cilantro prefers moist, well-drained soil with a pH of 6.2 to 6.8. In temperate areas, cilantro may grow year-round, as it can tolerate a light frost. In areas with lots of scorching hot sun, cilantro can be part of your shade gardening plan. If cooler weather is the norm, cilantro can be planted out in the open. If plants receive too

Cilantro

much sun and heat, they will bolt (go to seed). Since the seeds are also edible, this isn't necessarily a bad thing, but it will really slow down leaf production. At first, it is a good idea to start new plants every three to four weeks. After a while, the plants will develop an ongoing cycle. Plant seeds ¼" deep and 6"-8" apart. Keep the soil moist until plants are 2" tall and then water as needed, depending on weather, soil, and growth. Mature plants tend to be about 20" tall.

Young cilantro plants can be pinched back for bushier growth and more foliage, or they can be allowed to run wild. It's your call. Personally, I prefer the running wild version. I believe that this allows the survival of the fittest to create a forever patch of cilantro in my yard with minimal effort on my part.

While coriander seeds can be stored for a good long while, cilantro leaves do not dry well. Unlike many other herbs, which get a stronger flavor when dried, cilantro leaves tend to lose most of their flavor. To make the most of your cilantro crop, trying canning some salsa or cilantro pesto.

CILANTRO PESTS AND DISEASES

Cilantro plants may have trouble with common garden pests. These insect pests can often be managed with insecticidal soap. If you see wilt, leaf spot, or mildew, make a point of removing diseased plants and keeping the area clean for a season or two, to dry things out.

Many beneficial insects, both pollinators and predators, are attracted to cilantro's umbel-shaped flowers. The USDA Extension reports that California lettuce growers have discovered that planting cilantro, along with Alyssum plants, in their fields attracts predatory hoverflies, whose larvae can eat 150 aphids a day!

CILANTRO TRIVIA

Something weird about cilantro—not everyone tastes it the same way. To some people, cilantro is the perfect addition to guacamole, Indian dal, and salsa. To others, cilantro tastes soapy or rotten. Weird, right? Taste studies have found that identical twins agreed on the flavor of cilantro 80% of the time, while fraternal twins only agreed 50%.

Popular culture claims that eating cilantro can help remove heavy metals from your system, but research does not back that up. Cilantro may have the ability to reduce gastric ulcers and stabilize blood sugar, but more research is needed. Until scientists sort all that out, go out and put some coriander seeds in your yard and enjoy the flavor!

Cumin

Zones 10—12
Sun exposure: full sun
Ideal soil temperature: above 50°F

Cumin's pungent aroma has made it a popular spice since ancient times.

Kept on Egyptian tables the way we use salt and pepper, cumin is said to provide many different health benefits, though there is zero scientific proof for any of those claims. There are still plenty of other good reasons for growing your own cumin.

Cumin

Cumin's umbrella-shaped flowers make it easy to identify as a member of the carrot family. Other common garden umbellifers, or Apiaceae, include carrots, celery, dill, parsnips, and fennel. Like other umbellifers, cumin flowers attract many beneficial insects, such as hoverflies and pollinators.

Native to the Middle East, cumin (*Cuminum cyminum*) grows best in hot, dry regions and is very drought tolerant. It takes three to four months of hot weather to reach maturity. If temperatures drop, leaves will turn purple. Cumin is very susceptible to frost damage.

THE CUMIN PLANT

Cumin seeds look a lot like caraway seeds, being oblong with ridges. Those ridges are oil glands. Cumin plants grow 12"-20" tall, with attractive, feathery leaves. Cumin seeds are contained in dried fruits called achenes.

HOW TO GROW CUMIN

If you have the heat, you can grow cumin. Seeds should be planted ¼" deep and spaced 8" apart. These plants are very delicate when they first germinate and do not perform well in heavy clay soil. They prefer loose, sandy soil with good drainage, which makes them an excellent choice for raised beds. The ideal pH is 6.8 to 8.3.

CUMIN PESTS AND DISEASES

Cigarette beetles, drugstore beetles, mites, root knot nematodes, and tobacco caterpillars may cause problems for cumin. Fusarium wilt may also strike your cumin plants, along with the usual plant diseases.

Cumin plants

Cumin seeds are frequently included in birdseed mixes, so this plant has spread globally. Once established, this annual plant readily self-seeds an area.

Dill

Zones 2—11
Sun exposure: full sun
Ideal soil temperature: above 65°F

Dill's delicate fronds and distinct aroma make it a useful addition to your landscape.

Dill (*Anethum graveolens*) is an herb that is related to celery and is known for elevating pickled cucumbers, asparagus, garlic, and green beans to new heights. Did you know that dill oil, extracted from seeds, stems, and leaves, is used to make soap?

HOW DILL GROWS

Dill can reach a height of two to four feet, making it only slightly smaller than fennel, which has a similar feathery growth. Dill's leaves are wider and firmer than fennel's. Flowers are white or yellow umbels that attract beneficial insects. Dill seeds look like tiny brownish-gray orange slices. Once dill begins producing seeds, leaf production is over and the plant will soon die. Worry not, dear gardeners! Dill reseeds itself so easily that you are nearly assured of a new crop from seeds that fall to the ground. To collect seeds for kitchen use or future crops, remove seed heads and hang them upside down over a bowl or in a pillow case. Seeds will fall when they are mature and the flower head can be added to the compost pile to feed next year's generation!

Dill seeds and fronds

HOW TO GROW DILL

Dill is a biennial that is normally grown as an annual. Dill does not transplant well, so site selection is your first step. Dill prefers lots of sun, though partial shade can be tolerated. Shadier sites will result in less bushy plants. You can easily grow dill in a container that is at least 12" deep. This will make room for dill's taproot. ("Fernleaf" is a dwarf variety best suited for containers.) Seeds should be planted ¼" to ½" deep and the soil kept moist until seedlings emerge. Seedlings should be thinned to 12" apart. Once plants are established, the soil should be allowed to dry out between waterings. Side dressing plants with aged compost during the growing season will provide important nutrients. (Side dressing simply means dumping an amendment around a plant and watering it.)

DILL PESTS AND DISEASES

Dill has very few pests, thanks to the volatile oils that give it its flavor. Tomato hornworms and parsley caterpillars may be seen and can be handpicked. *Bacillus thuringiensis* (*Bt*) or insecticidal soap can be used to treat severe infestations. Dill is relatively disease-free.

HARVESTING DILL

Many dishes are enhanced by dill leaves, simply snip off what you need. You can also dry dill leaves for later use by placing cut leaves between cloth napkins or paper towels, laid on top of nonmetallic screens and storing in an airtight container. Dill leaves can also be frozen. You can keep harvested leaves fresh by wrapping them in a damp paper towel and refrigerating them for up to a week in a sealable container.

Growing dill for yourself is easy and rewarding. Give it a try.

Edible Flowers

Bright, cheery colors, delicate textures, and you can eat them!

Edible flowers have been part of the human diet since, well, since there have been people!

Did you know that carnation petals have been used as one of the ingredients in the French liqueur, Chartreuse,

Carnations (Darkone) CC BY-SA 1.0

since the 17th century?

Let me first share a story from my early trials with edible flowers. My dear sister decided to marry an Australian sailor and asked me to make her wedding cake. It was a lovely tiered white cake with yellow borders. I decided to add some stunning yellow flowers I saw outside. My sister's reaction of horror was not what I expected—until she explained that the Angel's Trumpet flowers I used were extremely poisonous. Needless to say, the flowers and the frosting came off. So...

WHEN IN DOUBT, DON'T

Before you go popping random blossoms in your mouth, you need to know that some flowers can make you sick, and others can kill you. If you are even remotely unsure about a plant, do not eat it. Sometimes there is a fine line between edible and inedible. For example, regular garden variety pea flowers and shoots are edible and delicious, while fragrant sweet peas (*Lathyrus odoratus*) are poisonous. Some varieties of daylilies are edible and others are not. The same is true for phlox and geraniums. Make sure you know what you have before tasting it.

Also, chemical sprays and car fume residue can be toxic, too. Chemical pesticides, herbicides, and insecticides should not be used on flowers that will be eaten. Never eat flowers from commercially grown plants, as there is no way to know for sure what has been applied to or used in growing these plants. Now that I have reminded you to be careful, let's see just how many flowers in your garden are edible.

EDIBLE HERBS

All herb flowers are edible. Basil, chives, cilantro, garlic, dill, lavender, marjoram, mint, oregano, rosemary, sage, savory, and thyme flowers can all be used to add an extra depth and a touch of color to many different dishes. You can also eat the flowers of anise hyssop, angelica, bee balm, burnet, chervil, fennel, ginger, and lemon verbena.

EDIBLE FLOWERS

There are a surprising number of edible flowers. All members of the viola family, which includes Johnny-jump-ups and pansies, and the dianthus family, of carnation fame, are edible. Here are other edible flowers, with just a little description of what to expect:

- Begonia, tuberous (*Begonia x tuberosa*) - citrusy leaves, stems, and flowers
- Begonia, waxy (*Begonia cucullata*) - slightly bitter leaves and flowers
- Borage (*Borago officinalis*) - cucumber flavor
- Calendula (*Calendula officinalis*) - spicy or peppery petals; Poor Man's Saffron
- Carnations (*Dianthus caryophyllus*) - sweet, nutmeg-flavored petals
- Chicory (*Centaurea cyanus*; Bachelor's buttons) - sweet, clove-flavored blooms
- Chrysanthemums (*Chrysanthemum coronarium*) - tangy, peppery petals; tangy new leaves
- Clover (*Trifolium sp.*) - brightly colored new flowers are sweet, licorice-flavored
- Crocus, autumn (*Crocus sativus*) - stigmas are saffron; unsure about the edibility of petals, so don't
- Dandelion (*Taraxacum officinalis*) - young flowers taste like honey; used to make wine
- Day lily (*Hemerocallis sp.*; other varieties not edible) - petals taste like sweet lettuce; flowers can be stuffed; new shoots reminiscent of asparagus
- Fuchsia (*Fuchsia x hybrida*) - brilliant, acidic blooms; berries are also edible
- Gladiolus - remove anthers; flowers of nondescript flavor good for stuffing

- Hibiscus (*Hibiscus rosa-sinensis*) - dried flowers for tea; cranberry-favored flower petals
- Honeysuckle (*Lonicera japonica*) - honey-flavored flowers; berries are highly poisonous
- Impatiens (*Impatiens wallerana*) - sweet flowers
- Johnny-jump-ups (*Viola tricolor*) - mild wintergreen flavor
- Linden (*Tilla spp.*) - honey-flavored flowers; heavy consumption can cause heart problems
- Marigold (*Tagetes tenuifolia*) - another Poor Man's Saffron; citrusy
- Nasturtium (*Tropaeolum majus*) - peppery flowers
- Pansy (*Viola x wittrockiana*) - petals are mildly sweet; entire flowers taste like wintergreen
- Peony (*Paeonia lactiflora*) - petals can be parboiled or used fresh; mildly sweet
- Phlox, perennial (*Phlox paniculata*; NOT annual phlox) - spicy petals
- Primrose (*Primula vulgaris*; Cowslip) - mild flavor; used in salads and to make wine
- Roses - all rose flowers are edible; flavor depends on variety
- Scented geraniums (*Pelargonium sp.*; NOT Citronelle variety) - lemony, spicy, or citrusy
- Sorrel (*Rumex acetosa*) - lemony flowers
- Violets (*Violata odorata*) sweet, perfumed flavor

EDIBLE FRUIT TREE FLOWERS

The flowers of many fruit and nut trees are also edible. Apple, apricot, peach, pear, and plum blossoms can be used to add color and a delicate complexity to many dishes. When using these flowers, be sure to only use the petals, and not the stamens or pistils. Because they contain low levels of cyanide, apple blossoms should be eaten in moderation. Citrus blossoms are very pungent and should be used sparingly. Leftovers can be added to floral arrangements, so that you can still enjoy the aroma.

You probably already eat several vegetable flowers: artichoke and broccoli for example. While eating the flowers of your vegetable plants reduces your crop yield, it can be a nice way to try something new. There are several different vegetable plants with edible flowers:

- Arugula (*Eruca vesicaria*; Garden Rocket) - mild piquant flavor
- Mustard (*Brassica sp.*) - flowers, young leaves can be eaten; some people are allergic
- Okra (*Abelmoschus esculentus*) - cranberry-citrus flavor
- Pea blossoms and shoots (*Pisum sp.*; NOT ornamental sweet peas) - taste like peas!
- Radish (*Raphanus sativus*) - radish flavored!
- Scarlet runner beans (*Phaseolus vulgaris*) - tasty, crisp pods add brilliant color
- Squash blossoms - use male blossoms and remove the stamens; excellent for stuffing

WAYS TO USE EDIBLE FLOWERS

While it is easy to sprinkle petals into a salad for a splash of color and flavor, there are many other ways to incorporate edible flowers into your diet:

- Petals can be stirred into butter, for a decorative spread.
- Small flowers can be painted with egg white and sprinkled with sugar, to decorate cakes and other desserts (these candied flowers can also be frozen for later use).
- Add to whipped cream or ice cream.
- Petals look lovely in fruit salads.

- Petals can be added to soups, stews, or risotto.
- Steep petals into tea, wine, or simple syrup.
- Small flowers can be frozen into ice cubes or used to decorate ice cream or sorbet.
- Whole flowers can be used to hold sweet or savory stuffings or mousse.

PREPARING EDIBLE FLOWERS

Edible flowers should be picked just before using and thoroughly rinsed off. This will help remove dust, frass, microorganisms, and any surface chemicals that may have blown in or been applied. Taste the flowers before using them, so that you know what flavor you are adding to your food.

Remove the pistils and stamens from most flowers. The only exceptions are violas and Johnny-jump-ups. In these cases, the other parts add good flavor. If you detect some bitterness in any edible flower, you may need to remove the white base of the petals. This is commonly needed when working with carnations, chrysanthemums, day lilies, and roses. How many edible flowers do you have in your garden?

Ginger

Zones 9—12
Sun exposure: full sun, partial sun
Ideal soil temperature: above 70°F

Ginger rhizome (Frank C. Müller) CC BY-SA 3.0

Ginger's sweet bite makes it an excellent addition to many favorite foods, and it can be candied for a special treat. This distant cousin to the banana tree and sibling of turmeric can be grown at home!

THE GINGER PLANT

Ginger was one of the first spices to be exported from the Orient and it is a fascinating plant. As a plant family in its own right, ginger (*Zingiber officinale*) is cousin to turmeric and cardamom.

The ginger we eat is not actually a root. It is a rhizome. Rhizomes are modified, underground stems that put out lateral shoots and adventitious roots. Ginger plants do not have aboveground stems. Instead, they grow much like the grass in your lawn, with leaves rolled together at the base of the plant to form pseudostems, except that they can grow three to four feet tall! Equally tall floral stems emerge directly from the rhizome. Flower buds start out green and then turn white and pink before opening up into mature flowers. Mature flowers can be pale yellow, deep purple, or brilliant red, depending on the variety.

HOW TO GROW GINGER

Ginger needs loose, nutrient-rich soil, so it is best grown in containers. This makes it easy to bring indoors as temperatures drop in winter, as well. Most grocery store ginger "roots" are treated with chemicals that prevent them from sprouting, but not always. While I normally warn against planting grocery store foods, due to the potential risk of introducing a safe-to-us-but-bad-for-plants disease, your ginger will, most likely, be growing in a container, so it's not really an issue. Rinse off the ginger and place it in a container filled with potting soil, just under the soil line. Keep the soil moist but not soggy to encourage growth. Being from the tropical rainforest, your ginger plant will need lots of warmth, moisture, and protection from intense sunlight. (Under the canopy, jungles are actually pretty dark!)

HARVESTING GINGER

While you can harvest ginger rhizomes at any time, it is best for the plant's long-term health if you wait until the aboveground portion withers, similarly to garlic. The desired portion of the rhizome is cut off and the rest of the plant can be returned to its container. The cut-off portion is then scalded to prevent it from sprouting. The older ginger gets, the tougher and drier the rhizome becomes. Ginger is a perennial plant, which means it keeps on growing. It may look as though it dies in winter, but don't be fooled. Unless your region is too cold for ginger, it will come back year after year. Each little nub on a ginger rhizome is a potential new plant.

GINGER'S SECRET TREAT

Inside a ginger flower, as with other flowers, are ovules, or perisperm. Traditionally, these tiny eggs offer a sweet, fragrant addition as a condiment. Just be forewarned, these perisperm are sialogogues, which means they make you salivate. Did you know that ginger flowers are also edible?

Why buy ginger shipped from around the world when you can grow your own?

Ginger ovules (Wikipedia) CC BY-SA 3.0BY-SA 3.0

Lavender

Zones 5—9
Sun exposure: full sun
Ideal soil temperature: above 65°F

Lavender has been used to soothe upset stomach, irritated skin, and bad hair days for more than 2,500 years.

Like other plants in the mint family, the essential oils found in lavender have sedative, antiseptic, antimicrobial, and anti-inflammatory properties. The word "lavender" comes from the Latin verb which means "to wash" or "to bathe".

Lavender flowers are used in sachets, soaps, linen spritz, soup, and frosting. These edible flowers can be candied and used to decorate baked goods, or added to teas, chocolates, and cheeses. Some people swear by lavender as an insect repellent, rubbing the leaves on skin or clothing. I don't know if it works but I imagine it smells better than bug spray.

That being said, the U.S. National Institutes of Health (NIH) does not recommend lavender for women who are pregnant or breast-feeding, or to pre-adolescent boys, due to potential hormonal prob-lems. For some people, lav-

English lavender

ender can cause skin irritation. And some people just don't like it. For those who do, this easy-to-grow perennial can add color to your landscape. Lavender also provides pollen and nectar for many beneficial insects, especially honey bees.

HOW LAVENDER GROWS

Being from a rocky Mediterranean region, lavender prefers hot, dry weather and loose, coarse soil. The root system tends to be significantly larger than the above-ground portion of the plant. These plants can live for 50 years and, being a mint, they will spread using underground runners, or rhizomes.

LAVENDER VARIETIES

There are over 35 species of lavender, with more than 250 named varieties. Generally, they are categorized as either "hardy" or "tender." Hardy English (or Dutch) lavenders (*Lavandula angus-tifolia* or *L. intermedia*) are the most commonly grown. These varieties can tolerate colder temperatures. Tender lavenders include Spike, Wooly, Egyptian, Spanish, and my all-time favorite, French lavender. Tender lavenders generally cannot handle frost. If an especially cold period is expected, tender lavenders can be protected with a cloth cover or an umbrella. When shopping for lavender, be sure to look at the label for the botanical name, so you know what you are getting.

How to Grow Lavender

Lavender can be grown from cuttings, layering, or root division. Before installing a new lavender plant, however, you need to select a good site. Lavender does best where there is plenty of air flow, loose soil, and sunlight. Also, these plants will spread, so you may want to put them in large containers. Container planting is particularly useful in areas with cold winters, as you can move plants into protected areas for the winter.

Because air is so important to lavender, be sure to work the soil so that it is loose enough to dig into it with your hands before planting. Also, keep mature size in mind. Some varieties can reach 5' across. Lavender prefers slightly alkaline soil, with a pH between 6.7 and 7.3.

Lavender uses a lot of phosphorus, so bone meal is a good soil amendment if your soil test indicates a lack. (This is highly unlikely west of the Rocky Mountains.) Mindful weeding during the first two years of a lavender's life will go a long way toward ensuring a healthy, long-lived plant.

Lavender Pests and Diseases

Lavender grown in compacted soil with poor drainage will commonly end up with root rot, black mold, and other fungal diseases. Top dressing around lavender plants with aged compost or wood chips can improve drainage over time. You can also mulch around lavender with light-colored stones or oyster shells, which reflect more sunlight up into the plant. This will help reduce the chance of fungal disease. (If your soil already contains plenty of calcium, the stones are a better choice.)

You may occasionally see frothy areas on your lavender plants. These are caused by spittle bugs. If spittlebug infestations become troublesome, simply spray them off with a hose. They are not usually a significant problem.

LAVENDER WINTER CARE AND PRUNING

Pruning French lavender

Many people think their lavender has died over the winter, but this is rarely the case. In early autumn, simply cut back the green portion of the plant until only a couple of inches of green remain. This will help your lavender look nicer during the winter and it will stimulate lush growth in spring.

Some lavender plants fall open in the middle, in a behavior known as "sprawling." This happens when the weight of new growth is more than the plant can support. In the wild, this is a great behavior because it allows new shoots resting on the ground to generate new plants. In your landscape, however, it won't look as nice. You can prevent sprawling by pruning back 1/3 of the plant in spring, then pruning back 1/3 of the new growth that follows. This will create a nice shape and it will help the plant remain upright and full.

HARVESTING LAVENDER

Lavender should be harvested when the florets first open. Snip off flowers just above a leaf pair to encourage new growth. Long-stemmed hardy varieties can be bundled and hung upside-down in a dark place to dry. Shorter-stemmed tender varieties, which tend to lose their flowers as they dry, can be threaded and hung in a pillowcase, so none of the flowers are lost. I use my guest room closet for drying lavender. It stays dark and I like to think that the aroma is soothing to overnight guests.

Lavender is a lovely addition to stumperies, rock gardens, and sensory gardens.

Preparing French lavender for drying

Lemon Balm

Zones 4—9
Sun exposure: full sun, partial sun
Ideal soil temperature: above 65°F

Summer iced teas, winter colds, and many fruit and fish dishes are all made better with lemon balm. This easy-to-grow perennial herb is a member of the mint family, which means it is a rugged, tenacious, and fragrant addition to your foodscape.

USING LEMON BALM

Also known as cure-all, sweet balm, and honey plant, lemon balm adds a soothing lemon flavor to teas, tinctures, and steam. Traditionally, lemon balm has been used to treat digestive upset, anxiety, cuts, and insect bites. Scientific research has demonstrated that lemon balm does provide some significant benefits (besides making a great cup of tea). It has been shown to help treat indigestion, irritable bowel syndrome, thyroid disease, Alzheimer's disease, ADHD, and high blood pressure. Lemon balm reduces the pain, spread, duration, and recurrence of cold sores (*herpes labialis*), and it helps regulate weight gain. According to The National Institutes of Health, drinking lemon balm tea improves memory and cognitive performance.

How's that for a cup of tea?

Lemon balm (Nabokov) CC BY-SA 3.0

How to grow lemon balm

Once lemon balm is established, it will readily self-seed, so choose a site that has room for it. Individual plants can reach two feet in height and width. It can also spread vegetatively, where twig ends touch the ground and develop roots. Unlike many other members of the mint family, lemon balm does not spread using stolons (runners). Regular trimming will keep lemon balm plants healthy and attractive. You can also grow lemon balm in a container. My in-ground lemon balm has always stayed rather low-growing and has been pretty year-round (even after frost!) with just a little bit of trimming. Lemon balm normally dies back in winter above-ground, but comes back in spring.

Lemon balm seeds require light and warmth (70°F) to germinate, but the mature plants prefer some afternoon shade. Lemon balm prefers rich, moist soil with good drainage, and a pH of 6.0 to 7.0. Unlike other herbs, lemon balm loses much of its flavor when dried, so fresh is better. Some people use lemon balm in a pesto recipe.

Lemon balm attracts honey bees!

The scientific name of lemon balm, *Melissa officinalis*, is a reflection of how much it attracts honey bees. The word "Melissa" is Greek for bee. Small flowers, which can be white, pink, red, or yellow, appear each summer, packed with nectar. Many beekeepers throughout history have planted lemon balm near their hives. Whether you keep honey bees or not, attracting them to your garden is sure to improve pollination and production.

Add lemon balm to your garden, landscape, or balcony for healthier bees and a happier you!

Marigolds

Zones 3—9
Sun exposure: full sun, partial sun, partial shade
Ideal soil temperature: above 70°F

Pot marigolds are edible flowers that add color and attract honey bees to your garden.

American marigolds are not edible, but they have a place in your garden.

MANY FACES OF MARIGOLDS

Most marigolds sold in the U.S. are members of the *Tagetes* genus. Tagetes, or simply "marigolds", are native to the Americas.

Known for their pungent smell, Tagetes marigolds attract and kill destructive nematodes. They may, or may not, deter deer, rabbits, voles, and other garden pests.

Pot marigolds (Berdan) CC BY-SA 3.0

Pot marigolds (*Calendula officinalis*), or calendula, will not protect your plants from herbivores or nematodes, but they are very useful. You can tell them apart because pot marigolds have slightly hairy leaves that grow in a spiral around the stem. Tagetes marigolds have alternate leaves. In both cases, these sunny yellow and orange members of the sunflower family create lovely borders that bloom throughout most of the year.

POT MARIGOLDS

People have been growing and using pot marigolds as food and medicine for centuries. Pot marigolds are short-lived perennials, typically grown as annuals. They normally grow 18"-30" tall, with 2" flowers.

Pot marigold flower petals have a tangy, peppery flavor. Traditionally added to German soups and stews, pot marigold is used in herb butters and cheeses, to garnish deviled or scrambled eggs, in fish dishes, and with steamed vegetables. Pot marigold flower petals add color and tang to salads. Marigold flower petals are also known as Poor Man's Saffron. Added to the water used to cook rice, the rice is turned yellow. Farmers feed marigolds to chickens to make the yolks a deeper yellow. One variety of pot marigold, "Mexican Mint", has the flavor of tarragon. It is also known as Texas tarragon. Pot marigold petals can be used to make a delightful tea.

Pot marigolds also have medical merit. Research has shown that tinctures of pot marigold are used today to treat skin irritations and burns, speed healing, and to control bleeding. That being said, some people are allergic to pot marigolds, so be cautious.

In addition to looking lovely as a border plant, pot marigolds will attract honey bees and other pollinators to your garden. Unfortunately, they will also attract several types of moths, whose larvae feed on many popular garden plants.

HOW TO GROW MARIGOLDS

Both types of marigolds are easy to grow from seed and they tend to be drought tolerant. Start seeds in small pots, only lightly covered with soil. The curved seeds are actually dried fruits, called achenes. Keep the soil moist, but not soggy, until germination occurs. Then, move plants to a sunny location with good drainage. Your marigolds may need protection from scorching summer afternoon sun, and they can be grown in containers. Marigolds readily self-seed.

MARIGOLD PESTS AND DISEASES

While these plants are relatively trouble-free, they may become infected with Alternaria leaf spot, aster yellows, charcoal root rot, cottony soft rot, cucumber mosaic, gray mold, Pythium root rot, southern blight, spotted wilt (from the tomato spotted wilt virus), and stem rot.

Many of these diseases can be prevented by providing good drainage and air flow, so top dress soil regularly with organic matter and space plants with mature sizes in mind.

So, do you know if your marigolds are edible or not? This poem may help:

> Tagetes are death to nematodes
> Armies of alternate leaves, our native marigolds
> While edible Calendula
> Can ease a burn or rash, spiral leaved pot marigolds

Marjoram

Zones 9—10
Sun exposure: full sun
Ideal soil temperature: above 65°F

Marjoram is a soft-spoken cousin of oregano. This tender perennial herb grows well on sunny windowsills, in containers, or tucked away in a quiet corner of the garden. The Greeks and Romans used marjoram as a symbol of happiness, and it's sure to put a smile on your face.

Marjoram leaves have been a culinary herb for a long time. It is slightly milder and more piney than its more boisterous cousin, oregano. Marjoram is used to make herbes de Provence and za'atar. Marjoram also attracts many beneficial insects, including butterflies and bees, with its tiny white, pink, and lavender flowers.

AN HERB BY ANY OTHER NAME

Marjoram (*Origanum majorana*) has been around long enough to have several names to differentiate it from oregano (*O. vulgare*), including sweet marjoram and knotted marjoram. Oregano is also known as wild marjoram. Other varieties of marjoram include pot marjoram, also known as Cretan oregano (*O. onites*), hardy or French marjoram, which is a cross between marjoram and oregano, and showy marjoram, or showy oregano (*O. pulchellum*).

Marjoram growing in an herb tower

GROWING MARJORAM

Marjoram is best started in pots. Seeds should be covered only lightly with soil. Keep the soil moist until seeds germinate, being careful not to wash them into a corner of the pot when watering. Marjoram prefers full sunlight and loose soil. Plants should be spaced 18" apart.

As a member of the mint family, marjoram spreads underground using rhizomes. This makes them a good ground cover. It can also make them invasive. Marjoram has semi-woody stems that lend themselves nicely to cascading out of hanging pots, or as a low shrub. While technically an evergreen, cold temperatures will cause them to lose their leaves and frost will kill the above-ground portion. One way to protect your plants and keep the garden attractive in winter is to cut the plants back to ground level and cover with a winter blanket of mulch. Come spring, those delicious new leaves will come right back for another year. Marjoram prefers alkaline soil, never needs fertilizer when grown in the ground, and it rarely needs watering once established.

MARJORAM PESTS AND DISEASES

Whiteflies and spider mites are common problems for marjoram. Those tiny sap suckers leave behind speckled, bleached-out leaves that don't look at all appetizing. You can fight back with a spray bottle filled with insecticidal soap or diluted horticultural oil. (Dormant oil is too heavy.) All the usual pests may also try feasting on your marjoram plants.

Though rarely affected, fungal diseases such as dodder, damping off, downy mildews, powdery mildew, rust, and botrytis blight (gray mold), can occur on marjoram.

HOW TO HARVEST MARJORAM

Just as your marjoram plants begin to flower, snip off the upper portions and hang them in a shady spot to dry. Garages work well. Guest room closets work even better. I like to believe that the gentle aroma helps guests enjoy a restful sleep. That might just be me. Try adding marjoram to your garden or landscape today for many years of fragrant, delicious beauty.

Mint

Zones 5—9
Sun exposure: full sun
Ideal soil temperature: above 70°F

While walking across Spain in 2016, I came upon an albergue (something like a hostel) where a woman was using a rid-ing mower. There wasn't any grass, but the air was filled with a sweet, powerfully refreshing smell. Rather than caring for a lawn, this family had a yard filled with mint!

THE MINT CLAN

The mint clan (*Lamiaceae*) is huge, with more than 7,000 species. It has grown alongside humanity since prehistory.

The mint clan includes a surprising number of familiar herbs and other plants: basil, oregano, thyme, sage, bee balm, lemon balm, lavender, savory, and even your desktop coleus plant and the mighty teak tree are all members of the mint clan, along with lamb's ears, hyssop, self-heal, catmint, salvia, horehound, chia, skullcap, wild bergamot, and bugleweed. Mints, on their own,

Peppermint flowers (Sten Porse) CC BY-SA 3.0

are also rather diverse, with 13 to 24 species, depending on who you ask.

MINT PLANTS

Mints are perennial plants that spread using rhizomes. Some would call them invasive. In fact, some mints are so invasive that they are illegal to grow in some areas. (I grow mine in containers.) Mint leaves have glands that produce volatile oils that make them taste and smell so wonderful.

Most mint plants have square stems. Flowers grow on spikes, and are generally a lovely blue or purple. If you look closely, you will see that mint flowers have four stamens and five fused petals, with two petals pointing up and three petals pointing down. Mints can tolerate drought and poor soil, making them an excellent choice for difficult areas.

MINT VARIETIES

Peppermint (*Mentha x piperita*) is a hybrid between spearmint (*M. spicata*) and water mint (*M. aquatica*). Water mint thrives in acidic wetland areas of Europe, western Asia, and northern Africa, and is now naturalized around the world. Traditionally used in South Africa to treat depression, water mint has been found to contain naringenin, an MAO inhibitor. Spearmint, of chewing gum fame, got its name because of its pointed leaf tips. The volatile oils and menthol of spearmint have made it a popular addition to toothpaste and baked goods. It can also be used as an insecticide against moths. Spearmint prefers partial shade, but can be grown in full sun to nearly full shade. (Did I mention how rugged mint plants are?) Because peppermint is a hybrid, it does not produce seeds and can only be propagated vegetatively.

Peppermint leaves are dark green with reddish veins, and they contain more menthol than spearmint. There are several different peppermint cultivars to choose from. My favorite is "Chocolate Mint." If you chew a leaf, fresh from the plant, you'd swear you were eating a peppermint patty. And no calories!

Other peppermint cultivars include apple, banana, ginger, lemon, pineapple, orange, grapefruit, lavender, and lime mints. Needless to say, I am intrigued!

HOW TO GROW MINT

Mint is super easy-to-grow. It prefers partial shade but can grow in full sun, given easy access to moisture. Plants will grow 12"-36" tall, but they can be mowed regularly to keep them short. (And it smells amazing when you do!)

Mint is best grown from cuttings. Simply make sure there is a node somewhere on the stem, cover it with soil and keep it moist until new growth emerges. Because of its preference for moisture, peppermint and other mints will need to be irrigated regularly during summer, just let the soil dry out between waterings. As rugged as this plant is, once it becomes established, it is pretty difficult to kill. They may start slowly, but then there's no stopping them!

MINT PESTS AND DISEASES

The same volatile oils that give peppermint it's refreshing flavor also work to deter many other common pests, including mosquitoes! Mint root borers and webspinning spider mites are common mint pests, along with many common garden pests, but they are not normally much of a problem. Also, beneficial insects, such as the spider mite predator (*Neoseiulus fallacis*) will fight off more common pests without any effort on your part. All you have to do is avoid using broad spectrum pesticides. Some fungal diseases may occur, especially on older plants. Young mint plants grow slowly, so competition from weeds can be a problem.

HARVESTING AND USING MINT

You can snip off fresh stems or leaves anytime for immediate use. For drying or distillation, leaves and flowers can be harvested as soon as flowers begin to open. Peppermint's cooling properties have made it popular topical treatment for muscle pain, tension headaches, and itching. There is even research that demonstrates peppermint is able to provide some relief for irritable bowel syndrome. The aroma of peppermint has also been shown to improve memory and alertness! This is a truly useful plant that takes little care.

Too much peppermint can cause skin irritation or heartburn, but you'd have to use an awful lot of it. Also, some people are allergic to peppermint, but it's rare. If you take medications for heart conditions, high blood pressure, or to decrease stomach acid, you should use peppermint with caution. (Did you know that peppermint scent is used in plumbing and construction to help locate leaks? I didn't either.)

You can beat the summer heat with a spray bottle filled with water and just a few drops of peppermint oil. (It's easy to make your own peppermint oil. Simply fill a container with a light oil—I use extra virgin olive oil - and a bunch of peppermint leaves. Cover and allow it to sit for a few days. Strain out all the solids and that's it. You have your very own peppermint oil!)

If you ever eat too much, nothing helps ease discomfort faster than a cup of strong peppermint tea.

Mint juleps anyone?

Oregano

Zones 4—8
Sun exposure: full sun
Ideal soil temperature: above 65°F

Italian cuisine simply wouldn't be the same without the heady aroma and complex flavors of dried oregano leaves.

Oregano (*Origanum vulgare*) is a member of the mint family. Like other mints, oregano is a hardy perennial herb that has a place in any plot or container garden. Oregano is also known as wild marjoram, being a close cousin to sweet marjoram (*O. majorana*). The two herbs are interchangeable in cooking.

OREGANO VARIETIES

The variety of oregano grown determines its flavor. The most commonly sold variety, *Origanum vulgare*, is relatively bland, as are *O. onites* and *O. syriacum*. *Origanum v.* 'Kent Beauty' has a lovely trailing growth habit, making it perfect for hanging gardens and containers. For the best culinary flavor, try planting one of these oregano varieties: *O. v.* subsp. *hirtum* (most popular), *O. v.* 'Compactum' (excellent flavor), *O. v.* subsp. *glandulosum*, *O. v.* subsp. *virens*, *O. v.* subsp. *viridulum*, or *O. v.* subsp. *vulgare*.

HOW TO GROW OREGANO

Oregano prefers hot, dry, sunny locations and well-drained soil. It can be grown indoors or out and is best grown in containers. While you can grow oregano from seed, it is easier to propagate oregano using cuttings and root division. In cold areas, oregano is grown as an annual. Plants should be spaced 12"-18" apart in full sun. Water culinary varieties moderately. Ornamental varieties will need little or no water.

Greek oregano 'O. v. hirtum'

Oregano thrives in soil with a pH between 6.0 to 9.0. Fertilizer is generally not needed. Plants can grow from 8"-30" in height and width, creating a bushy shrub or a trailing growth, depending on the variety. Oregano flowers are bluish-purple or white.

Oregano benefits from regular pruning. While plants are still small, pinch off tops down to a leaf node to encourage a bushier growth and to prevent legginess. In winter, established plants can be cut back to ground level. Since oregano is food, think twice about using any chemical pesticides.

Oregano has been used in folk medicine for a very long time, but there is no scientific proof that it actually helps treat anything. Research is being conducted, however, on oregano's usefulness as an antibacterial and against liver cancer.

OREGANO PESTS AND DISEASES

Common pests and fungal diseases may cause problems on oregano. Good air flow and proper watering make a big difference in oregano health. Too much water can cause root disease. Allow plants to dry out between waterings.

HARVESTING AND STORING OREGANO

Leaves of oregano provide the best flavor if harvested before the plant goes to flower. Simply grab a handful of stems and cut below your hand, rinse off any dust or bugs, shake off the excess water, pat dry and gently wrap the bundle with a rubber band. Hang in a cool, dry, shaded area until completely dry. Unlike basil and rosemary, oregano really gets its flavor punch during the drying process, so fresh use isn't recommended. Once the leaves have dried out completely, they can be removed from the stems by rolling them between your hands over a sheet of wax paper. Store in a dark, dry location in an airtight container. Properly dried and stored oregano can last for a year.

Parsley

Zones 2—11
Sun exposure: full sun, partial sun, partial shade
Ideal soil temperature: above 65°F

Parsley —it's not just for restaurants any more.

As a kid, I always turned a suspicious eye toward that sprig of greenery on my plate. My mother urged me to try it, so I did.

Unfortunately, my young taste buds were not impressed. The mildly bitter bite of parsley was not my idea of delicious until many years later. Now that my taste buds are older and wiser, the refreshing tang of parsley adds a bright balance between flavors, cleanses the palette and spices things up. If that weren't reason enough to add parsley to a landscape, parsley packs one heck of a nutritional punch and, hey, it looks nice in the garden!

Parsley is a central Mediterranean plant. It makes an excellent shade garden or container plant. You can even grow it on your kitchen windowsill for easy access and nice color if you have strong enough sunlight.

Parsley is related to celeriac and celery, which explains its Latin name (*Petroselinum crispum*), which means "rock celery", but it's a heck of a lot easier to grow than celery. Parsley prefers well-drained soil that is kept moist, but my plants seem to grow under just about any conditions. In spite of my heavy clay soil, I have several parsley plants that thrive under roses, trees, and shrubs. Research has shown that parsley also repels asparagus beetles, making it a good companion to asparagus and tomato plants.

Parsley growing in the top of a rain barrel

Growing parsley does require some patience if you are starting from seed. Seeds should be planted ½" deep, 6" apart, and they can take four to six weeks to germinate. Germination rates are pretty high, so growing parsley from seed is the most cost-effective method. While you're at it, plant some extras and give young plants to family and friends as gifts.

In tropical areas, flat-leafed and curly parsley are grown as annual herbs. In more temperate regions, parsley is biennial. Biennial plants take two years to go from seed to seed, but some of my parsley plants keep on growing for another year or so. In addition to leaf parsley, there is a variety called Hamburg root parsley (*P. crispum radicosum*). Root parsley is grown for the taproot, which looks, cooks, and eats like a white carrot. (I may have to try that!)

Parsley plants allowed to go to seed provide habitat, pollen, and nectar to honey bees and many other beneficial insects, some swallowtail butterflies, and even goldfinches. You will probably also end up with many free, randomly placed parsley plants next year!

If flavor and looks weren't reason enough to grow your own parsley, the CDC says it's a nutritional gold mine. They ranked parsley at #8 as a food that reduces chronic diseases, such as cancer, coronary disease, and osteoporosis. To learn more, check out the U.S. Dept. of Agriculture's nutritional analysis website that allows you to look up the nutritional value of pretty much any food. Just 10 sprigs of parsley provides 22% of the RDA for vitamin C and 200% of vitamin K.

It's pretty. It's durable. It's good for you. And it tastes good. Where will you plant your parsley?

Rosemary

Zones 8—10
Sun exposure: full sun
Ideal soil temperature: above 75°F

When it comes to perennial herbs, rosemary is one of Italy's finest. Rosemary is a fragrant woody herb. Honey bees love it, too!

ROSEMARY'S NEW NAME

Until very recently, everyone thought rosemary was in the mint family. As such, it was given the Latin name *Rosmarinus officinalis*. Genetic research has shown us that rosemary is, in fact, a type of salvia. Rosemary's new Latin name is *Salvia rosmarinus*.

GROWING ROSEMARY

Rosemary thrives in hot, dry regions. It takes little to no care and very little water. You can grow it in containers, indoors or out. Or you can put it in the ground where it will grow into a shrub. This drought-tolerant perennial can be sheared into decorative shapes, used as a fragrant hedge, or allowed to fill an area naturally. Once rosemary puts down roots, you will get decades of delicious color and fragrance.

Its purple, pink, blue, or white flowers provide pollen and nectar for honeybees and other pollinators. Rosemary grows best in slightly alkaline pH (7.0-7.8), well-drained soil. The easiest way to grow rosemary is to take six inches of new growth from an established shrub and covering it with soil. Keep it moist and roots will appear.

Rosemary

According to intercropping research, the astringent characteristics of rosemary are able to repel cabbage loopers, carrot flies, Mexican bean beetles, slugs, and snails.

Very few pests or diseases bother rosemary. Spittlebugs may be found on rosemary but they are easily displaced with a spray of water from the hose.

Saffron Crocus

Zones 6—9
Sun exposure: full sun, partial sun
Ideal soil temperature: below 60°F

The golden threads of saffron currently sell for $130 an ounce. That works out to over $2000 a pound. And you can grow your own. For free.

While you can certainly find less expensive saffron, there's no denying that it is one of the world's most expensive spices. One of the reasons for these prices is that harvesting the threads is very labor intensive. Also, it takes approximately 4,000 flowers to create one ounce of saffron threads.

What is saffron?

First, a quick flower review: the male part is called the stamen, which is made up of the anther and filament. The stamen usually surrounds the female part, or the pistil. The pistil is usually in the center of a flower and is made up of the stigma, style, and ovary. Saffron threads are the dried stigmas of a specific crocus flower species.

Farmed primarily in Iran, saffron crocus plants prefer full, blistering sun in the summer, heavy rains in spring, and they can tolerate a surprising amount of cold in the winter. The two things they don't like are shade and

Saffron crocus with three yellow stamen and three dark orange saffron threads

soggy soil. Saffron crocus flowers are sterile, which means they cannot produce viable seeds. Instead, crocus plants reproduce by creating corms. Corms are similar to bulbs. Each corm lives for only one season, but each one can produce up to 10 cormlets. Cormlets are usually small and brown, covered with a fibrous coating called a "corm tunic."

How to grow saffron crocus

Plant your saffron crocus (*Crocus sativus*) bulbs in June in a sunny, well-drained location. Keep in mind that these plants will continue to propagate potentially for decades. Crocus corms should be planted three to six inches deep, depending on the variety, with the pointy end up. Once a bed of saffron crocuses is established, these cormlets will need to be dug up and divided every so often, to prevent overcrowding.

Important Crocus Note
Spring blooming crocus are not the same thing and should not be eaten. Other fall-blooming plants that are advertised as crocus are actually a type of lily (*Colchium*) which is very poisonous. If you see six threads, instead of three, do not eat it.

Saffron crocus pests and diseases

Squirrels. Of course, squirrels. Also, rats, moles, birds, nematodes, and other bulb eaters can damage crocus corms in the ground. The only diseases that seem to affect crocus are rust and corm rot.

In mid-autumn, purple blooms will begin to emerge. Each morning, check your crocus plants for new flowers. Within each flower, you will find three golden saffron threads. Gently pluck them from the flower and place the threads in a paper envelope so that they can dry in darkness. I keep my saffron threads in my spice cabinet, where it is nearly always dark and dry.

These unobtrusive flowers spend most of their year underground. Come fall, dark green spikes emerge, followed by lovely purple blooms, and a jackpot for your spice cabinet. Put some in this year for yourself!

Sage

Zones 4—8
Sun exposure: full sun, partial sun
Ideal soil temperature: above 65°F

Sage (*Salvia officinalis*) is the popular breakfast sausage and turkey stuffing herb.

Since ancient times, sage (a member of the mint family) has been used to ward off evil, improve fertility, combat the Plague, sooth bug bites, cure snake bite, and calm nervous conditions. Whether it actually does any of these things is beside the point, once the smell of sage emerges from your kitchen.

Culinary sage

Sage is a perennial culinary herb that can be grown outdoors in any area with a Mediterranean climate (and indoors everywhere else). Sage is a rugged, forgiving plant that grows very well in containers. It has a long growing season and, being an evergreen, can withstand colder temperatures than more delicate herbs, such as basil. Unlike many herbs, sage leaves retain their flavor even after the plant flowers.

SAGE VARIETIES

There are several varieties of sage. Some can grow as large as two feet in all directions, while other cultivars are more compact. Some varieties have a more spreading character, making them a fragrant ground cover. You can even plant pineapple sage, which really does smell like pineapple! Sage leaves are normally grayish-green, but they can also be yellow, purple, rose, or cream colored. Leaves are somewhat crinkled (rugose) on top. The underside of the leaves is nearly white and fuzzy. Sage flowers can range in color from purple and blue to white or pink. These edible flowers make nice additions to salads and they can be candied as cake decorations.

HOW TO GROW SAGE

Sage can be grown from seeds, cuttings, or layering. Growing sage from seed is a slow process. It can take up to two years to reach full size. It's a pretty plant, if you are not in a rush. Seeds should be planted 1/8" deep and the soil kept moist until sprouting begins. Allow the soil to dry out between waterings once the true leaves appear. Sage can also be propagated with cuttings or layering. Layering simply means tipping an established stem downward until it touches the soil. Instead of growing new leaves, roots should begin to appear at each of the buds.

Like most herbs, sage prefers a sunny location with excellent drainage. Too much water is really the only threat to sage plants, as most insects find sage's aromatic flavor distasteful. Sage prefers a pH of 6.0 to 7.0.

Mature plants should be spaced two to three feet apart. Planting sage near carrots and cabbage can be beneficial by deterring cabbage loopers and cabbage worms. Also, the flowers attract pollinators and the plants themselves make lovely additions to the landscape, whether you enjoy the flavor or not.

Summer Savory

Zones 1—11, when grown as an annual
Zones 5—11, when grown as a perennial
Sun exposure: full sun, partial sun, partial shade
Ideal soil temperature: 70°F to 85°F

Summer savory is an herb that deserves more attention.

It has a unique earthy flavor similar to marjoram, thyme, and mint. It is commonly used in bean, fish, pork, barbecues, and poultry dishes. Summer savory is also a primary ingredient in herbes de Provence. The ancient Greeks believed that satyrs lived and frolicked in fields in savory. You may or may not see any satyrs in your savory patch, but it is still worth adding to your foodscape.

Summer savory (*Satureja hortensis*) is an annual cousin of (and sweeter than) perennial winter savory. It tends to grow to one foot in height and drapes nicely from containers. When your summer savory plants die off in winter, fear not! Summer savory readily self-seeds.

Native to southeastern Europe, summer savory

Summer savory

is slow to germinate but worth the wait. I grow summer savory in a tower. It also grows well in small containers and on sunny windowsills. Bees and other pollinators love the tiny white and lilac-pink flowers, and the flower heads end up tasting pretty amazing in meatballs!

HOW TO GROW SUMMER SAVORY

Summer savory prefers at least six hours of full sunlight, well-drained soil, and a daily drink of water. If the soil dries out too much, the plant will bolt and go to seed. Seeds need a little light to germinate, so only cover lightly with soil and use a mister to water until seedlings emerge. That should take two weeks. Place plants one foot apart. They can withstand light frost and will produce well into winter with just a little protection.

HARVESTING SUMMER SAVORY

Summer savory leaves can be used fresh or dried. Simply snip off what you need during spring and summer. As the growing season winds down, you can cut the plant off at ground level, hang it upside-down in a shady, dry space, and allow the leaves to dry.

Well, there you have it. Yet another easy-to-grow plant that you can add to your landscape.

Tarragon

Zones 5—9
Sun exposure: full sun, partial sun
Ideal soil temperature: 65°F to 85°F

Tarragon is a lovely licorice-flavored herb that requires very little care.

Traditionally used to flavor fish, chicken, and omelets, tarragon is a must-have ingredient when making Béarnaise sauce. It can also be snipped into salads, deviled eggs, potato salad, and enough other recipes to make growing this easy-to-care-for herb an easy choice.

TYPES OF TARRAGON

There are two types of true tarragon: French and Russian. French tarragon (*Artemisia dracunculus* var. *sativa*) is the culinary herb, while the Russian tarragon (*A. dracunculoides*) has no flavor. In both cases, the plants will grow up to 24" tall and 12" wide, with slender leaves and tiny green flowers that never open. The Russian leaves are somewhat larger than the French.

There is also a Mexican tarragon which isn't really a tarragon at all, but it does have the licorice-flavored leaves so it can be used as a replacement for French tarragon. Mexican tarragon is related to marigolds. To avoid planting Russian tarragon by mistake (as plants are sometimes mislabeled), have a 

Tarragon

taste. Unfortunately, many seeds are mislabeled, as well.

GROWING TARRAGON

Tarragon requires nothing more than occasional waterings and good drainage to provide lush growth. It is easiest to buy seedlings or to take divisions from established plants. Follow these steps to divide an older plant:

- Gently lift an established plant from the ground with a garden fork.
- Shake the soil from the roots.
- Look for roots with green shoots.
- Trim these root segments to fit into a four-inch pot filled with light soil.
- Place the pots where they will receive plenty of sunlight.

- Water to keep the soil damp for two weeks.
- The plants should now be ready for planting in the garden.

Tarragon performs well in containers for the first year, but it needs to be planted in the ground after that. The container limits root growth so much that the plants lose their flavor. Regular watering is the key to the production of tender new leaves.

Tarragon tolerates alkaline soil. Tarragon can be grown in full sun in cooler areas, or it can be added to an area with dappled sunlight or a shade garden in areas with really hot summer days.

Thyme

Zones 5—9
Sun exposure: full sun, partial sun
Ideal soil temperature: above 65°F

Thyme is a woody, aromatic evergreen herb from the mint family.

The ancient Greeks believed that thyme was a source of courage. In the Middle Ages, people put thyme under their pillows to ward off nightmares. Today, people slip sprigs of fresh thyme into their face masks.

In the kitchen, thyme is often crumbled into scrambled eggs, baked with chicken, or simmered in a favorite spaghetti sauce. Found in bouquet garni, herbs de Provence, and many Italian dishes, thyme's sweet, savory aroma can make even the simplest dish better. It smells nice when you walk by and brush it with your hand, too.

THYME VARIETIES

There are more than 50 varieties of thyme. There are ornamental thymes and culinary thymes. Some of the more popular edible varieties include:

- *Thymus vulgaris* - English thyme, Summer thyme, Winter thyme, French thyme
- *T. citriodorus* - Lemon thyme, Lime thyme, Orange thyme varieties
- *T. herba-barona* - Caraway thyme (a low growing variety that works well as a ground cover)

HOW TO GROW THYME

Thyme prefers hot, dry sunny locations. It grows best in well-drained, slightly alkaline soil. Thyme grows well in containers, especially unglazed pots that allow the soil to dry out completely.

Thyme can be grown from seeds, cuttings, or by dividing root clusters. If growing from seed, simply follow the directions on the package. Cuttings can be placed directly in loose soil. Root clusters should be placed with the crown (where the stem meets the roots) at the same level as the surrounding soil.

Thyme can grow into a lovely small shrub

Thyme plants should be watered regularly as they are getting established. After that, they need very little care. These hardy plants can withstand freezing winters and scorching summers. Pinch growing tips to keep plants bushy. If a thyme plant becomes too tall or leggy, it can be cut back by 1/3 in spring. Just be sure to cut above some new growth, or the stems may die.

THYME FOR INSECTS

Thyme's tiny fragrant flowers are big favorites among honey bees and other beneficial insects. According to companion planting claims, cabbage moths, tomato hornworms, and whiteflies are offended by thyme, but I haven't found any definitive proof.

Thyme oil has antiseptic properties that may combat minor bacterial and fungal infections. According to Medical News Today, washes made from thyme can help get rid of acne, and rubbing your skin with thyme may prevent mosquito bites. Even if it doesn't work, you'll smell delicious!

Turmeric

Zones 8—11
Sun exposure: full sun, partial sun
Ideal soil temperature: above 65°F

If you ever get the chance to grow your own turmeric, you really ought to give it a try. This distant cousin to the banana tree and sibling of ginger makes a lovely houseplant, as well as a nice addition to your spice collection.

Turmeric rhizomes

Before we learn how to grown our own, let's clear up a couple of things: pronunciation and medication. Many people mispronounce the word "turmeric" by leaving out that first "r" to make it "tumeric." The correct pronunciation is TER-mer-ic. As for medicinal properties, I've got some bad news—it doesn't have any. Wild, far reaching claims have been made about the medicinal qualities of turmeric, but scientific research has not been able to verify any of those claims. Studies are being conducted, and we may find that turmeric really does have some health benefits. Until then, let's just enjoy it in our curry and let that be reason enough to grow it.

Turmeric is frequently used in Asian cooking. It is a major ingredient in curry powder. It's bright yellowish-orange color has also made it useful as a fabric dye. The plant is an herbaceous perennial grown mostly for its nubby rhizomes that grow underground. The powdered turmeric you buy in the spice aisle is made from rhizomes that are boiled for 30 to 45 minutes, dried in an oven, and then ground into a powder.

THE TURMERIC PLANT

Turmeric is a tropical plant. As such, it prefers moist, warm temperatures (85°F to 95°F). If it isn't warm enough, your turmeric rhizomes will rot, rather than sprout. Seedling heat mats can be used to keep your turmeric toasty warm. Mature plants can grow three feet tall and the large green leaves make it a lovely houseplant. Just be sure it gets plen-

Wild turmeric (John Hill) CC BY-SA 4.0

ty of sunlight and an occasional misting. Once your turmeric plant has become established, and if it is particularly well suited to its location, it may send up a greenish-white stalk and you may even get some stunning pink flowers! What you're really growing, of course, is the lateral underground rhizomes.

HOW TO GROW TURMERIC

If you take a close look at one turmeric rhizome, you will see little nubs. Those nubs are buds. You can break a larger chunk into smaller pieces, just make sure each chunk has two or three buds. For each chunk of root, fill a medium sized container with rich, loose organic soil and place the root two inches below the surface with the buds pointed up. (If a nub has two buds, pointing in opposite directions, lay it down so that the buds point to either side and let nature do the rest.) Water it well, the first time, making sure the container drains properly. After that, water only when the top inch or so of soil has dried. Your turmeric plant will take seven to ten months to reach a harvestable size.

HARVESTING TURMERIC

Harvesting turmeric is a lot like harvesting potatoes. You really can do it at any time. The longer you wait, the bigger the bounty. Gently dig your fingers down into the soil, near the stem, and feel for the rhizomes. If they feel large enough, wriggle them loose and pull them up. Then, just take what you need and put the rest back in the soil for the next harvest! The rhizomes can be boiled and eaten like any other root vegetable. The leaves are often used as food wrappers for steaming, the same way corn husks are used to hold tamales.

Chapter Eleven

MELON FAMILY

Melons and squashes are a thick-skinned group. They grow on vines and keep their seeds in a line down the center of their fruit. Also known as cucurbits, this family includes pumpkins, cucumbers, gourds, and the ever-popular zucchini.

Melons and squash

These plants love hot weather and many of them have protective bristles. These summer crops are not picky about soil, but they grow quickly and need lots of water and nutrients. They also need good drainage and full sun.

Weedy cousins of the melon family include buffalo gourds and bur cucumber.

Cucurbit Cross-Pollination Myth

Garden folklore warns against growing squash, cucumbers, and melons near each other. The claim suggests that cross-pollination will occur, changing the taste of the produce. This is one of those "partly true, partly myth" stories.

First, when natural cross-pollination does occur, it only affects the genetic information held in next year's seeds and not the taste of the current season's produce. (Corn is the only exception to that rule that I know of.) Second, pollination can only happen with pollen of the same species. Cucumbers and melons are different species, so they will not cross-pollinate. What can happen is two different types of melon will cross-pollinate. That's how we got Crenshaw melons—Persian melons were crossed with casabas. Cucumbers, loofah, and watermelons only cross-pollinate with themselves, so cross-pollination is only a concern if you are growing different varieties. Groups that can cross-pollinate include:

- Summer squash, such as yellow crookneck and zucchini, can cross-pollinate with acorn squash, gourds (except edible snake gourds), patty pan squash, and pumpkins
- Banana, buttercup, butternut, Hubbard, and turban squashes
- Armenian cucumbers, cantaloupe, casaba, honeydew, and snake melons

These groups are all variations on the same species and can cross-pollinate. The current year's fruit will be what you expect. The seeds for next year's crop might be something different. If you save seeds, you may end up with something really unique growing next year. Sometimes it will be edible and sometimes it won't. Oddly shaped fruit and poor taste are usually the result of too much fertilizer, too much irrigation, or damp weather, and not weird cross-pollinations.

HOW TO HAND POLLINATE CUCURBITS

One common problem with squashes and melons is poor pollination. This is especially true for pumpkins. You can pollinate by hand for a bigger crop. To hand pollinate, you need to know the difference between male and female flowers. It's not hard.

Male butternut squash flower

Female butternut squash flower

Male flowers open earlier in the growing season. They have a stalk that grows in the center of the flower. This stalk is the anther. If you touch the anther and your finger comes away dusted in yellow, it is ready to use for hand pollinating. Just cut the male flower off and remove the petals to create a pollen paintbrush.

Female flowers contain an ovary, which looks like a small ball at the base, outside of the petals. Male flowers do not have this. Once female flowers begin to open, simply touch your pollen paintbrushes to the nubby bits (stigmas) in the center of the female flower. If pollination is successful, the ovary at the base of the flower will begin to swell, ultimately becoming a mature squash or melon.

MELON FAMILY PROBLEMS

In addition to the usual troublemakers, bugs attracted to this plant family include cucumber beetles, false chinch bugs, leaf-footed bugs, melonworm moths, pickleworms, seedcorn maggots, squash bugs, squash ladybugs, stinkbugs, and wireworms.

Many cucurbit diseases are related to overhead watering, inconsistent watering, and disease-carrying aphids.

Cucurbit Diseases

angular leafspot
bacterial leaf blotch
bacterial wilt
blossom end rot
cucumber vein yellowing
cucurbit aphid-borne yellows
cucurbit yellow stunting disorder
curly top
mosaic virus
potyviruses
scab
sudden wilt

Cucamelons

Zones 7—10
Sun exposure: full sun
Ideal soil temperature: above 70°F

Cucamelons may look like tiny watermelons, but there's nothing sweet about them.

Also known as Mexican sour gherkins, mouse melons, and pepquinos, cucamelons (*Melothria scabra*) make a fun addition to children's gardens and they look nice in a salad.

Before you jump on the cucamelon bandwagon, however, let's talk about taste.

A WORD ON THE CUCAMELON FLAVOR

It is difficult, at first, to put your mind's expectation of a watermelon aside, when biting into a cucamelon. And this is too bad, because cucamelons don't taste anything like watermelon. The flavor is more akin to a tangy cucumber crossed with a fava bean. If you expect watermelon, you probably won't like it. If, instead, you can bite into these grape-sized fruits with an open mind, you may end up with a new garden favorite!

CUCAMELON PLANTS

Native to Central America and Mexico, cucamelons need warm to hot temperatures to get started, and plenty of sunshine to keep them going. Once established, your cucamelon plants will continue to produce fruit well into autumn.

Cucamelon

Cucamelons plants produce both male and female flowers, so they can pollinate themselves.

HOW TO GROW CUCAMELONS

Trellised cucamelon plants

Seeds should be planted 1" deep and 6"-10" apart. Cucamelons are more rugged and drought tolerant than cucumbers, but they are slow getting started. Like cucumbers, cucamelons grow best in rich, slightly acidic soil.

After seedlings emerge, thin plants to every 12". Fairy-like vines can grow 10' long, so they need to be given something to climb. Keeping your cucamelons off the ground will help reduce slug feeding and fungal diseases, though pests and diseases of cucamelon are practically unheard of.

Be sure to save a few of the fruits that fall to the ground on their own as a source of seeds for next year. Cucamelons also have tuberous roots that can be dug up in fall and stored over the winter in your garage, to be replanted in spring.

Cucumbers

Zones 4—11
Sun exposure: full sun
Ideal soil temperature: above 70°F

Originally from South Asia, cucumbers have found their way into gardens around the world. Botanically, cucumbers (*Cucumis sativus*) are classified as berries. This is because they are the fruit of a single ovary.

CUCUMBER VARIETIES

There are many types of cucumber: slicing, pickling, gherkins, bush, burpless, and seedless. Seedless cucumbers develop fruit without being pollinated. These cucumbers are usually grown in greenhouses. All the other types of cucumbers are self-incompatible. This means they cannot pollinate themselves and you will need more than one cucumber plant. While any cucumber can be pickled, pickling cucumbers are bred for size and shape. They have bigger bumps, too.

Cucumber plant with fruit

HOW TO GROW CUCUMBERS

Cucumbers love rich soil with a pH of 5.5 to 6.5. Seeds should be planted 1" deep and 6"-10" apart. After seedlings emerge, thin plants to every 12". Cucumbers need lots of sunlight. Cucumbers grow on creeping vines that can be trellised onto tomato cages, along fences, cattle panels, or on a teepee made from bamboo poles. Keeping your cucumbers off the ground will help reduce insect damage and fungal diseases.

CUCUMBER PESTS AND DISEASES

Cucumbers have the same problems as other members of the squash family. Squash vine borers, cucumber beetles, and squash bugs will all try to sink their tiny mouthparts into your delicious cucumbers, so keep a lookout.

CUCUMBERS AND BITTERNESS

Sometimes, cucumbers taste bitter. We used to think that water stress was the only culprit. Now we know that lower than normal temperatures can cause bitterness. So can temperature fluctuations greater than 20°F, or when they are stored next to other ripening vegetables. So, protect your cukes and keep harvesting!

Melons

Zones 3—11
Sun exposure: full sun
Ideal soil temperature: 75°F to 85°F

Sweet, juicy melons are a gardening favorite. They are easy to grow, productive, and delicious. It just wouldn't be summer without slicing through the hard outer rind of a melon to enjoy the sweet, refreshing fruit within.

The melon clan

Within the melon clan, there are several different groupings (by genus) of some familiar, and some not so familiar, melons:

- Winter melon (*Benincasa hispida*) - cooked as a vegetable in India and Asia
- Watermelon (*Citrullus lanatus*) - enjoyed for more than 4,000 years! (Its wild cousin, Egusi, has inedible flesh but the seeds are an important food source in Africa
- Horned melon (*Cucumis metuliferus*) - has spikes!
- Muskmelon (*Cucumis melo*) - includes cantaloupe, casaba, honeydew, and canary melons

How melons grow

Like their cousins in the squash family, melons grow on vines. Unlike other vegetables crops, however, each vine has both male and female flowers. The male flowers generally appear first and usually only last for one day. Melon pollen is very sticky, so wind pollination does not occur. Honeybees are needed to carry the pollen from one flower to the next. If there are not enough honeybees in your area, you may want to reach out to your local beekeepers guild. Very often, they are happy to have a new place to put their bees! Or, you can use a fine paintbrush to transfer the sticky pollen to the female flowers, or you can break off a male flower, remove the petals, and apply the pollen that way. Female flowers can be identified by the miniature fruit (ovary) at the base of each blossom.

Melon plant

HOW TO GROW MELONS

Melon seeds are big and easy to work with. They really love hot weather. Prepare the planting area by digging compost into the soil and creating hills. Each hill should be approximately 4 feet square. Plant 3 to 5 seeds, 1" deep and 2" apart, into the middle of each hill. Water the area well. Once your seeds have sprouted and grown into seedlings with a few sets of leaves, snip the smallest plants off at ground level, rather than thinning by pulling them out. This lets the remaining plant's roots and helpful soil microorganisms stay undisturbed.

Melons need to be watered every two or three days during the peak of summer. Sometimes even more. Regular watering can help prevent the fruit from splitting open. Side dressing melon plants with aged compost during the growing season also improves both crop quantity and quality. Side dressing simply means putting compost next to the plants and watering all those yummy nutrients into the surrounding soil. Easy and effective.

You may want to add a layer of straw or sawdust under your melons to get them up off the ground. This helps prevent rotten areas, and insect and fungal infestation. Melons can also be grown in containers, towers, or straw bales, and trellised. The fruit itself will need personal hammocks if you use a trellis. You can tell a melon is ready to harvest when you see a slight crack around the stem where it is attached to the fruit. This is called the "full slip" stage. Crenshaw, casaba, and some honeydew varieties do not develop a slip. Casaba and honeydew melons can be stored for several weeks, while other varieties are best eaten right away.

Did you know that melons are actually berries? Let's take a closer look at a couple of melons that may surprise you.

Cantaloupes

Cantaloupes are a unique type of muskmelon. And American cantaloupes aren't actually cantaloupes at all.

TYPES OF CANTALOUPE

In the U.S., cantaloupe have a strongly textured, or ribbed, rind and bright orange flesh. This North American variety (*Cucumis melo* var. *reticulatus*) is not technically a true cantaloupe.

North American cantaloupe

In Europe, where true cantaloupes are grown, you will find melons with green or orange flesh and less pronounced ribbing. The European variety is called *C. melo* var. *cantalupensis*.

Whichever type of melon you decide to grow, you are sure to enjoy the fruits of this labor!

HOW CANTALOUPES GROW

Cantaloupes are vining annuals that love heat. Temperatures between 85°F and 95°F are ideal, and these plants can tolerate temperatures as high as 104°F. Cantaloupe's bisexual flowers are mostly pollinated by bees, so a healthy bee population is important for a good melon crop. Whereas a single bee visit is enough to pollinate other crops, cantaloupes are fickle and may need 10 to 15 bee visits before pollination is completed.

Cantaloupes can be grown in all types of soil, as long as there is good drainage. To grow your own cantaloupes, wait until temperatures are well above 60°F. Plant seeds 3"-6" deep in loose mounds. Mounds should be 3' apart and in full sun. Keep the mound moist, but not soggy, until germination occurs.

Cantaloupes are moderate

European cantaloupe

feeders, which means a top dressing of aged compost after germination is probably all that is needed. (Of course, you should still conduct a soil test to make sure your plants have access to all the nutrients they need.)

CANTALOUPE PESTS AND DISEASES

Proper plant spacing and the use of a trellis can prevent many of these diseases by improving air flow. Fruits grown up a trellis will need to be supported with hammocks. Melons growing on the ground should be protected with a layer of straw or some other material that gets them up off the soil.

Heavy rain (or over-watering) can cause fruit split.

Cantaloupe Problems
cucumber beetles
green peach aphids
root knot nematodes
seed-corn maggots
squash bugs
wireworms
belly rot
cucumber mosaic
monosporascus root rot
watermelon mosaic
zucchini yellows mosaic

HARVESTING CANTALOUPES

Cantaloupes are ready for harvest at "full slip" stage. Cantaloupes should be eaten as soon as possible after being harvested, as they tend to lose moisture more quickly than many other members of this family. If you end up with a bumper crop of melons, your best method of preservation is to try your hand at canning some preserves. Cantaloupe pairs nicely with peaches and nectarines. And be sure to save seeds for next year's crop!

The majority of the world's cantaloupe crop is grown in China and shipped around the world. Believe me when I tell you that harvesting a fresh melon from your yard is a very satisfying and delicious experience. And halved cantaloupes make lovely ice cream bowls.

Watermelons

What summer picnic would be complete without watermelon? Sweet, refreshing, and adaptable, watermelon is another easy-to-grow addition to your foodscape.

HISTORY OF WATERMELON

Watermelons were cultivated 5,000 years ago, in Egypt. Watermelon seeds were even found in King Tut's tomb! But ancient watermelon ancestors were not the bright red, sweet fruits we know. The original watermelons tasted pretty awful. They were bitter and hard. People grew them anyway, because these melons could hold water for weeks and even months, if stored properly, hence the name.

Watermelon as depicted in a 17th century painting by Giovanni Stanchi CC BY-SA 4.0

Five thousand years ago, that was a really big deal. As plumbing became a thing, watermelons had to up their game. Over time, and with selective breeding, they became the sweet summer picnic favorites that we love.

HOW TO GROW WATERMELON

Watermelon plants (*Citrullus lanatus* var. *lanatus*) can take up some space. Vines may grow 10' long and the leaves are large. Plant watermelon seeds 1" deep in groups of 6-10 seeds. These seeds should be planted in hills that are 3-4 feet apart. These hills are mounds of loose, rich soil 2' in diameter.

Once seedlings emerge, save the best three and snip the others off at ground level. Mulch around the plants to reduce weeds and retain moisture. Individual watermelons can be grown in a container, but it should be large—at least five gallons. They can also be grown up trellising or on stock panels, but each melon will need a hammock.

Baby watermelon (Fred Hsu) CC BY-SA 3.0

Watermelon seeds will not germinate below 70°F. Row covers can be used over seedlings to protect them from pests and to retain some heat. Watermelons prefer a soil pH of 6.0 to 6.8. Watermelons do require a significant amount of water to produce fruit, but avoid getting the leaves wet to prevent fungal disease. If the leaves wilt in the afternoon, don't worry about it. If they stay wilted into the evening, check moisture levels. Once fruit starts to appear, you will want to lift it up off the ground with some straw. This reduces the chance of belly rot. Reduce watering just before your watermelons ripen to increase sugar levels and intensify the flavor.

If you add watermelon plants to your foodscape this summer, enjoy the fruit this year and save some seeds for next year's crop!

Seedless watermelon production began in the 1990s. Seedless watermelons happen because plant breeders do two things. First, they take the normal 22 watermelon chromosomes and double them, using a chemical process. Then they pollinate female flowers of plants with 44 chromosomes with male plants that have 22 chromosomes. The resulting offspring have 33 chromosomes and are highly unlikely to have viable seeds.

Now you know.

Squash

Zones 2—11
Sun exposure: full sun
Ideal soil temperature: 65°F to 75°F

Squash plants produce a lot of food. They grow best in hot, dry summers. Squash are heavy feeders and they need lots of water, but they repay your efforts with abundant harvests.

Summer squash (Stearns Farm CSA) CC BY-ND 2.0

HOW SQUASH PLANTS GROW

Squash plants have very large leaves with bristles on the under-side. The stems are tubular and also have bristles. Most winter squash vines can get very long, while summer squashes have a bushy, mounding growth. In both cases, these plants can take up some room, so don't plant more than you have room for in the garden.

HOW TO GROW SQUASH

You can always leave last fall's squash, melon, or pumpkin on the ground. It will go through the natural cycle of withering, collapsing, rotting, resting, and sprouting. Or, you can start with seeds. Squash seeds are large and flat and should be planted 1" deep.

Squash plants do not respond well to transplanting, so it is best to start them where you want them. Also, the squash family is temperature sensitive. Seeds will not sprout if the soil isn't warm enough. Any seeds that start under less than ideal conditions end up using too many resources just to stay alive. They rarely grow into healthy, productive plants.

Since these plants take up some room, squash are often grown in hills. These hills are usually 6"-8" high and 12"-24" wide. Hills are mounds of loose soil amended with aged compost or manure. These hills improve drainage and the soil warms more quickly.

Depending on the variety, these hills can support one to four plants. Squash seeds planted in rows should be 18" to 30" apart, also depending on the variety. Squash can also be grown in containers or raised beds. In arid regions, you can use inverted hills, or shallow areas. This makes watering easier, but it may increase problems with pests and fungal disease. Wherever you start your squash seedlings, you will want to snip the rejects off at soil level. This protects the remaining roots and important soil microorganisms.

Squash plants are heavy feeders. You can help them stay

healthy and productive by top-dressing around plants with aged compost or fish emulsion. Avoid applying extra nitrogen. Nitrogen stimulates leaf growth, not fruit.

During the peak of summer, afternoon wilting is normal and not cause for concern. If they haven't perked up by morning, they need more water. Squash needs to be watered deeply once or twice a week, depending on the weather. Mulching around plants can reduce the need for water. It also stabilizes soil temperatures and reduces competition from weeds.

As fruits grow, give them a bed of straw. This reduces soil contact and the potential for fungal disease. Gently turning your squash can keep colors and growth even, and it lets you see if any problems are lurking underneath.

SQUASH PROBLEMS

Water-stressed squash will taste bitter. This bitterness is caused by toxins that can be potentially dangerous. Don't let this scare you off, just be sure to water your squash plants regularly. This will also help prevent blossom end rot.

Squash are subject to all the normal garden pests and diseases, and a whole lot more. If you made a list of all the pests and diseases that affect squash, you might wonder how these plants survive at all. But they do. In fact, they thrive! But it's always a good idea to know what might happen, so you can nip it in the bud before things get out of hand.

Squash Diseases
belly rot
charcoal rot
cucumber mosaic
Fusarium crown and foot rot
Phytophthora fruit and crown rot
root rot
squash mosaic
white mold
zucchini yellow mosaic

First, inspect your squash plants regularly. If you see a small hole in a squash stem, slit it open lengthwise a little to see if the problem is squash vine borers. Borers can be removed by hand. Then, lay the cut stem on the ground and cover it with soil. If you're lucky, new roots will start to grow, giving your plant more water and nutrients.

Common squash-specific pests include cucumber beetles (which carry wilt disease), darkling beetles, driedfruit beetles, false chinch bugs, mites, redhumped caterpillars, seed corn maggots, squash bugs, stinkbugs, whiteflies (cucurbit yellow stunting disorder carriers), and wireworms. If you live in the southeastern U.S., melonworm moths and pickleworms may also be a problem. Placing row covers over seedlings and dusting plants with diatomaceous earth can reduce pest damage organically.

Squash plants are vulnerable to several bacterial, fungal, and viral diseases. When watering squash, try to avoid getting the leaves wet. Wet leaves are prone to fungal diseases. Soaker hoses are a convenient way to water squash plants.

Environmental conditions, such as irregular watering, can cause blossom end rot, bitter fruit, and blossom drop.

If all that weren't enough, molybdenum deficiencies can cause a condition known as yellows. Yellows eliminates squash fruit set and generally kills the plant. Sporadic watering and insufficient calcium can also cause blossom end rot. Soil tests from a reputable lab are the best way to learn what's in your soil.

Despite all those threats, you'll probably still end up with more squash than you know what to do with.

In the plant world, reproduction is the name of the game. The more often you harvest the fruit, the more fruit your plants will produce. Squashes should be harvested by cutting the vine with a sharp knife about one inch above the fruit. Do not twist or yank at it, as this can damage the plant.

There are two types of squash: summer squash and winter squash. This has nothing to do with when they are grown. Instead, it is more about when they are eaten. Winter squash have hard outer shells. This makes them easy to store. Summer squashes have thin, tender skins and are usually eaten (or preserved) while immature.

Summer squash

There are two main types of summer squash: zucchini and yellow, but these are divided up into several different varieties:

- Green zucchini - the classic
- Yellow (or golden) zucchini - no tapering, straight cylinder
- Romanesco zucchini - stays tender even when it reaches horse leg proportions
- Straightneck yellow - tapers at the stem end
- Crookneck yellow - tapers at the stem end with a crook
- Pattypan - scalloped disks
- Cousa - shorter and stubbier than zucchini
- Zephyr - a cross between yellow crookneck and yellow acorn
- Eight ball - a spherical zucchini

Summer squash prefers a sunny location with loose, well-drained soil and a soil pH of 5.8 to 6.8.

Adding aged compost around your squash plants is nearly always a good idea, just avoid adding too much nitrogen. Too much nitrogen will encourage plenty of leaves but very little fruit.

One nice thing about summer squash is that it can be harvested at any stage in its development. Simply cut the stem and enjoy the fruits of your labor! Once you've harvested a summer squash, you can add it to stir fry, salads, soups, stews, or just nibble on it while reading a good book. Odds are, another one will be ready to harvest in a day or two. Summer squash is particularly sensitive to ethylene gas, so you will want to keep them away from bananas and other ripening fruits.

Summer squashes are best harvested young and eaten fresh. Because squash is a low-acid food, it cannot be safely canned on its own. Even using a pressure canner to preserve summer squash is no longer considered adequate.

YELLOW SQUASH

Yellow squash offers a sweet, buttery harvest and they are easy to grow.

Once temperatures stay at or above 60°F, seeds can be planted 3'-4' apart, if planting in rows. Another option is to plant 4-5 seeds, spread 3" apart, in hills. Keep only the best seedling for each hill, snipping off the others at soil level.

Yellow crookneck squash

Fruit production should start 60 days after planting. If your plants are not producing, use a moisture meter to make sure they are getting enough water.

The fruit is bright yellow (making it easy to find, come harvest time) with thin skin that may be smooth or bumpy. If there is a hook at the stem end, we call it crookneck. Yellow squashes without the hook are called straightneck.

Fruits are produced near the base of the plant and should be harvested when they are 4"-7" long and 2" in diameter. Like other summer squashes, yellow squash will get tough if allowed to grow too large. Harvesting frequently also spurs the plant to produce more fruit.

ZUCCHINI

Zucchini is a summer squash that can sneak up you.

Large, prickly (edible) leaves shade the ground. They also hide the occasional zucchini, allowing it to reach horse leg proportions. Everyone has a story of the monstrous zucchini they swore wasn't there the day before. It happens. When it does, stuff it with sausage and onions and bake it, or make some Chocolate Zucchini Cake.

According to Guinness World Records, the longest zucchini

on record was more than eight feet long and the heaviest weighed in at over 64 pounds. Imagine stuffing one of those monsters! In Britain, these epic squash are called "marrows", but zucchini are generally harvested when much smaller and younger.

There are several types of zucchini

Zucchini is a very forgiving and productive plant. You can grow zucchini in large containers, raised beds, or in the ground. Seeds germinate best at 70°F-95°F. You can plant seeds individually or in hills. Individual plants should be spaced three feet apart.

Winter squash

Pumpkin pie, pumpkin pudding, pumpkin bread, and the ever-popular Halloween jack-o-lantern are all autumn favorites. Did you know that most canned pumpkin puree is actually squash?

Pumpkins and other winter squash share enough characteristics as to be indistinguishable according to the FDA. Huh. How about that? No matter. Growing pumpkins and other winter squash is very rewarding and easier than you may think.

It takes a lot of water to make a winter squash. During fruit set, each plant should receive approximately 1" of water per week. (One inch of water is equal to 0.623 gallons per square foot.) Since winter squash are shallow-rooted, it is not a good idea to disturb the soil. If you only have a small space, winter squash can be trained up a trellis.

Fortuna white pumpkin plant

Depending on the size of the fruit, you may need to provide hammocks as support.

Winter squash are ready to harvest when the rind is firm and the stem is shriveled. You can leave them to cure on the vine or cut them off and store them in a cool, dry location with good air flow. Garages work nicely. After your winter squash has cured, it will remain edible for several months.

BUTTERNUT SQUASH

Harvest from two plants

The bright orange flesh of butternut squash is a primary ingredient in rich, creamy soups, substantial casseroles, and delicious pies.

Butternut squash grows best in full sun, but it seems to perform just as well in partial shade in areas with especially hot summers. (I grow my butternuts under a nectarine tree and they both seem happy about it.)

Butternut squash is a deep-rooted plant, making it well suited to areas experiencing drought.

PUMPKIN

After temperatures have reached a steady 70°F, pumpkin seeds are planted in hills. Each pumpkin plant can take up to 50-100 square feet, given the opportunity. You can also redirect vines along walkways, lawns, or fences.

Plant 4-5 seeds in each hill. If you have room for multiple hills, they should be spaced 4'-8' apart. After your seedlings are 2"-3" tall, select the best two or three for each hill and snip the rejects off at soil level. If you are growing pumpkins in rows, seeds should be planted 6"-12" apart in rows that are 6'-10' apart, thinning seedlings to one plant every 18"-36".

Keep your squash watered and mulched and you are sure to get an abundant crop.

Pumpkin fun in the garden

In time, even pumpkins get wrinkles

Chapter Twelve

ONION FAMILY

Members of the onion family (*Liliaceae*) usually have long, vertical leaves, a leafless flower stalk (scape), and flowers with six petals (or multiples thereof). Leeks, garlic, chives, shallots, and asparagus are all members of the onion family. (Who figured out that asparagus is a member of this family? Actually, asparagus is a distant relation with shared ancestors, but they're close enough to be included here.)

All of these crops are best planted in late summer and early fall in areas with mild winters. In regions with cold winters, spring planting gives these plants time to grow to full size. In either case, these plants can be grown in full or partial sun or partial shade.

If you see wild onions or rain lilies growing in your landscape, the onion family will love your yard.

A variety of onions (Colin) CC BY-SA 3.0

ONION FAMILY PROBLEMS

All families have problems and onions are no exception. In addition to the normal pests and diseases, members of this group are also under threat from bulb mites, leek moth larvae, onion eelworms, onion flies, and onion maggots. Additional diseases to watch for include bacterial soft rot, garlic mosaic, rust, pink root, white rot, basal rot, and several botrytis infections.

Most onion diseases are related to excessive moisture. Proper irrigation and allowing the soil to dry out between waterings are your best defense.

Asparagus

Zones 3—10
Sun exposure: full sun, partial sun, partial shade
Ideal soil temperature: 75°F to 80°F

April is an excellent time of year to start planting asparagus. Now, growing asparagus is not a task for the impatient. You will not get a crop the first year. You won't get a crop the second year, either. However, those succulent stalks are certainly worth the wait. Plus, once they start producing, you will continue to get harvests for many years.

Asparagus was offered to the Egyptian gods more than 5,000 years ago, and people have been enjoying it ever since.

ASPARAGUS LIFE CYCLE

Unlike many of our vegetable crops, asparagus grows from crowns, which are food storage rhizomes. The familiar spears, left to their own, will open up and grow into ferny branches that can reach 4'-5' in height. Asparagus leaves are actually modified stems, much like conifers. The root system is adventitious. Yellow to greenish-white flowers emerge and become red berries when fertilized.

DO NOT EAT ASPARAGUS BERRIES.
They are poisonous to people.

HOW TO GROW ASPARAGUS

Before you starting planting asparagus, give the site some thought. Asparagus plants may take a few years to really start producing, they will continue to produce for 20-30 years or more! Asparagus loves raised beds in full or partial sun, and lots of compost-rich soil. Asparagus does not compete well against weeds, so be sure to keep the asparagus bed weed free. Mulching will help a lot.

One-year-old crowns are the best way to start. Dig a trench 12" deep in the bed and place asparagus crowns 18" apart. Spread the roots out, cover with soil and water, but do not fill in the trench. Watch for new growth. As shoots begin to appear, add more soil, repeating until the trench has been filled. If you want to grow asparagus from seed, the seeds must be germinated between damp paper towels and then gently transferred to soil.

Purple asparagus!

Keep the asparagus bed consistently moist, but not soggy. While spears may appear the first year or two, force yourself to ignore them. Allow the plants to go through their annual cycle. This will help them develop a strong root system, necessary for long-term production.

ASPARAGUS PESTS AND DISEASES

Asparagus is susceptible to Fusarium wilt and asparagus rust. Remove and discard diseased shoots. Aphids can also become a problem. To get rid of the aphids, simply spray the plants with a hose.

Harvesting asparagus

By the third year, you should be able to harvest some, but not all, of the spears. They taste the best when they are 5"-7" tall. Cut or snap the spears off at or near ground level. By late spring or early summer, your asparagus harvesting season is done. Allow any spears that come up to complete their normal cycle.

If you want white asparagus, you will need to blanch them. That means covering them with soil, newspaper, or some other material that will halt photosynthesis as they grow.

If you end up with a bumper crop of asparagus, you may be tempted to eat it all. That might be a bad idea. Eating a lot of asparagus can make urine smell pretty awful. Instead, the shoots can be pickled and stored for a long time They taste particularly good in a Bloody Mary.

Chives

Zones 4—8
Sun exposure: full sun, partial sun, partial shade
Ideal soil temperature: above 65°F

No self-respecting baked potato would consider its raiment complete without freshly snipped chives. Chives can elevate even the simplest dish and they look lovely, growing on a windowsill.

Chives (*Allium schoenoprasum*) are edible perennial bulbs. Their tender green spikes are frequently offset by purple spherical blooms that are equally edible. Many beneficial insects are attracted to the flowers, as well. Plant them once and they will provide many years of flavorful beauty.

HOW TO GROW CHIVES

Chives are so easy to grow that they are an excellent children's activity. Chives prefer well-drained soil with a pH of 6.0 to 7.0 and full sun. I have had chive plants perform equally well in partially shaded clay. This herb is tenacious - I've even had chive plants return after being decimated by chickens. Plant seeds ¼" deep and water well. Light is

Chives

not needed, at first, but seeds must be kept moist and at a temperatures of 60°F to 70°F to germinate. Chives make excellent container plants and they transplant easily, once seedlings are 4"-6" tall. Established plants can and should be divided periodically to avoid overcrowding. To divide a chive plant, gently dig the entire plant out of the ground and pull it apart into smaller clumps, or you can leave it in the ground and sink a shovel down through the middle, removing a portion to be transplanted elsewhere. You will want at least five to ten bulbs in the clump to be moved. Once established, your chive plants will readily self-seed.

CHIVE PESTS AND DISEASES

The only pest I have seen on my chives is an infrequent visit from individual slugs. Damping off disease, powdery mildew, and pink root are also said to attack chives, but not in my experience. I think, in this case, the chive plant is the anti-pest. In fact, European gypsies traditionally hang bunches of dried chives to ward off evil and illness!

HARVESTING CHIVES

Snip off however much you will be using, as close to the base as you can without damaging the rest of the plant. If your chive plant starts looking worn out, especially in late winter, you can cut the entire plant to a height of two to three inches to stimulate fresh growth. If you harvest more chives than you need, you can snip them into small bits, lay them between layers of cloth or paper towel to dry and then store in an airtight container.

Herbs are excellent additions to an edible landscape or a windowsill garden, and chives are the easiest of the edible herbs to grow. Get yours started today!

Garlic

Zones 4—9
Sun exposure: full sun
Ideal soil temperature: 55°F to 75°F

Who doesn't love garlic? Add some melted butter and you can make just about anything taste amazing. What's even better—it's easy to grow!

Cousin to onions, shallots, chives, and leeks, garlic is a member of the Allium family. So why talk about garlic in the middle of August? Most of us gardeners are currently dealing with an overabundance of tomatoes, zucchini, and cucumbers, but fall will be will be here before you know it.

Garlic

Rather than let your valuable garden real estate go fallow, you can chop up plant material, as plants end their productive cycle, and use this valuable resource to prepare your winter crop beds. Lay the material on top or dig it in a few inches. By the time October rolls around, the worms will have created the perfect growing medium for your garlic.

HOW TO GROW GARLIC

Garlic can be grown in containers, shade gardens, on balconies or windowsills, or in traditional garden rows. As a bulb, it is a resilient plant that can fit into practically any landscape. While you can grow new plants from a garlic purchased at the grocery store, you are better off buying starts from a reputable grower. Grocery store garlic is safe to eat, but it may harbor diseases that can harm future crops for many years.

Freshly harvested and braided garlic

Garlic comes in two basic forms: hard-neck and soft-neck. The soft-neck variety stores better, but the hard-neck variety produces bigger cloves that are easier to peel. When you are ready to plant, simply separate the cloves from a garlic and plant them approximately six inches apart and 1" deep, with the root end down and the pointy end up. That's it!

GARLIC LORE

Garlic has been cited as a cure-all and demon-repellant, among other questionable attributes, but science has shown that garlic really does repel aphids, cabbageworms, codling moths, Mexican bean beetles, peach borers, and even slugs and snails. In my book, that makes garlic worthwhile simply as a natural pest and disease inhibitor. Of course, I love to eat garlic, so I would plant it anyway!

Harvesting garlic

Unlike onions, whose leaves are a tube, garlic leaves are flat. When the leaves start to turn yellow and fall over, gently remove your garlic plants from the ground, dust off the dirt, and put them in a shady spot for a couple of weeks. If you feel inspired, you can then try braiding your garlic crop, but I have found that it's a lot harder than it looks!

Be sure to save your very best garlic for planting in the following fall. Over time, your garlic crop will be become better acclimated to your microclimate and produce even better harvests!

Leeks

Zones 2—11
Sun exposure: full sun
Ideal soil temperature: 70°F to 75°F

Leeks have a nice delicate flavor, but they can get pretty pricey in the grocery store. Luckily for us, they are easy to grow!

Unlike other members of the Allium family, such as garlic and onions, leeks do not form bulbs underground. Instead, leeks grow an edible stem that can be up to 2" in diameter. Like garlic, the leaves are flat. Leeks are commonly paired with potatoes, but they can also be steamed, roasted, or baked to stand on their own.

Leek cultivars

There are two basic types of leeks. Short-season leeks are planted in spring and harvested in late summer and early fall. Hardy long-season leeks are also planted in spring, in the north, but not until late summer in warmer areas. These leeks are not ready for harvesting for at least 100 days, which means they are ready for use through winter.

How to Grow Leeks

Leeks are biennial plants that are grown as annuals. You can start leeks from seed or by replanting the white base of an existing leek. If you use the base of a leek purchased from the grocery store, be aware that you may be introducing destructive pathogens into your garden.

The base should be planted much deeper than you might expect: 4"-6" deep. This is how part of the stem stays white, because it is blanched underground. Blanching means keeping certain parts of a plant white by blocking sunlight.

If you use seeds, plant them ½" deep and 6" apart. If you start seeds indoors, be sure to harden them off before planting them in the ground or in tall containers outside. You can also buy seedlings from your local garden store, but they will need to be gently untangled from each other before replanting—they look like unmown grass in the pot. Seedlings should then be transplanted deeper into the soil than they were, up to where the green stems begin, for a longer, more drought resistant edible. Once the seedlings are as big around as a pencil, bank soil or mulch around each plant to continue blanching the base.

Leeks

Leeks prefer cooler temperatures, so fall and winter are the best time to grow leeks in areas with hot summers. Leeks enjoy full sun and well-drained soil, but the two components that make the biggest difference in growing leeks are water and nitrogen. Leeks are heavy feeders, so planting them near peas or beans will provide an extra boost of nitrogen early in the growing process, followed with aged compost. Leeks have shallow roots so regular watering is needed for plants to reach full size. Water stress will significantly reduce yields. The soil should be moistened to a depth of 18" every week. Mulching around plants can reduce weeds, add nutrients, and cut water needs.

Onion rust and onion white rot are the most common problems encountered when growing leeks.

Onions

Zones 6—9
Sun exposure: full sun
Ideal soil temperature: 50°F to 90°F

Onions are not roots, even though they grow underground.

The layered sphere we call onion is a bulb. Edible onions form when shortened underground stems are surrounded by fleshy leaves, called scales. People have been growing onions (*Allium cepa*) for 7,000 years.

One of the nicest things about growing your own onions is that they can be eaten at any stage of development. Early green shoots are called scallions, or spring onions, while mid-stage development crops are called summer onions. Onions are a cool weather crop. Hot weather will cause onions to go to seed, or bolt.

ONION VARIETIES

There are three common varieties of onion: white, yellow, and red. White and yellow onions are commonly sautéed or caramelized. This releases sugars that make them taste sweet. Red onions are more often used fresh, in salads and when grilling.

Onions are also classified according to the number of day-hours it takes to trigger the development of a bulb:

- Long-day (L) onions - need 14 hours of daylight or more, planted late winter, not suitable to regions with hot summers
- Indeterminate-day (I) onions - need 12 to 13 hours, planted in fall, may work in hot regions
- Short-day (S) onions - need 11 to 12 hours, best choice for areas with hot summers and mild winters

Some onions have been bred to be smaller. These are called boiler, pickler, or pearl onions. The term "pearl onion" is incorrect because pearl onions are an entirely different species. True pearl onions are more closely related to leeks than to common onions, and they do not have layers, more similar to garlic.

HOW TO GROW ONIONS

Onion seeds are relatively short-lived when compared to other seeds. You can grow onions using transplants or onion "sets". Onion sets are seeds that were sown in early summer, but so close together that they could not continue their development. Onion sets tend to bolt, rather than creating onion bulbs. Transplants are one or more seasons older than sets and usually available in garden stores in mid- to late autumn. If growing seeds, cover them only lightly with soil.

Red onions

Frequent thinning is necessary for a good onion harvest. Onions are heavy feeders, so it's a good idea to add aged compost to the planting area a couple of weeks ahead of time. You can expect to harvest mature onions in 12 to 18 weeks. Successively planting more onions can give you an ongoing crop of fresh, tasty onions. Generally grown as an annual, this biennial edible can reseed itself in your landscape indefinitely, given the opportunity, so choose a well-drained spot that gets plenty of sun.

Onions about to flower next to radishes in full bloom

CURING ONIONS

Onions are mature when the tops die back naturally. When the top half of mature stems have turned brown, stop watering. When the lower stem begins to turn yellow, carefully dig them out of the ground. After they have been dug up, they need time to cure, or dry. This reduces the risk of rotting. Harvested onions can be braided, laid out flat, or placed in nets for several days to dry out properly.

ONIONS IN THE LANDSCAPE

Due to their ability to self-propagate, onions and their cousins make useful foodscape plants. Keeping mature plant sizes in mind, you can create attractive mixed plantings that can be lovely and useful.

Mature onion plants can grow three feet tall, with impressive spherical flowers that attract hoverflies and other beneficial insects. Wide-leafed leeks are slightly shorter and can stay in place for several months before they must be harvested. Narrow-leafed garlic is more seasonal, providing green spikes for several winter and spring months, followed by browning that some find messy. The browned tops can be bent over and hidden from view behind spiky, clumping chives that tend to stay green year-round, offering up miniature versions of the onion flowers.

WHY DO ONIONS MAKE ME CRY?

Onions contain protective enzymes that are released as an acid gas when cut. That's what burns your eyes and causes you to tear up when cutting onions. And you can ignore all those great ideas about how to avoid the burn: bread in your mouth, sunglasses, lemon juice…none of them work. If you really need respite from onion burn, freeze or refrigerate your onions before cutting, or cut them under or in front of a fan.

Scallions

Zones 6—9
Sun exposure: full sun
Ideal soil temperature: 50°F to 90°F

The crisp, slender stalks of scallions are easy to grow and they take up very little space in a garden or on a windowsill.
Scallions, also known as green onions or spring onions, can either be immature onions before they set bulbs (spring onions), or a specific variety of Allium that never forms significant bulbs.

SCALLIONS IN THE GARDEN

Scallions can be grown in window boxes, indoor planting containers, hanging planters, or in the ground. They can be grown in full sun or they can be used in shade gardening. The spiky forms of newly growing scallions add a pretty accent to many plantings.

How to Grow Scallions

Seeds can be started at any time of year and seedlings can be grown indoors or out. Seeds should be heavily planted, ½" deep. Scallions can be grown in clumps, so there is no need to thin transplants. Scallion seeds require moisture to germinate and they can take a month to get started. Keep the soil moist

Scallions

and be patient. Like other onions, scallions have a shallow root system, so proper irrigation and frequent, gentle weeding are important. Scallions are heavy nitrogen feeders, so feed regularly with fish emulsion, blood meal, or alfalfa meal. Planting a new batch of scallion seeds every three weeks will keep you supplied with scallions year-round. Also, each time you snip the base off a scallion, those roots can be replanted to grow a new scallion!

Shallots

Zone 4—8
Sun exposure: full sun
Ideal soil temperature: 50°F to 90°F

Shallots are a type of onion. Until recently, shallots were classified as their own species, but we now know that they are, in fact, members of the onion family, along with scallions, chives, leeks, and garlic. Slightly milder in flavor, shallots add a special touch to your cooking and, yes, cutting them up will make you cry.

Types of Shallots

Shallots are believed to have originated in Central or Southwest

Asia. There are several types of shallots, but the two most well-known are the popular, red-skinned shallot (*Allium cepal*), and the more flavorful French Gray shallots (*A. oschaninii*).

How shallots grow

Shallots are a type of bulb. Rather than growing a single bulb, the way onions do, or as a single head with several cloves, the way garlic grows, shallots create clusters of identical daughter bulbs, called offsets. Covering each bulb is a protective layer of papery tissue that can range in color from golden brown to crimson red. The flesh can be off-white, tinged with magenta or green. Shallots are very tolerant plants. They can handle bright, hot sunlight or partial shade, and they will grow in soil pH from 5.0 to 6.8. Shallots love phosphorus, but they cannot tolerate poor drainage. Shallots that sit in soggy soil will rot.

Red-skinned shallots (Ask27) CC BY-SA 3.0

How to grow shallots

October and November are the best times of year to plant shallots in the mild areas. You can start with seeds, but I urge you to try using those offshoots, commonly called "starts" for faster results. Prepare the bed by top dressing with aged compost. The looser the soil is, the better. Then, simply press the root end of each bulb into the soil, leaving the shoulders of the bulb above ground. Space plants 6" apart. Rows should be 10" apart. Do not mulch heavily on top of the bulbs as this can interfere with initial growth. Straw works well.

In spring, as your shallot begin to develop bulbs, give them a nutritional boost with aged compost or a well-balanced organic fertilizer. Shallots use an inch of water a week, so be sure to irrigate regularly during dry spells.

If flower stalks emerge, remove them. Continue watering and weeding your shallots until the tops of the leaves begin to turn yellow and fall over.

Shallots grow very well in containers and look lovely on windowsills, especially when so many other plants are dormant. When you harvest a shallot plant, cut the leaves an inch or two above the bulb and allow the bulb to dry in a cool, dark area. If cured properly, they can be stored for up to six months. If you leave some of your shallot plants to continue their life cycle, you can collect your own offshoots for the next season's crop.

Shallots can be pricey in the store, but they are easy to grow at home.

Chapter Thirteen

SUNFLOWER FAMILY

The sunflower family (Asteraceae) is a cheery group. All members have brightly colored compound flowers and shallow roots, and many make their way to the dinner table. Artichokes, Echinacea, lettuce, escarole, chamomile, tarragon, and chicory are all part of the sunflower family. So are dandelions, marigolds, cardoons, and salsify. These plants are best started in spring, under full or partial sun, in loose soil. They have very few pests and they tend to attract pollinators and other beneficial insects.

That being said, artichoke plume moths, cabbageworms, squash bugs, and sunflower bud moths may cause occasional problems. Diseases of this group include angular leafspot, crown gall, cucumber vein yellowing, and scab.

If you already have dandelions, sneezeweed, or cornflowers, you may as well give the sunflower family a try.

Artichokes

Zones 3—11, when grown as annuals
Zones 7—11, when grown as perennials
Sun exposure: full sun
Ideal soil temperature: 70°F to 80°F

Artichokes are a ritualistic food that require patience, good conversation, and a nice glass of wine to be truly appreciated.

Modern artichokes (*Cynara cardunculus* var. *scolymus*) evolved from the cardoon. Cardoons are still grown for their stalks and immature buds. Artichokes found in grocery stores today tend to be larger and tougher than is ideal. Growing your own lets you enjoy a more tender and flavorful artichoke. As an added health benefit, artichokes contain more antioxidants than most other vegetables.

'Artichokes' by Karen Bacica (www.facebook.com/karenbacicafineart)

The artichokes we eat are actually spiny, immature flower buds. Each artichoke is made up of a cluster of hundreds of smaller flowers, protected by modified leaves called bracts. Once these flowers bloom, the meaty bracts and the base, or heart, are too tough to eat. The lovely purple flowers are nice to look at, though.

GARDEN SPACE FOR ARTICHOKES

Artichokes can be grown practically anywhere, but they are large plants, averaging 4'-6' across, so be sure to give them room to grow. They prefer cool, moist summers (or relatively shady spots) and mild winters. The majority of the commercial crop is grown in the central, coastal areas of California.

Artichoke bud (Jamain) CC BY-SA 3.0

While most artichokes are grown as annuals, they can be grown as perennials, producing edible buds for four to five years. Under the right conditions, you may be able to harvest as many as 30 artichokes per plant per year. Mature artichoke plants will also give you baby artichoke plants. To get the most out of this crop, it is important to

Artichoke flower

provide light, nutrient-rich soil, and plenty of water in summer.

ARTICHOKE VARIETIES AND PROPAGATION

Artichokes are either green or purple. Traditionally, they are a warm weather crop that is propagated vegetatively or by seed, depending on the variety. Vegetative propagation refers to division and root cuttings. To divide an artichoke plant, simply wait for new growth to appear in spring. Sink a shovel between the new shoot and the parent plant, lift the new growth with the shovel and transplant it elsewhere. Root cuttings can be taken from established plants and placed in moist soil. They will create a new stem and become independent plants. Varieties that perform better through vegetative propagation include Italy's large purple Romanesco, Spain's medium green 'Blanca de Tudela', and Peru's 'Spinoso e Inguano'.

If you live in a colder region, it is important that you select a cold-tolerant variety. Heirlooms, such as 'Violetta Precoce', 'Green Globe', or 'Romanesco' are very temperature sensitive and will not grow well in northern regions. 'Opera' and 'Imperial Star' are better choices for colder areas. 'Green Globe' and 'Imperial Star' perform the best in Zone 9.

Since artichokes have deep taproots, they are not well suited to containers. They are best planted directly in the ground. Artichoke seeds should be sown ¼"-½" deep when temperatures are expected to be 70°F-75°F for a few weeks. Artichokes are heavy feeders, so side dress each plant with fertilizer or aged compost at the beginning of the growing season. Plants will need 1/10 of a pound of nitrogen at each feeding. Blood meal works well, and it has no fillers.

ARTICHOKE PESTS AND DISEASES

At the end of each growing season, many pests can be thwarted by cutting the stems to ground level and covering with mulch. Artichoke curly dwarf is a viral disease that causes stunting and dark, necrotic (dead) spots. To avoid this problem, use only disease-free stock. Botrytis, or gray mold, is a fungal disease that occurs after extended periods of warm, wet weather.

Harvest your artichokes when they are about the size of an apple for the best flavor and tenderness.

A funny side note about artichokes: the fleshy leaves contain a chemical, called cynarine, that inhibits taste receptors, making water and other things taste sweeter! Did you know that artichokes are used to make tea and liquor? Now you know.

Chicory

Zones 3—8
Sun exposure: full sun, partial sun, partial shade
Ideal soil temperature: 55°F to 70°F

Chicory root coffee may stir you to wax romantic, with dreams of beignets and jazz, but these rugged roadside weeds have a lot to offer.

Blue chicory flower (Alvesgaspar) CC BY 2.5

Chicory is not a single type of plant. Instead, it is its own tribe within the sunflower family. Members of the chicory clan are woody biennials, often grown as annuals. They have pretty blue composite flowers. Occasionally, the flowers can be white or pink, but this is rare. Flowers appear all summer and into autumn. Chicory leaves are normally toothed or lobed. The stems are tough and hairy, with a groove running lengthwise. Chicory plants can grow 10"-40" tall. Like their cousins, the dandelions, chicory plants have an irritating milky sap called latex.

If you see wild chicory growing, the soil is probably compacted. Luckily, chicory's deep taproot helps break up that compacted soil, plus it's drought tolerant.

CHICORY'S BITTER TRUTH

It's true. Chicory can be bitter. Some people like it and some don't. Apparently, we evolved to dislike bitterness to avoid being poisoned. Sounds fair. As a result, we now avoid many healthy foods.

Speaking of healthy foods, we all know how important it

is to eat our fruits and vegetables. A certain animated sailor has been telling us, for decades, to eat our spinach. You may be surprised to learn that chicory contains twice as much nutritional goodness as that other salad standard.

Chicory contains powerful compounds called polyphenols. In 2013, the Journal of Nutrition published research showing that adults who consume 650 mg of polyphenols each day tend to live longer and better than those who don't. This is because those compounds protect our cardiovascular systems, fight cancer, and reduce inflammation. One cup of chicory contains 235 mg of polyphenols, twice the amount found in spinach!

CHICORY AS FOOD

Chicories are highly versatile plants. Their slightly bitter leaves are used in salads, the buds can be blanched in boiling water, and the taproots are frequently roasted and ground up as a coffee substitute. Your chickens will love it, too.

The leaves of chicory plants that have been stressed tend to be more bitter. You can reduce the bitterness by irrigating regularly, or changing the cooking water a few times. If you want to harvest chicory root for a Big Easy beverage, you'll want to gather them before the flowering stems emerge. These roots can also be cooked and eaten the same as carrots or parsnips, ground into flour and used to make bread, and some brewers add chicory to their beer recipes. How's that for versatile?

Chicory

CHICORY CONFUSION

The chicory tribe has lent itself to a lot of confusion over the years. Wild chicories go by many names: cornflower, bachelor's buttons, coffeeweed, hendibeh, blue daisy, and wild endive. But that's not the confusing part. Like other family connections, the chicory clan includes radicchio, Belgian endive (pronounced on-DEEV), and frisée. How are those related?

It ends up that chicory is divided into two major groups: the endives and the chicories. (See where the confusion starts?) To complicate matters, those groups are subdivided further. The endive group splits into escarole and curly endive, or frisée, and the chicory group splits into a root group and a leaf group. This might help:

> **Chicory (*Cichorium*)**
> endive (*C. endivia*)
>   escarole (*C. endivia latifolium*)
>   curly endive, or frisée (*C. endivia crispum*)
> chicory (*C. intybus*)
>   roots (*C. intybus sativum*)
>   leaves (*C. intybus foliosum*)

Before we look at the differences between these groups, let's learn about their similarities.

HOW TO GROW CHICORIES

Chicories are cool season plants that prefer plenty of sunlight but can be grown in partial shade. They look nice on balconies, too! In warm regions, chicories can be started in late summer, and again in early winter. These plants are tolerant of and made sweeter by a light frost. Plants prefer a soil pH of 5.0 to 6.8.

Prepare the seed bed by top dressing with aged compost.

As your chicories grow, side dress with more aged compost. This will provide valuable nutrients, retain moisture, and slow weed growth. Chicories require consistent moisture for the best flavor and the least amount of bitterness.

Seeds should be planted ¼" deep and thinned to 12"-18" apart. Plants growing too close together are more likely to bolt. If you allow them to go through their full life cycle, the flowers will attract pollinators and you will find salad greens turning up everywhere that it can grow. Most chicories mature in 85 to 100 days, depending on conditions.

CHICORY PESTS AND DISEASES

Despite chicory's rugged nature, all the usual pests and diseases will try taking advantage of your chicories, along with darkling beetles, but serious damage is rare once plants are established. Apparently, the bitterness that makes chicories so healthy for us also makes them undesirable to pests. You can use brassica collars to protect seedlings from cutworm damage and row covers to block many of the other pests.

Diseases specific to the chicories include bacterial soft rot, bottom rot, leaf rot, Rhizoctonia blight, Septoria blight, and white mold. You can prevent many of these diseases by employing good cultural practices. Narrow-leaved varieties seem to have no serious diseases.

Chicory is one of those plants that can grow like a weed. Once established, you can pretty much ignore it until you decide to harvest whatever part you have a hankering for. Even the flowers are edible!

Now, let's look at the differences between endives and chicories and their cultivars.

Endives

If you eat salads, soups, or burgers, escarole and curly endive are excellent additions to your garden. Endives look pretty, they tolerate both heat and cold, and, if allowed to go to seed, will decorate your yard with dozens of rosette-shaped edible plants for years to come.

ESCAROLE

Escarole (*C. endivia latifolium*) is a "bitter green" endive that looks like lettuce, but packs a powerful nutritional punch. Grown since Egyptian times, escarole is a rugged, versatile plant. And no Italian wedding soup would be right without it.

Escarole makes a nice edible border

Lightly sautéing or braising escarole is the best way to bring out its sweetness. Escarole does not freeze well, but many of the recipes that use it do, so cook some up and freeze it for later use. In fact, it is easier to find recipes for escarole than growing tips. But grow it we shall!

Unlike it's curly-leaved sibling, escarole has broad, flat leaves that form an open head with a yellow to white center. The degree of greenness in the leaves is an indicator of its bitterness. The chemicals that create that bitterness are said to aid digestion.

When plants are five to six inches tall, you can remove outer leaves any time you like, or cut the entire plant off at ground level. Leaving the root system in place will feed important soil microorganisms that help our plants thrive. More often than not, new leaves will grow from this stump.

CURLY ENDIVE, OR FRISÉE

The thing I like best about growing curly endive (*C. endivia crispum*) is that I don't have to think about it. It's always there (except for during the peak of summer) and I don't have to do anything for it.

Narrow, curly dark leaves form a loose head or a rather prostrate rosette that grows in my lawn, around my ornamentals, under my fruit trees, in containers, and pretty much anywhere a seed landed after my original crop bolted. I'll never have to buy curly endive plants or seeds again!

Curly endive

Grab a packet of mixed endives today and get them started. Your salads will taste better and your foodscape will have that much more to offer!

Chicory chicory

The *intybus* half of the chicory world is grown for either roots or leaves. These plants all share the same characteristics as other chicories, but they have some unique attributes that deserve mention.

BELGIAN ENDIVE

There is a reason why Belgian endive (*C. intybus sativum*) is so expensive in the stores. Also known as French endive, odds are pretty good that you can grow your own, if you have the time.

Belgian endive, left to its own devices, can be quite bitter. The Belgian endive you see in the grocery store has been blanched to reduce that bitterness.

It ends up that the chlorophyll plants use to make food from sunlight also makes chicories bitter. Blocking the sunlight, or blanching, for two to three weeks before harvesting gives the plants their delicate white color and removes much of the bitterness. To blanch Belgian endive, wait until the plants are 4"-

5" tall and the leaves are dry (to avoid rotting), tie a string around each plant, and place a large planter or bucket over each one. Commercially grown Belgian endive is planted very close together, creating a blanching environment, but it's tricky.

Did you know that Belgian endive is grown twice? Before blanching takes place, you have to grow the root. Then you grow the head. If you simply put a Belgian endive seed in the ground and water it, you will get what looks like all the other chicory plants.

In the case of Belgian endive, a seed is planted and allowed to grow normally. Then the top portion is removed, the root is refrigerated (vernalized) and then replanted, and then grown in the dark. This forces the plant to respond as though it has gone through a winter. As a result, the head it produces is very tightly wrapped, pale, and tender.

To grow your own nutty, crunchy, slightly bitter winter greens, follow these steps:

Belgian endive (Bff) CC BY-SA

Belgian endive plants (Rasbak)
CC BY-SA 3.0

- In spring, plant Belgian endive seeds (110-140 days before your first hard frost) in loose, well-drained soil with a pH of 6.5 or higher.
- When plants are 3" tall, thin to a 4" spacing.
- Allow the plants to grow through summer, feeding them gently but not with too much nitrogen, which can result in too much leaf growth and not enough root.
- In late autumn, when roots are 1½" in diameter, carefully dig them up and put them in a protected spot, out

of sunlight, for a couple of days to cure.

- Cut off the leaves, leaving 1" above the crown.
- Put the roots in cold storage (your refrigerator will work) for at least two weeks.
- Replant the roots in trays or containers in a dark room or under a cover that will block the light and water as needed.

Three to four weeks later, you will have your very own Belgian endive crop. Simply snap the head off and there you have it! Each root only produces one head, so the old root can be fed to your chickens or added to the compost pile. Be sure to try my recipe for Pear Feta Bites. It's always a party favorite!

RADICCHIO AND SUGARLOAF

Radicchio

Sugarloaf chicory (Adaptive Seeds)

The chicories grown for their leaves (*C. intybus foliosum*) include radicchio and sugarloaf chicory. Sugarloaf chicory looks a lot like Romaine lettuce, but with a toothed edge. Also known as sugarloaf borca and green radicchio, plants mature into football-shaped heads that can be grown and cut, year after year. Like other chicories, sugarloaf chicory is more bitter than most salad greens. These loaves of green are often braised or grilled before eating, to reduce the bitterness and to bring out more of their sweetness.

Sugarloaf chicory and radicchio can be grown from seed, or you can let them self-seed and go a little wild. Ultimately, you can also propagate these greens using division.

In most parts of the country, sugarloaf chicories and radicchios are planted in late spring and early summer for autumn and early winter harvests. They are very drought tolerant plants but will taste better with regular irrigation. They grow best in loose soil with good drainage, making them an excellent choice for raised beds. Plants mature in 80 days, on average.

Jerusalem Artichokes

Zones 3—9
Sun exposure: full sun
Ideal soil temperature: 65°F to 90°F

Jerusalem artichokes are a type of sunflower with an edible tuber.

Having nothing to do with Jerusalem and very little to do with artichokes, these members of the sunflower family are native to the eastern half of North America. There is debate over the source of the name Jerusalem (which may be a corruption of the Italian word for sunflower, girasole), the "artichoke" portion of the name comes from the flavor shared by these two plants. Other people claim these tubers taste more like chard, only sweeter.

Also known as earth apples, sunroots, Canadian truffles, or sunchokes, Jerusalem artichokes (*Helianthus tuberosus*) have provided an attractive dietary staple to many indigenous peoples. Now naturalized in Europe, thanks to the colonists who sent tubers home, Jerusalem artichokes have been out of favor in the U.S. until recently.

Jerusalem artichokes look like their cousins, the sunflowers, growing 6'-15' tall. The bright yellow flowers are somewhat smaller. The tubers look a lot like turmeric and ginger. Long and bumpy, these tubers can range in color from brown to white, or purple to red, depending on the species and growing conditions.

Growing Jerusalem artichokes

To grow your own Jerusalem artichoke crop, begin by selecting a site. Remember, these plants are going to be around for a long time, and they can become rather tall. Unlike many other plants, sunchokes seem to enjoy being clumped together, but they should still be planted 8"-12" apart. Create soil mounds over the plantings, 2"-3" deep, and water regularly, allowing the soil to dry out between waterings.

Starting with a single Jerusalem artichoke tuber, you will eventually find your garden

Jerusalem artichoke plant with flowers (Paul Fenwick) CC BY-SA 3.0

overrun with these perennials. Each plant can produce 75-200 tubers every year. That works out to about 5 pounds. Left unharvested, each of those will produce tubers of their own. To some, that's a good thing—others may feel differently. Since tubers left in the ground for too long tend to get woody and inedible, and they can become invasive, they are good candidates for large containers or raised beds. Grown in containers, Jerusalem artichokes will need to be watered deeply, once a week, throughout the summer. Staking may be needed to keep them from toppling over, or you can grow them along a fence or against a building.

Harvesting Jerusalem artichokes

As the leaves, flowers, and stems begin to die back at the end of the growing season, usually in autumn, you can dig up the tubers and allow them to dry, unwashed, for storage. Sunchoke stems can be chopped and used for mulch or left whole and used to make a pole bean teepee next spring. Any tubers that will be saved for next year's crop are simply placed back in the growing bed, along with some aged compost, and the cycle begins again.

Surprisingly low in starch, Jerusalem artichokes contain a type of carbohydrate sugar, called inulin, which gives them an underlying sweet taste. While the human gut cannot digest inulin, bacteria farther down can, so some people may experience a certain "airiness" after eating sunchokes. If they are not bothersome to you, they also

Sunroot tubers (H2ase) CC BY-SA 3.0

provide a lot of good nutrition. Or, if you prefer, you can ferment your Jerusalem artichoke crop to make brandy, the way they do in Germany.

As an older native plant, sunchokes have very few pests or diseases to worry about. So, mark your calendar to start Jerusalem artichokes in spring, and start preparing the planting space today!

Lettuces

Zones 2—11
Sun exposure: full sun, partial sun, partial shade
Ideal soil temperature: 70°F to 85°F

Lettuce may not look like it has much to offer, but this member of the sunflower family can provide good food, ground cover, and color!

Lettuce is a biennial garden staple that finds its way into most burgers and lays the foundation for nearly every salad ever made. With half of the world's lettuce being grown in China, and numerous cases of *E. coli* and *Salmonella* poisoning from

236

bagged salads, lettuce should be one of the first garden plants you try. Fresh lettuce is cheaper, tastier, safer, and far better for the environment than anything that has been shipped from half-way around the world.

HISTORY OF LETTUCE

The ancient Egyptians took advantage of a certain type of weed whose seeds contained a lot of oil. Over time, those weeds became domesticated and the edible leaves started being used for food and medicine. The Romans gave lettuce its Latin name, *Lactuca sativa*, for the white latex (*lactuca*) that drips from cut stems. (*Sativa* means cultivated.) Seeds were saved from favored types, ultimately creating nearly 150 varieties of lettuce.

Lettuces look lovely between rose bushes!

LETTUCE VARIETIES

Lettuce generally grows as a crisphead, loose leaf, or romaine form, but there are seven cultivar groups:

- Oilseed lettuce is grown solely for its large, oil-packed seeds.
- Stem lettuce is grown for its stalk and used primarily in Asian cooking.

- Iceberg, or crisphead, lettuce is mostly water, with few nutrients, but it ships and stores well.
- Romaine lettuce, of Caesar salad fame, contains high levels of folic acid.
- Loose leaf, cutting, or bunching lettuce comes in many shapes and colors.
- Bibb, Boston, or butterhead lettuce is a sweet, loosely formed head (perfect for Lettuce Wraps!).
- Summercrisp, or French crisp, is a cross between crisphead and loose leaf, but larger and sturdier than Bibb.

Romaine Notes

Your Caesar salad wouldn't be the same without romaine. Romaine is also called "cos" for the Greek island of Cos, where it was grown extensively.

Romaine is a nutritional powerhouse, high in folate, which has been shown to boost male fertility and reduce depression for everyone. The CDC ranks romaine as the 9th healthiest food you can eat to prevent chronic disease. It tastes pretty good on a burger, too!

Loose leaf lettuce leaves may be smooth, frilly, curled, notched, or scalloped. Leaf lettuces contains plenty of vitamin K, which helps promote bone strength.

HOW TO GROW LETTUCES

Lettuce plants prefer full sun, but they can grow just fine in shade gardens, too! In spite of their taproots, lettuces do not need particularly large or deep containers to provide you with fresh leaves for your sandwiches and salads. You can grow lettuces on bright windowsills, in containers, in a traditional garden, or scattered throughout your landscape. Wherever you grow lettuces, you'll be glad you did.

Lettuce seeds are really tiny, so don't try planting outside on a windy day. (Yep, I learned that one the Hard Way.) Seeds only need to be covered with ¼" of soil, but they must be kept moist until they germinate. Misting is a good way to keep seeds moist without knocking them

Romaines and other lettuces grown in a doubly raised bed

into your neighbor's yard. Vermiculite works, well, too. Water thoroughly at first and then as needed to prevent wilting.

Spacing between plants depends on the variety. If you plant new seeds every few weeks, in succession, you will get a continuous harvest. Loose leaf and romaine lettuces can be harvested in a cut-and-grow method, in which outer leaves are removed as needed and the plant is allowed to continue providing edible leaves for the entire growing period. You can also wait until the head is full size and then cut it off an inch or so above soil level. You might be surprised to see the plant will start producing another head!

BOLTING

Once temperatures start rising, your lettuce plants will probably bolt, or go to seed. You can tell this is happening because your docile, rounded lettuce plants will suddenly send up a spike from the center that looks very sun-lettuce-like. If you allow this to continue, and I urge you to do so, your lettuce plant will become too bitter to eat, but it will produce flowers and seeds for future generations. You

Bolting red leaf lettuce

can let them fall where they will, or you can wrap bags around flowering heads to collect seeds. I now have an attractive food-scape, with all sorts of lettuces growing in all sorts of places. Unless it's the peak of summer, you can create a fresh salad with a variety of lettuces simply by walking around your backyard!

LETTUCE PESTS AND DISEASES

Aphids are a lettuce plant's worst enemy, with snails and slugs being a close second. In addition to all the other usual pests, rabbits, voles, and uncaged chickens will all be attracted to your lettuce plants.

White mold can sometimes be a problem, too. For the most part, though, lettuce grows so quickly, that you are bound to have plenty, in spite of the pests.

Finally, any packet of lettuce seeds that you buy will have far more seeds than you will be able to use in a growing season. Solution: swap seeds with friends and neighbors!

Planting lettuces near garlic and chives is said to reduce aphids, but I don't know if that's true.

Sunflowers

Zones 2—11
Sun exposure: full sun, partial sun
Ideal soil temperature: 70°F to 85°F

Sunflowers hardly need description, but there is a lot more to these giant flowers than meets the eye.

Sunflowers (*Helianthus annus*) come in lots of sizes. Some types of sunflowers grow as a single fat, hairy stalk with a massive flower on top, while others grow several branches with smaller flowers. Some dwarf varieties are only two feet tall, while others can reach twelve feet or more!

If the happy blooms and tasty seeds weren't reason enough to add them to your garden, sunflowers also attract many beneficial insects. Honey bees, lacewings, butterflies, hoverflies, and parasitic wasps enjoy the nectar, pollen, and prey insects found on and near sunflowers. Sunflowers will also attract tiny wrens and finches. These birds are very fond of eating the wide, spade-shaped leaves. Local squirrels and seed eating birds can become problematic, but you can always plant a few extras near the fence.

Dwarf sunflowers

ANCIENT HISTORY AND SUNFLOWERS

Sunflowers are native to North America. Recent research has shown that they were also growing in Central America way back into antiquity. According to researchers at the University of Cincinnati, "sunflowers were domesticated thousands of years and hundreds of miles apart" making them an interesting topic in human history. In the 1500s, Spanish conquistadores banned the use of sunflowers in Mexico, believing that they were aphrodisiacs. More currently, sunflowers are one of the world's top oil producing plants. Each year, nearly 45 million tons of sunflowers are grown worldwide.

HELIOTROPISM

Heliotropism refers to a plant's ability to track the sun across the sky. Sunflowers are masters of heliotropism. But it's not a simple matter of evaporation on the sunny side that moves these behemoths. Instead, they use hormones, called auxins, and an internal circadian clock to track the sun. During the night, they turn their west-facing blooms back toward the east, in anticipation of the dawn. Scientists were surprised to discover that bringing outdoor sunflowers indoors, with a constant overhead light source, the plants still went through their east to west cycle for a few days. It was also found that certain genes tell the east side of these plants to grow more quickly during the day, while the west side grows more at night. As they mature, this movement slows, leaving most sunflowers facing east, rather than west. The reason? It ends up that eastward facing flower heads heat up more quickly than their westward neighbors. This added warmth attracts five times more beneficial insects, for better pollination and pest protection!

SUNFLOWERS AND CHILDREN

Sunflowers grow quickly, and often to impressive heights, making them an excellent choice when gardening with children. If you plant sunflower seeds properly, you can create a fort, maze, or magic castle right in your own back yard! Or, to watch germination as it happens, place sunflower seeds inside a clear glass with a dark colored sponge. Place the seeds between the glass and the sponge and add water. Before you know it, the magic happens!

If you turn the seeds different ways, you can see for yourself how the roots always go down and the stem always goes up. Then take your sunflower sprouts and add them to a salad or plant them in the garden! In either case, they make a healthy snack and provide your children with a sense of ownership.

HOW TO GROW SUNFLOWERS

Most sunflower plants are grown from seed. Sunflowers need lots of sun, water, and nitrogen, but they are less picky about soil than many other plants. Seeds can be started in small containers and then transplanted, or they can be directly sown into the garden or landscape, after the last chance of frost has passed.

Seeds should be planted 1" deep and watered daily until they sprout. Seedlings will need an inch of water each week. For optimal growth, space your sunflowers 2' apart. Dwarf varieties only need 6". Seedlings often need protection from birds, squirrels, slugs and snails. Sunflowers can take up to 3 months to reach full size. Sunflowers do, occasionally, need staking.

Sunflower seeds contain a chemical that is toxic to grass plants, so you should harvest the seeds before they start falling on your lawn or near other members of the grain family.

You can also plant sunflowers much the way Native Americans did, using the Three Sisters Method, by replacing corn with sunflowers. The squash or melon leaves will shade the ground around your sunflowers and pole beans will climb the stalks and provide a nitrogen boost before they go to seed themselves.

SUNFLOWER PESTS AND DISEASES

Sunflowers tend to be sturdy plants that fend for themselves rather well. Keep a lookout for ant trails going up the stalks that can indicate an aphid problem. Sticky barriers can be used to block the ants, which makes the aphids more vulnerable to their natural enemies. Along with all the garden variety pests and plant diseases, your sunflowers may have to deal with dried fruit beetles, carrot beetles, some foliage-feeding caterpillars, leaf beetles, and the dreaded sunflower bud moth. Fungal diseases, such as crown gall, can be a problem, but this occurs more in agricultural fields than in backyard gardens.

HARVESTING SUNFLOWERS

Once your sunflower head has reached full size, it will probably be bent over and surprisingly heavy. Before removing the head from the stalk, use your fingernail to nick out a few seeds and open them up. Are the seeds plump? If not, give them some more time. You certainly don't want to harvest a head of empty shells! Seeds have normally reached maturity around the same time the petals start to fall from the flower. You can protect immature heads from birds with netting or large paper bags.

Once the seeds have reached maturity, cut the stem an inch or two below the flower head. If you stroke the face of the flower head with your hand, dozens of tiny dried bits (pappus) will fall away. Give your sunflowers a quick rub to dislodge potential pests and to remove these bits. Seeds can be allowed to dry in the head, or they can be rubbed loose over a newspaper or old sheet.

Sunflowers arrange their seeds with mathematical precision

Save several of the largest, healthiest looking seeds for next year's crop. After that, allow seeds to dry out completely before storing in an airtight container. You can also salt and/or roast your seeds. If you suspect seed pests, freezing your sunflower seeds will kill off any eggs that may be lurking in the shells. Sunflower seeds stored in the refrigerator or freezer are good for a year, while raw seeds stored at room temperature are only good for two to three months. Roasted, shelled seeds have a shelf life of three to four months, and unshelled roasted seeds can last four to five months.

SUNFLOWER TRIVIA

Sunflower oil can be used as a horticultural oil, but I definitely prefer it as sunflower butter on toast or in place of peanut butter in cookies. Yummy!

One variety, the giant whorled sunflower (*Helianthus verticillatus*), was first seen in 1892. Then it was believed to be extinct until 1994 when it was discovered by Vanderbilt University student, Jennifer Ellis. The giant whorled sunflower is currently listed as an endangered species and is only found in Alabama, Georgia, and Tennessee—the birthplace of the sunflower species.

245

Chapter Fourteen

TOMATO FAMILY

Tomatoes, potatoes, and eggplant may seem like an unlikely trio, but they are all members of the nightshade family, along with tomatillos, bell peppers, chili peppers, groundcherries, and tobacco.

Flowers have five petals, leaves are alternate, and the fruit is a berry. These plants love moist, nutrient-rich soil and full sun, with frequent irrigation. While parts of these plants can be toxic, we have long enjoyed the fruits of their labors.

If nettle, jimson weed, or thorn apples grow in your landscape on their own, this group will thrive!

Tomatoes, peppers, and eggplant are all members of the nightshade family
(Horticulturalist RJ) CC BY-SA 4.0

PROBLEMS IN THE NIGHTSHADE FAMILY

These plants are especially prone to Verticillium wilt and Fusarium wilt when crop rotation is not used. Bacterial spot, blossom end rot, cankers, corky ringspot, curly top, foamy canker, and tomato spotted wilt are other diseases specific to the nightshade family.

Bagrada bugs, Colorado potato beetles, corn earworms, hornworms, leaf-footed bugs, leaf rollers, lygus bugs, Oriental fruit flies, stinkbugs, tomato fruit worms, tomato psyllids, and treehoppers can also infest your plants. Nematodes can also be a problem.

Eggplant

Zones 9—12
Sun exposure: full sun
Ideal soil temperature: 75°F to 90°F

Eggplant is a tasty member of the nightshade family.

Cousin to tomatoes, potatoes, peppers, and tobacco, eggplant (*Solanum melongena*) grown in tropical areas is a perennial. Everywhere else, it tends to be a large annual. Your eggplant bush can grow to be five feet tall, but most are closer to two feet tall.

Botanically, an eggplant is a berry. This is because it is a fleshy fruit, without a stone, that grows from a single ovary.

Eggplant with eggs
(Horticulturist RJ) CC BY-SA 4.0

Within that fleshy fruit are many tiny black seeds. These seeds taste bitter because they contain nicotine alkaloids. Don't worry, though. You would have to eat 20 to 40 pounds of eggplant to get the equivalent nicotine found in one cigarette.

HOW TO GROW EGGPLANT

People have been growing eggplant since prehistoric times. It's that easy. Originally from Asia, eggplant needs heat. Seeds can be started indoors a month before your last frost date. The seeds are small, so do not plant more than ¼" deep. With plenty of heat and moisture, your seeds may germinate in as little as 7 days. Be sure to harden off your plants before installing them outside. They will need a spot with plenty of sun and good drainage. Eggplant prefers slightly acidic soil (pH 5.5 to 7.0), so acidification may be necessary in areas with alkaline soil. Plants should be spaced 18"-24" apart. They will need a lot of water and regular feeding. Reduce competition with weeds by mulching around plants. Eggplants are available in several sizes, colors, shapes, and patterns, plus there are early maturing varieties. Time to give 'em all a try!

Three types of eggplant (J.E. Fee) CC BY 2.0

EGGPLANT PESTS AND DISEASES

Pretty purple eggplants
(Joydeep) CC BY-SA 3.0

Lygus bugs will join the ranks of garden pests attacking your eggplant. Foamy canker, mosaic, root rot, tomato spotted wilt, and Verticillium wilt are common eggplant diseases. Eggplants are also susceptible to a condition called "shoe stringing". Shoe stringing describes the way leaves become thin and leathery, with a chewed-up appearance. The cause is unknown at this time.

HARVESTING EGGPLANT

Your eggplants are ready to harvest when the flesh does not spring back when pressed. Do not pull or twist fruit to remove it—this can damage plants. Instead, snip the stem just above the fruit. Eggplants have the best flavor when they are eaten within 24 hours of being picked. And they are best left on the kitchen counter and not in the refrigerator.

According to 13th century Italian folklore, eating an eggplant can make you go crazy. That claim was repeated in 19th century Egypt, when it was said that insanity was "more common and more violent" when the eggplant is in season in the summer.

There are many theories about the insanity claim. Personally, I think it may have something to do with the abundance of food your eggplant plants can produce.

Groundcherries

Zones 8—11
Sun exposure: full sun
Ideal soil temperature: above 75°F

I always assumed that groundcherries grew underground. Having never eaten one or seen one, I decided to learn the truth about them.

Also known as Inca berries, golden berries, and Cape gooseberries, groundcherries are not gooseberries at all. Like tomatoes, however, they are berries. Groundcherries taste like strawberries crossed with pineapple.

Groundcherries (*Physalis*) get their Latin name from the papery bladder that surrounds the fruit. This bladder is made from the calyx. (The calyx is the green sepals that form around the base of a flower.) The common name refers to the way fruits are harvested, once they fall to the ground. There are over 75 species, all of which are native to the tropical Americas, including tomatillo (*P. philadelphica*). There are both edible and inedible members of *Physalis*. Chinese lantern (*P. alkekengi*) is an orna-mental, inedible groundcherry that can become invasive.

GROUNDCHERRY PLANTS

Groundcherry plants look very much like tomato plants, but the stems are sturdier. The leaves can be oval, triangular, or lance-shaped. Like other nightshade plants, the bell-shaped flowers have five petals, with yellow, green, white, or purple centers. These bushy plants are often grown as annuals, but can be perennial, under the right conditions. The fruit is the size of a cherry and can be orange, green, yellow, or purple, with a structure much like tomatoes.

Groundcherries

HOW TO GROW GROUNDCHERRIES

If you can grow tomatoes, you can grow groundcherries. These plants like a lot of sunshine and hot temperatures. They perform well in poor soil and can be grown in containers. Start seeds in small pots 6-8 weeks before the last frost date, planting them ¼" deep. Keep the soil moist. Seeds should germinate in 7-10 days. Like tomatoes, groundcherries will sprout roots from their stems, so seedlings should be planted deep enough to bury the first or second stems. This will give them a better root system. These plants get bushy, so be sure to give each plant the room it is going to need. Plants should be at least 2' apart. Irrigate regularly and be sure to top dress around the plants with aged compost. Groundcherries are heavy feeders.

GROUNDCHERRY PESTS AND DISEASES

Like their cousin, the tomato, groundcherries are susceptible to hornworms and stinkbugs, along with more common garden pests. Many of these can be thwarted with row covers. Groundcherries are resistant to many diseases, but they may be affected by Alternaria, curly top, Fusarium wilt, tobacco mosaic virus, and Verticillium wilt.

HARVESTING GROUNDCHERRIES

Immature fruits are not edible. After the husks have dried and become papery, the fruit will drop to the ground. This is the fruit you should harvest. The husk is not edible and should be added to the compost pile. Groundcherries are commonly eaten fresh, or used to make jams, jellies, sauces, and pies. The fruit can also be dried like a raisin, or used in salads.

Once you have grown groundcherries in your foodscape, it is not uncommon to find them growing on their own the next summer. These tiny packets of sweet, fruity flavor are a delight! They have become a family favorite that we now plant every spring.

Peppers

Zones 9—11
Sun exposure: full sun
Ideal soil temperature: 75°F to 85°F

Sweet or hot, bell-shaped or elongate, all peppers are members of the nightshade family.

People have been growing peppers for several thousand years. Native to the Americas, peppers (*Capsicum*) are now grown all around the world.

PEPPER VARIETIES

Peppers are usually classified as sweet (bell) or hot (chili). In Singapore, India, and Australia, the bells are called capsicum. All peppers start out green. If left on the vine long enough, different varieties may turn yellow, red, orange, or purple. Depending upon who you ask, there are 20 to 27 species (and hundreds of varieties) of peppers. There are five domesticated Capsicum species:

- *C. annuum* - Anaheim, banana, bell, cayenne, jalapeño, ancho/poblano, chipotle
- *C. baccatum* - Bishop's crown, wild baccatum, Brazilian starfish, peppadew
- *C. chinense* - Bhut jolokia, bonnet, Carolina Reaper, habanero, naga, Trinidad
- *C. frutescens* - Tabasco, Xiaomila, Kambuzi, Siling labuyo
- *C. pubescens* - rukutu, luqutu, Manzano peppers

Bell peppers

HOW TO GROW PEPPERS

Peppers love warm weather. In fact, there's no sense starting pepper seeds early, because they won't germinate. Even if they do, they won't grow well. To get a head start on the growing season, many gardeners use seed heating mats. The soil needs to be 70°F to 84°F for peppers to really get going.

Peppers prefer loose, loamy soil (or even sand), making them a good choice for raised beds or containers. Seeds should be planted ¼" deep. Ultimately, you will want to space plants 18"-24" apart. When thinning, snip unwanted plants off at soil level to avoid disturbing other plants' roots. At first, the soil should be kept moist but not soggy. Soggy soil can cause damping off disease and several other problems. All peppers

Thai pepper plant
(Daniel Risecher) CC BY-SA 3.0

are self-pollinating, but crops are significantly larger when other pepper plants are nearby.

Peppers need nighttime temperatures that are at least 50°F to 55°F, to prevent blossom drop. You can improve a seedling's root system by removing any growth from the bottom third of the stem and burying those nodes below the soil surface, the same way you might for tomatoes. These nodes will produce roots, giving your plant access to more water and nutrients. Water deeply, right away, to help the soil settle, removing air pockets, and keeping the roots moist. And be sure to label your plants!

Pepper plants benefit from a thick layer of organic mulch placed around, but not touching, each plant. Plants should be side-dressed with nitrogen about once a month for healthy leaf growth. In August, you can increase feedings to once every two weeks.

Note: if you plan on saving seeds from your peppers, be sure to keep different varieties away from each other, as they will cross-pollinate.

PEPPER PESTS AND DISEASES

Like many other of our favorite food plants, peppers are in big demand in the insect world. Some birds may want to take a bite, as well.

Sunburned pepper

Most pepper diseases are of the standard fungal variety. Use seeds designated with a letter "V"—this indicates resistance to Verticillium wilt. Regular irrigation will control blossom end rot.

Sunburn, or sunscald, can also be a problem on pepper plants. While too much nitrogen can cause excessive vegetative growth and not much fruit, the opposite causes a different set of problems. Low nitrogen levels can reduce leaf coverage to the point that fruit is damaged. Row covers can be used to reduce sun exposure, once fruit set has occurred.

HARVESTING PEPPERS

Each pepper has a color that indicates it is ready to be picked. Read your seed packet or check online or at your local library to learn more about specific varieties. While most jalapeños are harvested when green, the flavor becomes sweeter as the fruits mature and turn red.

One of the most common mistakes gardeners make when harvesting peppers is that they do it too soon. If your peppers feel thin-skinned, give them some more time.

Chili Peppers

If you like your food spicy, chili peppers are a garden necessity.

Hot pepper plants are small shrubs with striking red, orange, or yellow fruits, depending on the variety. These plants look great in a landscape and they can provide you with peppers all summer long.

Cubanelle Peppers

WHY THE HEAT?

The reason chili peppers are hot is because they contain capsaicin. Capsaicin is found, in varying degrees, in nearly all peppers. Sweet bell peppers contain little to no capsaicin. Powerfully hot peppers are used in Africa to keep elephants out of gardens and other crops. Birds, on the other hand, do not have those particular pain receptors, so they are largely responsible for the spread of wild pepper plant seeds. Before we learn about different varieties of hot peppers and how to grow them, a word on Scoville heat units.

SCOVILLE HEAT UNITS

Scoville heat units (SHUs) are used to measure perceived heat or spiciness, as a function of capsaicin levels. The American Spice Trade Association (ASTA) uses high-tech chromatography and some crazy math to measure the relative pungency of a sample. A Scoville heat unit ends up being one part capsaicin per million units of dried pepper. Since it matters just how dry a sample is, people trained to taste hot peppers add their subjective data. (Who knew that was a job?)

Tabasco sauce rates 3750 SHUs, while sriracha sauce ranks in with 2,200 SHUs. Choose your peppers accordingly and be sure to wash your hands with plenty of soap and warm water after handling hot peppers and their seeds before you do anything else. Seriously.

Make a little space in your spring planting schedule to start some chili pepper plants for yourself and your friends.

Scoville Heat Units

PEPPER VARIETY	SHU
Pure capsaicin	16,000,000
Pepper spray	5,000,000
Carolina Reaper	2,200,000
Trinidad Moruga Scorpion	2,000,000
Trinidad Scorpion Butch	1,400,000
Naga Viper	1,300,000
New Mexico Scorpion	1,200,000
Ghost Pepper	1,000,000
Red Savina Habanero	450,000
Orange Habanero	275,000
Scotch Bonnet	250,000
Datil	200,000
Thai	75,000
Cayenne, Bishop's Crown	40,000
Manzano	21,000
Serrano	16,000
Jalapeno	5,500
Poblano, Anaheim	1,500
Banana pepper	250
Bell pepper	0

Paprika

There are far too many foods that seem out of reach when it comes to growing them at home. Paprika is a perfect example. Let's take the mystery out of paprika.

Ever since learning how easy it is to grow edibles at home, I keep finding foods that make my landscape look more interesting and my meals more delicious. I decided to see if I could grow my own paprika. It ends up I can, and so can you!

The paprika we buy in stores is simply dried and ground up sweet peppers (*Capsicum annuum*). In some

Red and green Bishop's crown peppers

cases, the peppers are smoked over oak wood or roasted. Tomato peppers (*C. annuum* var. *annuum*) are the most common ingredient, but pretty much any pepper can be used.

TYPES OF PAPRIKA

Paprika is classified as sweet or hot. Sweet paprika is made from the flesh, or pericarp, and only half of the seeds are used. Hot paprika includes some of the seeds, stems, white part (placenta), and calyces (flower sepals) of sweet peppers along with chili peppers and cayenne peppers, for extra flavor and heat. Most of the paprika you buy in the store is a Hungarian sweet recipe, but cooks and aficionados take paprika more seriously than that. According to *The Complete Book on Spices and Condiments With Cultivation, Processing and Uses*, there are several grades of Hungarian paprika:

- Delicate - mild, rich flavor; light to dark red
- Exquisite delicate - slightly pungent; most commonly

exported; bright red
- Pungent exquisite delicate - more pungent than exquisite delicate
- Rose - strong aroma; mild pungency; pale red
- Semi-sweet - blend of mild and pungent paprikas; medium pungency
- Special quality - mildest; very sweet; deep bright red
- Strong - hottest; light brown

Spanish paprika (pimentón) is classified as mild (pimentón dulce), mildly spicy (pimentón agridulce), and spicy (pimentón picante). How about we create a new set of categories: store-bought and homegrown? While practically any peppers can be used to make paprika, Hungarian and Spanish varieties are the most common. Hungarian peppers tend to be 2"-5" long, oblong to pointy, and thin-walled. These peppers are mostly mild with only a few exceptions. Spanish peppers are larger, ranging 5"-9" long, thick-walled, and more susceptible to disease.

Your paprika peppers are ready to harvest when they develop full color. Since different varieties are different colors, you need to read that seed packet or plant label.

HOW TO PREPARE PAPRIKA

Depending on whether you prefer sweet or hot paprika, you may want to incorporate those other, hotter peppers or remove most of the seeds and pith for a sweeter paprika. In either case, the peppers must be thoroughly dried. You can use a thread and needle to string your paprika peppers up to dry. You can also smoke them over oak, roast them in your oven, or use a dehydrator. Once they are completely dry, grind them up in a food processor or coffee grinder. Voilà! You have made your own paprika!

And guess what? You can use these peppers the same way you would any other, adding them to salads or snacking on them while enjoying your garden. Homegrown, homemade paprika makes nice gifts, too. Did you know that paprika peppers contain more vitamin C than lemon juice and that their flavor improves when heated? Now you know.

Potatoes

Zones 2—11
Sun exposure: full sun
Ideal soil temperature: above 45°F

Grocery store potatoes are cheap. But the plants are attractive and digging through the soil for potatoes for your supper just feels good.

FOOD STORAGE AND GEOPHYTES

Potatoes are tubers. Tubers are a type of geophyte. Geophytes are plant organs used to store food and water. They are also used in asexual reproduction. There are several types of geophytes: bulbs, corms, and everything else. That "everything else" is what

Potatoes

we call tubers. Potatoes and yams are stem tubers. Stem tubers emerge from modified stems. These stems can start out as stolons or rhizomes. Stolons are stems that grow at or just below the soil surface as "runners". These stems are converted into adventitious roots at the nodes and, what would have been a bud above ground, becomes a spud below. Rhizomes are runners that connect a parent plant to its offspring.

A MODIFIED STEM

The "eyes" seen on a potato are actually stem nodes. Within each potato you will find the same plant cells you would find above ground: vascular bundles, pith (spongy tissue), and cortex (outer tissue). Now here's the funny part. While our standard spud grows from stem tubers, sweet potatoes grow from root tubers. The internal cell structure is very different. Root tubers have no nodes. That is why sweet potatoes have a more elon-gated form. At one end, you will find

Potatoes grown in a raised bed with mustards and cabbages

crown meristem tissue, which grows into stems and leaves. At the other end, called the distal end, the tuber produces roots. But enough of that, let's start growing some potatoes!

HOW TO GROW POTATOES

While potatoes can certainly be grown from spuds bought at the grocery store, this is a bad idea. Foods bought in the store are safe for human consumption, but they are not guaranteed to be free from common garden pests and diseases. You are far better off buying certified pest- and disease-free seed potatoes.

The easiest way to grow potatoes is in a barrel or raised bed. You can even use a clean trash can with drainage holes added. If potatoes are planted in the ground, you will be finding rogue spuds for many years. Also, digging them up from the ground is, let's face it, work. Growing potatoes in containers makes harvest-ing significantly easier and they make nice summer patio plants!

To begin, fill the bottom of the container(s) with 4" of loose, moistened soil. Cut seed potatoes into 2" chunks, making sure that each chuck has several eyes. Small seed potatoes can be planted whole. Place the chunks 6" apart and cover them with 3" of moistened soil and repeat the process until the container is filled. Water lightly and be sure to place planters where they will get lots of sunlight.

Potatoes need loose, well-drained soil and frequent, light

watering. Never let potato plants sit in water, or they will rot. Potatoes use a lot of nitrogen and potassium, and they prefer acidic soil (as low as 4.8 pH).

At first, it will look as though nothing is happening. With time, water, and sunlight, those seed potatoes will send out roots and stems that will pull nutrients from the soil and create carbohydrates out of sunshine. (Don't you just love photosynthesis?) Before long, the container will be filled with lush, green growth. Aside from occasional watering and feeding (aged compost works great!), that's all you have to do until it completes the season's life cycle.

HARVESTING POTATOES

Eventually, the lush aboveground growth will start to die off. When it starts looking ragged, dump the contents of the container out on a tarp and remove the mature potatoes. Now comes the really cool part: mix the remaining soil with some aged compost and do it all again with the

Potatoes come in a variety of colors

immature spuds! I have been growing potatoes from the same batch of seed potatoes since 2011. To me, homegrown potatoes taste far better than store-bought spuds.

POTATO PROBLEMS

We've all heard about the Great Potato Famine. Over one million people died and another two million people abandoned Ireland. It was all because of potato blight. Potato blight makes potatoes rot in the ground. Other potato diseases include charcoal rot, corky ringspot, cucumber mosaic, curly top, leafroll, pink root, sclerotium stem rot, cankers, and white mold. Many of these diseases can be prevented with good drainage and proper spacing between plants. These practices will help prevent many of the other garden diseases, as well.

Common potato pests include all the usuals, along with potato psyllids, potato tuberworms, silverleaf whiteflies, Colorado potato beetles, Jerusalem crickets, and wireworms. But don't let these threats stop you from trying your hand at potatoes.

Tomatoes

Zones 5—12
Sun exposure: full sun
Ideal soil temperature: 80°F to 85°F

Prior to Halloween in 1548, Italy had no tomato sauce. Hard to imagine, isn't it?

Native to South and Central America, tomatoes have been cultivated for more than 3,000 years. And it is the promise of sun-warmed, sweet tomatoes that attract many people to gardening. Be forewarned. No store-bought cousin will ever measure up once you have grown your own!

Tomatoes on the vine

WHAT IS YOUR TOMATO TYPE?

Tomato plants are classified as either determinate or indeterminate. Determinate plants, also called "bush" tomatoes look like three to five-foot shrubs and all the tomatoes ripen within a four to six-week period. This is perfect if you plan on canning your bounty. It doesn't really work if you are growing tomatoes for fresh eating. Indeterminate tomatoes put out a continuous crop all summer and fall, providing a similar-sized crop, but spread out over time.

THE TOMATO PLANT

Commonly grown as annuals, tomatoes (*Solanum lycopersicum*) are actually perennial plants in their native regions. These members of the nightshade family, along with eggplants and potatoes, are self-pollinating. This means that honey bees and other pollinators can carry pollen from one flower to another, on the same plant, to cause a plant to create fruit. Of course, the more plants you have, the higher your pollination rates will be. Plus, you can never have too many tomatoes, right?

SHOPPING FOR TOMATO PLANTS

Spring garden shows and plant sales draw gardeners like moths to a flame. This is especially true when it comes to tomato seedlings. With so many varieties, colors, and sizes to choose from, we tend to get carried away. To be fair, who doesn't want to try growing that new black, striped, pear-shaped variety with a nice citrusy aftertaste? So we fill boxes, bags, and the backseat with countless new and old favorite tomato plants and head home.

As dreams of heirlooms and hybrids dance through your head, remember that tomatoes, like all other plants, can carry pests or disease. When you bring new plants home, be sure to place them in a quarantine area until you are sure they are healthy. And handle them gently as you transition them from greenhouse life to life in your yard. Give them some protected time to get used to the weather as you monitor for signs of problems.

HOW TO GROW TOMATOES

Tomatoes are easily grown from seed or cuttings. They grow best in the ground, but can also be grown in containers or raised beds. But starting too soon is a waste of time and seeds, because those won't thrive. Tomatoes can be started indoors six to eight weeks before your last frost date. Seeds should be planted ¼" deep. Keep the soil moist, but not soggy.

Germination of most tomato seeds usually takes five to ten days in warm weather. Colder temperatures slow the process. As your tomato plants get bigger, you may want to provide some support with tomato cages or stakes.

PINCHING YOUR TOMATO PLANTS

No, I don't want you to be mean to them—well, maybe a little. Pinching back excess growth can make more nutrients available to whatever is left and it stimulates flower and fruit production. On the other hand, if you take away too many leaves, your tomatoes can get sunburned. Yellow or green shoulders on otherwise red fruit is also a sign of too much sun exposure. Pruning tomatoes is a balancing act between sun protection, fruit production, and disease prevention. Prune your tomato plants so that they have two or more stems starting near the base of the plant. If you pinch your plants to make one central stem, they will produce fruit earlier, but at lower quantities.

You can give your tomatoes the best flavor by cutting back on watering a few days before harvesting. Called deficit irrigation, this concentrates the flavors and makes your tomatoes taste sweeter.

TOMATO PESTS AND DISEASES

Hornworms and blossom end rot are the two most common problems faced by tomato grow- ers. Blossom end rot is caused by an erratic calcium supply, which occurs whenever water- ing is irregular. (Get your soil tested to see what the calcium and other nutrient levels are be- fore adding amendments. Too much is just as bad as too little.) A regular watering schedule can reduce blossom end rot in tomatoes, as well as leafroll, cracked fruit, and catfacing.

Blossom end rot

Tomato hornworms are large and can devour an amazing amount of foliage before you even know it.

Along with your common garden pests, tomato-specific pests include blister mites, Eriophyid mites, green fruit beetles, Japanese beetles, leaf-footed bugs, oriental fruit flies, stinkbugs, treehoppers, tomato fruitworms, and tomato pinworms. Rats, voles, birds, and squirrels, too. Always squirrels.

Tomato diseases include tomato ring spot, tomato spotted wilt, Alternaria stem canker, tobacco mosaic virus (TMV), gray leaf spot, and stem blight, along with the usuals. Many of these diseases can be pre- vented with regular crop rotation.

Tomatoes grown from seed will devel- op a taproot. What is really strange is that tomatoes grown from

Hornworm

cuttings will not. They grow a fibrous root system instead.

Chapter Fifteen
TREE FAMILIES

A rose by any other name…just might be a peach tree. It's true!

The rose family (Rosaceae) includes a surprising number of popular fruit trees. Apples and pears, known collectively as pomes, are in the rose family. So are the stone fruits, along with raspberries and blackberries. Roses are edible, too. Rose hips, the seed balls that form under flowers, are used in jams, jellies, and tea. Rose water and syrup are used to add flavor to many Middle Eastern dishes, such as halva and baklava. But I digress.

Apples

Most members of the rose family and other fruit and nut trees are deep-rooted, woody perennials. They grow best in areas with loose soil, good drainage, and full sun. These plants have chilling requirements that must be fulfilled before fruit can be produced, so be sure to pick varieties and cultivars that match the chill hours expected in your yard.

Chill hours

We are all familiar with the buds and leaves of spring, the prolific growth of summer, and the harvest of autumn, but fruit and nut trees and shrubs (and strawberries!) are working through winter, as well. Colder winter temperatures are part of these plants' natural lifecycles. In preparation to survive potentially freezing temperatures, they produce a hormone that initiates a state of protective dormancy.

WHAT ARE CHILL HOURS?

Chill hours are an accumulation of temperatures between 32°F and 45°F. Somehow, plants keep track of this information. I have no idea how. But chill hours are so important that stations have been set up across the country to measure them. In this temperature range, the growth inhibiting hormone responsible for dormancy begins to break down. This allows trees and shrubs to begin producing buds which will ultimately become the leaves and flowers of spring.

If not enough chill hours are accumulated, flowers and buds will not form properly, which means you might not get any fruit. This can also extend bloom time, making delicate buds and flowers vulnerable to diseases, such as fireblight and brown rot. Different species need varying amounts of chill hours. Within each species, each variety has its own needs, as well. This is why learning about plants before you buy them is so important. For example, northern varieties of blueberries have chilling requirements of 800-1,000 chilling hours, while southern varieties may only need 150-200 chilling hours. Temperatures above 60°F can reverse chilling accumulations. There are two major models used to calculate chill hours. The Utah model provides chilling hours, while the Dynamic model provides chilling portions. They both take the same basic information into account.

YOUR LOCAL CHILLING HOUR STATION

Universities work in conjunction with the USDA to provide valuable information to farmers and orchardists. You can access this information online and over the phone to find out more about the cumulative chilling hours in your area. Depending on where you live, and how far you are from the nearest recording station, the information will be more or less accurate. Simply call your local Master Gardeners, Department of Agriculture, or university for more information.

Another way you can calculate your chilling hours is to go to www.wunderground.com/wundermap/ to find the recording station closest to you. Just click on the bubble and copy and paste the station number, and then enter that station number on the Get Chill website (getchill.net). This site can be slow sometimes, but the information is very good.

Do not trust your local box store to sell you the right one. Do your homework.

How to plant bare root trees

While you can eat a peach and then plant its seed, this doesn't always work out the way you expect. Like many other popular fruits, peach seeds do not necessarily produce offspring that taste as good or grow as well as the stock you buy at your local nursery. This is because most fruit and nut trees are grafted. Grafted trees have an aboveground part from one variety and a root stock from another variety. This is done to take advantage of one variety's ability to develop strong roots, while other varieties may taste better or be more pest or disease resistant. Also, your pit grown peach tree will not produce fruit for a few years, and some will never produce fruit. Fruit trees can be started from twig cuttings called scions, but most people opt for bare root trees from reputable suppliers.

Tree size characteristics

	Size	Time to maturity	Lifespan
Full	15-20'	20 years	50 years
Semi-dwarf	12-15'	5-8	15-25
Dwarf	10-12'	3-5	15-25

Most bare root stock trees are two or three years old. Bare root trees are best planted in winter and early spring, when temperatures are above 45°F. Choose a site that can accommodate the tree's full size and provide plenty of full sun and good air circulation. You can also grow dwarf fruit and nut trees in large containers.

Before planting, examine the root system for signs of disease or damage. These bits should be cut out. If your bare root tree is not going to be planted right away, it should be soaked in a bucket of water for two to twelve hours, but no longer. (Plants can drown, too, you know!)

When you are ready to plant, dig a hole that allows the roots to spread out freely. Be sure to not leave smooth edges in the hole. This can create an impenetrable barrier to young roots. You can help your tree get a better start by roughing up and scoring the edges of the planting hole and removing any grass or weeds that are growing within two feet of the hole.

Place the tree in the hole, making sure that the graft union (the place where the root stock joins the scion) is at least two inches above soil level. This is important. You should be able to see a slight flare of the trunk at the base. Planting trees too deeply is one of the easiest ways to kill them, though it may take a few years.

Add soil around the roots and water thoroughly, rather than tamping it down. Pressing down on the soil damages delicate root hairs needed by the tree to absorb water and nutrients. Watering, or mudding in, your tree removes air pockets that can dry roots out before they ever get a chance to grow while providing the water needed to recover from the planting ordeal.

It is a good idea to provide tree supports for your young tree. Whitewash the trunk and exposed branches each spring with one part white, interior latex paint and one part water to prevent sunburn damage. Just be sure to remove those supports after the tree is established, and avoid using supports that choke or rub against the bark.

Mulch around your new tree, keeping the mulch several inches away from the tree trunk, and water regularly until the root system has become established. The first two or three years, flowers should be removed, to encourage a strong root system. I know it's hard, but you'll thank me later.

Seasonal fruit and nut tree care

While each species has its own needs, we can make some generalizations about seasonal fruit tree care. These practices keep your trees structurally sound and productive, while reducing pest and disease problems. These trees are deciduous, which means they drop their leaves as temperatures fall. This makes it easy to prune in winter. The only exception to late season pruning are apricots and cherries, both of which are very susceptible to Eutypa dieback. These trees should be pruned when dry weather is expected. For all your other fruit and nut trees, this schedule of care should keep them healthy:

- Winter - prune for size and structure; remove dead, diseased, and rubbing limbs; remove shriveled fruits from the previous season (mummies); rake debris out from under tree; spray dormant oil to control scale insects, and aphid and mite eggs; apply fungicides, as needed; whitewash exposed branches.

- Spring - spray with fungicide when twig tips first green, when buds are pink, and then every 10 days until the rainy season ends; fertilize; water deeply every two to three weeks; thin fruit; install sticky barriers.
- Summer - fertilize; water deeply every two to three weeks.
- Autumn - after harvesting, fertilize using spring rates; remove mummies and fallen fruit; rake debris out from under tree; destroy or compost fallen leaves; apply dormant oil, Bt, or fixed copper, as needed.

FRUIT AND NUT TREE PROBLEMS

Because many of these plants are related, they share many of the same problems. In addition to your garden variety pests and diseases, your fruit trees will be susceptible to several other diseases and pest problems.

Rose Family Diseases

apple scab	Eutypa dieback
bacterial canker	leaf and cane spot
bacterial spot	mottle
botrytis	peach leaf curl
citrus blast	pear scab
crown gall	raspberry leaf curl
cytospora canker	shot hole fungus
dwarf virus	X-disease

Deer, birds, and other critters will try to enjoy your harvest before you do. Netting can help, but it's a pain to take off. Many varieties of caterpillar will also happily munch on fruit and leaves, so monitor your plants every few days in spring and hand pick those beasties. You can always feed them to your chickens.

Rose Family Pests

apple maggots	leaf-footed bugs
borers	leafrollers
codling moths	navel orangeworms
Eriophyid mites	pear psylla
Eugenia psyllids	plum curculio
fruit flies	raspberry horntail wasps
fruitworms	redhumped caterpillars
Fuller rose beetles	

Don't let all those threats discourage you from trying these amazing plants. They survive against the odds. Even notorious Brown Thumbs have been able to grow berries and fruit and nut trees successfully. You can, too!

LONG TERM REWARDS

The plants in this family are an investment in your landscape's future. You will not have a harvest the first year. You won't get one the second year, either. But in the long run, these plants can produce an annual bounty that goes on for decades.

Avocados

Zones 9—12
Sun exposure: full sun

Avocado trees are fascinating. Unlike most fruiting trees, which can be either self-pollinating or not, avocado trees are both and neither. Confused? Read on!

Avocado trees flower with a behavior called synchronous

dichogamy. Each flower is both male and female, but at different times. Also, there are two kinds of flowers: type A and type B. Type A avocados include Haas, Gwen, Lamb Haas, Pinkerton, Reed, GEM, and Harvest varieties. Bacon, Ettinger, Fuerte, Sharwil, Sir Prize, Walter Hole, Zutano, Marvel and Nobel are B avocados.

When an A avocado flower first opens in the morning, it is female for a few hours and then it closes. The next day, the same flower reopens in the afternoon, but this time it is male. When a B avocado flower opens for the first time, in the afternoon, it is female. Then it reopens the next morning as a male. Since a mature tree produces over one million flowers in a season and the flowers open on different days, there is no need for another tree for pollination to occur.

HOW TO GROW AN AVOCADO TREE

Many of us have used toothpicks on an avocado pit with dreams of a productive tree. You can make that dream a reality with these tips (and a lot of patience).

To start an avocado tree from seed, simply insert three or four toothpicks into the sides of the seed and suspend it, fat end down, over a glass

Sprouting avocado pits

of water. One inch of the seed should be submerged. In six to eight weeks, the stem and roots will emerge. To improve structural growth, cut the stem back to 3" when it reaches a height of 6"-7". When leaves reappear, move the young tree to a 10"-12" diameter pot filled with rich soil or to your yard. Be sure to leave the seed half exposed. Water frequently and give it plenty of sunlight. When the seedling reaches a height of 1', cut it back to 6". This will promote the growth of fruit-producing branches. It will take five to thirteen years to start producing fruit.

If you don't want to wait that long, plant a bare root tree. The best time to plant is March and April. Young avocado trees don't take up water very well, so summer months are too hot to start a young tree. Avocados are shallow rooted, which means most of the roots are in the top 6" of soil. Most trees fail because they are planted at the improper depth. Also, avocado roots are very sensitive to damage, so treat them gently as you fill the hole with nutrient rich soil. If the soil is heavy clay, elevate the tree a little bit, in a mound, to avoid drainage problems. The mound should be 1'-2' high and 3'-5' in diameter. Be sure that there is no lawn within several feet of the tree. Mulch will help retain moisture, just don't let it touch the trunk to avoid borers or fungal disease. Avocado trees prefer a soil pH of 6.0 to 6.5 for optimal growth.

Young trees need to be watered two or three times a week. Water heavily, but let the soil dry out between waterings. By the end of the first year, water once a week. A mature tree will use as much as 20 gallons of water a day during the peak of summer and they need a lot of nitrogen and zinc.

Avocado pests and diseases

Common avocado diseases include avocado root rot, bacterial canker, dothiorella canker, leaf blight, phytophthora root and crown rot, stem blight, sunblotch, and Verticillium wilt. Avocado lace bugs, latania scale, mealybugs, mites, nematodes, omnivorous loopers, orange tortrix moths, soft scales, thrips, and whiteflies will all be attracted to your avocado tree. Birds and squirrels will join in the feeding fray, so you may want to build a tree cage around part of your avocado tree. If you have the time and the space, growing an avocado tree in your yard can provide decades of the best guacamole ever!

Citrus

Zones 9—11
Sun exposure: full sun

The flowers of the citrus clan usually have a strong smell and there's no mistaking the heavy, oily skin of citrus. This skin provides moisture-holding protection from its subtropical origins. Hailing from Southeast Asia and Australia, modern citrus fruits evolved from small berries found on pummelo, citron, and mandarin orange trees. Crossing these three ancestors in different ways has led to the creation of oranges, grapefruit, kumquats, lemons, limes, mandarins, and those tiny delicious, loose-skinned oranges (calamansi).

Kumquats

CARING FOR CITRUS

Citrus trees and shrubs grow easily in warmer regions. They can be put in the ground or grown in containers. They prefer well-drained soil and as much sun as you can provide. Since the fruit is very heavy, it is a good idea to protect these trees from heavy winds. Citrus trees can produce for 50 to 100 years, so use care when selecting a site.

Citrus trees are relatively trouble free, when grown in an appropriate location. Pruning is normally limited to the standards of removing dead, diseased, and crossing branches. You will also want to remove vertical water shoots. Citrus tree trunks and the upper surface of exposed branches benefit from whitewashing, to prevent sun scald. Regular feeding will help your citrus tree stay healthy and productive. Each of the dosages listed below should be divided into two or three separate feedings:

- 1st year - 3 tablespoons of nitrogen per tree
- 2nd year - ¼ pound of nitrogen per tree
- 3rd year - ½ pound of nitrogen per tree
- 4th year - ¾ pound of nitrogen per tree
- 5th year and on - 1 pound of nitrogen per tree

Understand that ¼ pound of nitrogen is not the same thing as ¼ pound of packaged fertilizer. Assume, for example, that your 5-pound bag of fertilizer has an NPK of 10-5-2. This means that out of the 5 pounds, 10% of the bag is nitrogen, 5% is phosphorus, and 2% is potassium. (The rest is filler.) This works out to a ½ a pound of nitrogen, a ¼ pound of phosphorus, and 1/10 of a pound of potassium. In all likelihood, your citrus tree will not need those other nutrients, so they are best left out of the equation (especially until after you get a soil test). An easier way to feed your lemon and other citrus trees is to use blood meal or ammonium sulfate.

Blood meal contains 13.25% nitrogen, 1% phosphorus, and 0.6% potassium. To equal one pound of nitrogen, you would need to apply 7½ pounds of blood meal. Five pounds of ammonium sulfate will give you the same amount of nitrogen. Just remember that these feedings are totals for the year and that they should be spread out over three different feedings, ideally in April, June, and August.

Dumping too much water on your orange tree can lead to splitting. Heavy rains can do the same thing. Split citrus are usually not ripe enough to eat but they provide the perfect breeding ground for bacteria, fungi, and other pests. Like mummies, they should be discarded as soon as they are seen.

HARVESTING CITRUS

Knowing when to harvest your citrus can be tricky. Lemons and limes have distinct colors when they ripen, but Valencia oranges may still have a greenish tint to the skin when they are ripe. The only reliable way to tell if your fruit is ripe is to taste it. Unlike climacteric fruits, citrus does not continue ripening once they are removed from the tree. The best place to store your citrus is on the

Heavily laden (and poorly pruned) navel orange tree

tree. If you do pick more fruit than you can use (or a branch breaks, dumping two dozen oranges in your basket), you can store them for four to six weeks in the refrigerator. You can also treat yourself with some fresh squeezed orange juice or a lemon drop! Personally, I grate the zest from two oranges over some sliced beef, juiced four oranges, and stirred in some corn starch, soy sauce, ginger, and a pinch of Ghost Pepper for a delicious Spicy Orange Beef Stir-Fry.

Citrus trees are heavy producers. A mature tree can produce up to 300 oranges a year. Do the math and that comes out to more than 130 pounds of oranges!

CITRUS PESTS AND DISEASES

The biggest insect threat to your citrus tree is the Asian citrus psyllid. This new-to-the-U.S. pest can infect your tree with a fatal disease called huanglongbing, or HLB. If your citrus tree becomes infected with HLB, it must be destroyed by a professional—an experience both sad and expensive.

Before accepting citrus fruit, cuttings, or bare root stock from a fellow gardener, check with your County Extension Office to see if either of you live in a quarantine zone. And be sure to shop for citrus trees from reputable sellers who guarantee that their trees are pest and disease-free.

More common pests include a variety of scale insects and mites, Fuller rose beetles, glassy-winged sharpshooters, hoopla beetles, and katydids. Leafminers will burrow tunnels in citrus leaves, but the damage is mostly cosmetic, unless it becomes extensive.

Citrus trees are rugged, but they are still susceptible to many of the more common plant diseases, along with armillaria root rot, brown rot, citrus blast, exocortis, phytophthora-related diseases, and the Tristeza disease complex.

Figs

Zones 7—12
Sun exposure: full sun

Figs are believed to be the very first human attempt at agriculture, even before barley, wheat, and legumes, more than 11,000 years ago. In Aristotle's day, farmers and scientists had some interesting ideas about wild fig trees and farmed fig trees: it was believed that tiny wasps flew from the wild (fruitless caprifig) trees to the farmed female (fruited) trees to help them hang on to the fruit! If that weren't interesting enough, did you know that figs are not actually fruit at all? Read on!

These resilient trees thrive in areas with hot, dry summers and cool, wet winters. Originally from the Middle East and western Asia, figs are now found all around the world (except Antarctica, of course!) and with good reason. Forget the bagged, dried version of this healthful fruit. Plucking a freshly ripened fig from the tree and taking a bite is heavenly. If you decide you have too many figs to eat fresh, you can always dry your own!

HOW FIGS GROW

Figs (*Ficus carica L.*) are deciduous trees that can grow 30' tall. They tend to send out multiple trunks that create a tree that takes up some space. Fig wood can be weak, so pruning may be needed to keep the tree structurally sound, but not necessarily. Their wide, fragrant leaves provide nice shade, but you will want to avoid the sap as it contains a form of latex that can irritate your skin. Fig trees

Fresh figs

prefer sunny, well-drained locations and they are quite drought tolerant. Figs can also grow well in poor, rocky soil.

Figs reproduce several different ways. Naturally, birds and mammals that eat the fruit end up spreading seeds. Fig trees also send out aggressive roots, stolons, and suckers that can be used to create new plants. You can also bend a low-growing branch down to the ground, or a container, and hold it down with a rock or some wire. After roots emerge, the new growth can be separated from the parent plant. Most fig trees are purchased as bare root trees.

Botanically, fig trees are gynodioecious, which means they have hermaphrodite flowers and female flowers on separate plants. Unless you buy a self-pollinating variety, you will need more than one tree. Fig pollination is usually completed by tiny specialized wasps called *Blastophaga psenes*. (Aristotle was partly correct!) Fig flowers are hidden clusters found inside a hollow structure called the syconium. The fruit, which is not technically a fruit, is actually a scion, or infructescence. An infructescence is a fruit head made up of the ovaries from a flower cluster, often called a "false fruit" or a "multiple fruit," depending on the presentation. Within each fig "fruit" are several one-seeded fruits called druplets. Pineapple, wheat, and corn are other examples of infructescence.

Fig trees can be grown in large containers, but planting them in the ground practically eliminates the need for irrigation. Like grapes, fig trees have deep roots that allow them to get most of the water they need from the soil.

FIG PESTS AND DISEASES

Thrips, ants, green fruit beetles, dried fruit beetles, gophers, and birds are the only serious pests. Ants can be thwarted with a sticky barrier around the trunk. I have always found that netting is invaluable for protecting my fig crop. Eriophyid mites may not cause significant damage but they can carry fig mosaic. Sunburn protection is a good idea. Simply paint a 50:50 mix of water and white latex (not enamel) paint on exposed surfaces.

Some fig varieties produce two crops a year. The first, or "breba" crop, occurs in midsummer and the second, main crop ripens in late summer or fall. Be sure to allow figs to ripen on the tree. They will not continue to ripen once picked.

Add figs to your foodscape for decades of delicious fiber and welcome summer shade!

Persimmons

Zones 4—10, depending on the variety
Sun exposure: full sun, partial sun

Sweet, juicy persimmons are easier to grow than you might expect.

There are many good reasons for growing your own persimmon tree, the first of which is they are not particularly fussy about soil and they are nearly pest-free. You don't need to worry about chilling hours as much as with other fruit trees, and they bloom late enough in the season to avoid frost damage.

Persimmon is a large tropical tree. Mature persimmon trees can grow from 15 to 60 feet tall and 20 feet across, with a lovely rounded canopy. Leaves are both glossy and leathery on top, with a brown, fuzzy undersurface. These leaves will fall off in autumn, being deciduous, but that makes it easier to prune and manage the tree during dormancy.

Your first decision, when growing persimmon, is to decide which type you want.

Non-astringent persimmons look like squat tomatoes (Warren Leywon) CC BY-SA 4.0

TYPES OF PERSIMMON

Persimmons are actually the fruit of several trees in the *Diospyros* ('Zeus's wheat') genus. This group of trees is divided between valuable, dense ebony lumber (*Diospyros ebenum*, et al) and fruit-producing varieties. Within the fruit-producing group, there are some you can eat right away, and some you'd be better off waiting a while.

The North American native persimmon (*Diospyros virginiana*) tends to be smaller and seedier than its more popular Asian cousin (*D. kaki*). The Oriental, or Japanese persimmon is further divided into two groups: astringent and non-astringent. That astringency (read "pucker factor") is caused by tannins. Those tannins can make your mouth feel as though you just gargled with witch hazel, which I do not recommend. Generally speaking, the astringent varieties need to be fully ripe and soft before becoming sweet and delicious. With over 2,000 cultivars of fruit-producing persimmon trees, you have several to choose from, including:

- Oriental or Japanese persimmon (*Diospyros kaki*) - very sweet and soft, most popular
- American persimmon (*D. virginiana*) - native to the eastern United States; commonly used as root stock
- Black persimmon, black sapote, or chocolate pudding fruit (*D. nigral*) - interior white fruit turns black when ripe; native to Mexico
- Date plum, or lotus persimmon (*D. lotus*) - tastes like a combination of dates and plums
- Indian persimmon (*D. peregrina*) - green fruit turns yellow when ripe; used more in folk medicine than as food; native to northeast India
- Texas persimmon (*D. texana*) - entire fruit turns black when ripe; very sweet
- Velvet-apple, Mabolo, or Korean mango (*D. discolor*) - bright red fruit; native to East Asia

Note that native and Oriental persimmon trees will not cross-pollinate.

PERSIMMON FRUITS AND FLOWERS

Native persimmon trees are dioecious, meaning they have male or female flowers, but not both. If you have one of these, you will need two trees. Oriental persimmon trees have both male and female flowers. In either case, those flowers are relatively small, creamy white, with a large green calyx. The calyx is the cup-like structure seen at the base of a flower's petals and is the hard, dried leaves on top of a harvested persimmon. Botanically, a persimmon fruit is a berry because it is formed from a single fertilized plant ovary.

Fruits mature in autumn, staying on the tree into winter. Don't be fooled, however. Squirrels and rats have an uncanny ability to gnaw the insides out of your persimmons and other fruits from the side facing away from your windows. I have a friend who discovered, to her dismay, that every single piece of fruit, and there were many pieces of fruit, had all been hollowed out while she wasn't looking.

If you only have room for one persimmon tree, just make sure it is a self-pollinating variety. Both Fuyu and Hachiya will produce fruit without a second tree. California Rare Fruit Growers, Inc. suggests keeping persimmon trees away from eucalyptus trees. I'm sure there is a good reason, I just don't know what it is.

HOW TO GROW A PERSIMMON TREE

If you want to grow a persimmon tree from seed, you will need to put it in the refrigerator for a couple of months. This is called stratification and it mimics the effects of winter weather. Unlike other fruit trees, which are pretty much companionable to a wide variety of root stock grafts, persimmon trees are not as amenable. You are probably best off buying bare root stock from a reputable seller. Just be gentle with your young tree. The immature taproot breaks easily.

Persimmon trees perform best in soil with a pH of 6.0 to 6.5. If you need to acidify your soil, you need to know that altering pH is an uphill battle, requiring regular attention and effort. If you are determined, you can acidify your soil to make things more hospitable for your persimmon tree. The wood tends to be brittle, so provide protection from strong winds.

When planting a young persimmon tree, it is critical that the tree be planted at the proper depth. Then, cut the aboveground portion down to three feet in height and mud it in well. You will also want to provide sunburn and herbivore feeding protection. Deer, rats, squirrels, birds, and gophers will gnaw roots, stems, bark, or fruit, depending on the species. Even coyotes enjoy the occasional persimmon.

Regular irrigation will improve fruit size and quality, though the trees are somewhat drought tolerant. Mature trees will need 36"-48" of water each year, but they do not need a lot in the way of feeding. In fact, if you give them too much nitrogen, they will drop their fruit! Over-feeding, over-watering, and too much boron in the soil can cause blossom drop and young fruit drop. Top dressing with aged compost and mulching are better ways to go, unless a lab-based soil test tells you some important plant nutrients are missing.

PRUNING PERSIMMON

Persimmon fruit forms along the sides and at the tips of long, current-year stems. If those stems are too long, the branches are likely to break. During the dormant season, train your persimmon tree into a modified central leader or open vase system, removing any dead, diseased, or rubbing branches. Each year, you will want to perform light to medium pruning for size, structure, and air flow. Persimmon can also be pruned into a lovely espalier. Heavy fruit loads can cause branch loss, so fruit thinning is a good idea.

PERSIMMON PESTS AND DISEASES

While relatively pest-free, persimmons may occasionally be attacked by root nematodes, mealybugs, and scale insects. If you see ant trails, look more closely for signs of scale infestation. Sticky barriers can eliminate the protection provide by ants.

Diseases most likely to impact a persimmon tree include armillaria root rot, gray mold, leaf blight, leaf spot, and Phytophthora root and crown rot. Fusarium dieback may also occur. More commonly, nutrient deficiencies can cause a number of symptoms. Low iron causes leaf bleaching, insufficient calcium leads to leaf curling, and magnesium deficiencies cause brown spots on leaves. Sunburn damage is common, so whitewash exposed areas and keep trees well irrigated during the peak of summer.

You can speed ripening and reduce astringency by storing persimmons in paper bags. This traps the ethylene gas that make fruits ripen close to the fruit, at higher concentrations. Eaten fresh, in baked goods, as jam, or dried, the only down side to growing a persimmon tree is the super abundant crops that you will have to deal with each autumn. We should all have such problems!

Pomegranates

Zones 8—11
Sun exposure: full sun

Pomegranates grace holiday tables, a symbol of prosperity, but you can add them to your yard or balcony for some prosperity of your own!

'Pomegranates' by Karen Bacica (www.facebook.com/karenbacicafineart)

When I was a child growing up in the San Fernando Valley, there was an empty lot down the street. On that lot was a giant old pomegranate tree. It had grown up and out and down, almost like a willow, creating a magical circular space underneath. No one could see us from outside the tree, the growth was so thick! We would pick sun-ripened pomegranates from the outside of the tree and then enter our Secret Clubhouse, where we would tell stories and make wild guesses about growing up, as we munched on the sweet-tart fruity seeds. These healthful fruits are perfectly suited to growing in drought-prone areas. With a small initial investment of time, money, and water, your family can enjoy fresh pomegranates for many years to come.

POMEGRANATE VARIETIES

Before you buy a pomegranate tree, be sure that the variety you are buying is an edible and not an ornamental. There is no sense dedicating space and water to an inedible variety when you can have an edible one! Pomegranates grow in a variety of colors and sizes. Rinds can be red, yellow, pink, orange, green, and even black. Some varieties have seeds that are very hard, while others are softer. Both ornamental and edible types can be self-pollinating or cross-pollinated by hummingbirds and insects. It takes a pollinated flower up to seven months to produce an edible fruit.

Did you know that the fruit of a pomegranate tree is a berry? That's if you ask a botanist. Like other berry plants, pomegranates (*Punica granatum*) have spiny branches and delicious fruit.

HOW TO GROW POMEGRANATES

Pomegranate fruit and foliage

Pomegranates prefer full sun and hot summers, but they can handle some partial shade. They will founder in wet soil or full shade, so choose your site accordingly. Pomegranates can be grown from seeds, but it will take a few years before you get any fruit, and pomegranate seeds do not always grow true to the parent plant. Cuttings and bare root trees are better choices. Grafting does not work for pomegranates. Newly planted trees should be watered every day until you see new growth. Then water only once a week (assuming it doesn't rain). Keep weeds away with mulch, just be sure the mulch stays 6"-8" away from your pomegranate.

Pruning Pomegranate

Pomegranates are deciduous trees that can grow up to 30' tall and 15' wide (most are 6'-12' tall). Pomegranates produce fruit on second-year wood, so you will want to make sure that you leave some of the last year's growth when pruning. Pomegranates can be pruned as full-sized trees, hedges, or shrubs. They can also be grown in containers. You can even create bonsai and topiary from pomegranate!

Pomegranate Pests and Diseases

Like tomatoes and citrus, pomegranates are susceptible to citrus fruit split. Other diseases that can turn up include Alternaria rot, Armillaria root rot, Botrytis blight, and other fungal diseases, especially if plants are over-watered.

Common pests include whiteflies, fruit flies, ants, cotton aphids, mealybugs, soft scales, leaf-footed bugs, cherry leafhoppers, and the pomegranate butterfly.

Eating a Pomegranate

Those little seeds are tasty, but getting to them can be a pain. The easiest way I have found is to cut the fruit in half, hold one half peel side up, over a bowl, and beat the bejeezus out of it with a wooden spoon. The seeds fall out and the rest of it tends to stay put. It is easy to remove any other debris simply by adding water to the bowl: the fruit sinks and everything else rises. Ta da!

Pomes

Pomes are accessory fruits. Botanically, these fruits feature one or more carpels that are surrounded by the fruit we enjoy. Apples and pears are pomes, and so are loquats. These trees are beautiful investments in your landscape. Lovely pink blossoms in spring, lush, green growth in summer, and an autumn bounty. These trees will live and produce fruit for the next 25 to 50 years, depending on the size and variety you select.

When choosing pear and apple trees, first consider the amount of space you have available. Dwarf and semi-dwarf trees produce a lot of food without taking up as much space. It is far easier to pick fruit and care for your tree if it is a dwarf or semi-dwarf. On the other hand, standard sized trees live and produce fruit for twice as long.

Pears

Apple tree

Size isn't the only factor to consider. Since each variety has specific environmental needs, choosing the variety best suited to your yard can lighten your workload and boost production. Choose well.

These trees grow best in well-drained, nutrient rich soil with full sunlight. The best way to start growing pears or apples is with bare root stock.

SEASONAL POME CARE

Apples and pears are most productive if 15%-20% of each year's new growth is removed in winter. One or two months after the tree is covered with blossoms, thin fruit to one piece every 6". Mature trees are fertilized at a rate of 1½-2 pounds urea or 40 pounds manure in spring. In summer, fertilize young trees monthly using ¾ pounds urea or 20 pounds aged manure and spray for codling moth.

Heavily laden apple tree

Loquat

POME PROBLEMS

There are very few pests or diseases that will kill an apple or pear tree outright, but they have many attackers. The use of sticky barriers around the trunk will halt crawlers and climbers, but many pome problems are carried on the wind. Stem blight, fireblight and other bacterial blights, and scab are common diseases, along with all the usuals. Cedar apple rust can also occur if apples are grown near Eastern red cedar trees. Also, apples share a susceptibility to bacteria blast with lilacs and stone fruits.

Birds, rats, and squirrels are a constant threat to your crop unless trees are caged. And there's a new pest on the apple scene: chili thrips. Apparently, chili thrips have expanded their menu.

Apples

Zones 3—8, depending on variety
Sun exposure: full sun

Growing apples is highly rewarding, but don't try starting one from seed.

These particular fruit trees are what is known as "extreme heterozygotes," which means the offspring are very unlike the parent plants. Planting seeds from a Red Delicious apple will not produce apples that look or taste like a Red Delicious. This is why most modern apple trees are propagated from cuttings that are grafted onto sturdy root stock.

APPLE HISTORY

Apples (*Malus pumila*, aka *Malus domestica*) have a rich and varied history. They hold a place in nearly every culture and religion, being one of humankind's earliest attempts at tree cultivation. Wild apple trees (*Malus sieversii*), however, bear little resemblance to their domesticated progeny. Wild apple trees, still found in central Asia, can grow up 40 feet tall and the fruit is smaller and more tart than most people find palatable.

Most of the apples you see in the grocery store are crosses between *Malus pumila* and crab apples. To date, there are over 7,500 apple cultivars with various traits of skin color, texture, disease and pest resistance, juiciness, storage ability, and more. In 2010, the entire apple genome was mapped, with more than 57,000 genes identified. (Humans are estimated to have 30,000 genes—kind of makes you wonder, doesn't it?)

BARE ROOT APPLES

When selecting your root stock, keep in mind that some apple varieties require cross-pollination, while others are self-pollinating. If you only have room for one tree, you will want to be sure to select a self-pollinating variety or all you will get is summer shade. Bare root stock is generally planted in late winter or early spring.

Apple trees are generally classified as hardy or long-season. Long-season apples perform best in Hardiness Zones 5-8, while hardy apples prefer zones 3-5. Different varieties have different chill hour requirements. Most red varieties need more chilling hours than green and yellow apples. Red apples generally need 1200-1500 chill hours to fully develop their color and flavor. If your garden only gets 500 chill hours, you will want to select a variety that matches those hours. If you don't, you won't get fruit.

If you live in an area frequented by fog, you are going to see more russetting. Russetting is when the apple's skin turns brown and rough. It still tastes good, though.

Pears

Zones, 4—9, depending on the variety
Sun exposure: full sun

Luscious summer pears are one of the more difficult tree fruits to keep from squirrels, but the rewards, for many, are worth it.

Eight pear varieties (left to right): Bartlett, Red Bartlett, a different Red Bartlett, D'Anjou, Bosc, Comice, Concorde, and Seckel

People have been growing pears for more than 4,000 years and Bartlett pears have been the standard for over 200 years. European pears (*Pyrus communis L.*) hail from Western Asia and modern-day Iraq and Iran.

Pear varieties

Pears are categorized by the season in which they ripen. Summer pears have thin skins, ripen on the tree in summer, and most are small to medium, and the fruit is fine-textured. Winter pears feature gritty-textured fruit that ripen in autumn. Selecting the best cultivar for your Hardiness Zone, chill hours, and taste is much easier before you put a tree in the ground.

Pear Zones

- Bartlett - summer, early, yellow, long chill, 800 hours, zone 5-8
- Bella Di Guino - summer, earliest ripening
- Bosc - winter, russet, 700-800 hours, zones 4-9
- Buttria Precoce - summer, large tree and fruit
- Comice - winter, midseason, 200-600 hours, zones 5-8
- D'Anjou - winter, green, 800 hours, zone 5-8
- Kieffer - winter, fire blight resistant, yellow skin, crisp white fruit, 350-400 hours, zones 4-9
- Orcas - winter, yellow
- Red Clapp's Favorite - summer, red skin, tastes like a spicy Bartlett, zones 5-8
- Rescue - winter, large fruit, red-orange skin, smooth flesh
- Seckel - summer, natural dwarf, red russet fruit, fire blight resistant, 300-800 hours, zones 5-9
- Ubileen - summer, large fruit, zones 5-9
- Warren - summer, extra sweet, brown, tear-drop shaped

How to grow pears

Unless you select a self-fruitful variety, you will need at least two trees for fruit to set. Pear trees are best pruned into a Y shape.

They tend to grow very upright and need trimming to create a healthier, more spread-out growth. Pear fruits do not require as much thinning as apples and other fruits. You can leave two or three fruits per cluster without problems.

PEAR RIPENING

If you allow your pears to ripen on the tree, you will probably never get to enjoy one. Pears are a favorite food of squirrels and birds. I once lost an entire season's crop because the squirrels were willing to harvest the pears two days earlier than I was.

Knowing when a pear is ripe can be tricky. This is because pears ripen from the inside out. The easiest way to tell if it is time to harvest a pear is to use the Cradle Test. To do this, cup one hand under a pear and use the other hand to swing the fruit from its 6:00 position to a 9:00 position, with a twisting motion. If the fruit falls, it's ready.

Actually, pears taste better if they are harvested when they are mature but not fully ripe. Put them in the refrigerator for a few days, up to two weeks for summer pears, and three to four weeks for winter pears. After the fruit has been chilled, bring it back to room temperature and enjoy. By the way, don't bruise the fruit at any point in this process. As I said, growing pears is not an easy process. The sweet, juicy flavor of a fresh, properly ripened pear, however, is exquisite.

Find a spot in your landscape for one of these beauties, because plucking an apple or pear from your very own tree and taking a bite, well, it's just one of life's finer experiences.

Stone Fruits

Plums, nectarines, apricots, cherries, peaches, and almonds are all stone fruits. But so are olives, coconuts, mangoes, coffee, pistachios, walnuts, and black pepper. So what, exactly, are stone fruits?

The term stone fruit refers to all plants that produce seeds that are hard pits, called drupes or stones. Botanically, stone fruits are those that develop from a single carpel. Drupes are close cousins to berries, but that's another story.

Most stone fruits contain compounds which, when chewed up, generate hydrogen cyanide. Don't let that scare you off. This is mostly true of the seeds, not the fruit, and the amounts are too small to do anything but fuel sensationalists.

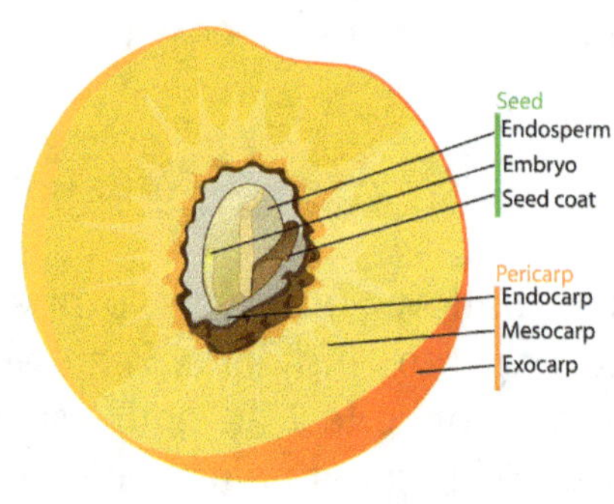

Diagram of a typical drupe, or stone fruit

A more common definition of stone fruits refers only to members of the *Prunus* genus, though this isn't entirely accurate. A plant can be a stone fruit without being a member of the *Prunus* clan.

PRUNUS PLANTS

The *Prunus* genus is part of the rose family, making plums, almonds, and all the rest distant cousins to loquats and soapnut trees. (Did you know that almonds, nectarines, and peaches are the same species? I didn't either.) There are both edible and ornamental stone fruits. Hawthorn, flowering cherries, and cherry laurels are ornamental stone fruits, but you may as well get fruit if you are going to invest time, water, and garden space on plants. When that food happens to be summer sweet peaches and apricots, well, all the better!

PROPAGATING PRUNUS

If you plant the pit from a grocery store stone fruit, you probably won't get offspring that looks, behaves, or tastes the way the first fruit did. This is because most bare root fruit and nut trees available today are a hardy root stock grafted onto a productive, flavorful fruit producer. Many of these plants are propagated by twig scions and cuttings taken from adventitious roots, to create clones. Because all of these fruit trees are members of the same genus, they can be grafted onto one another and produce edible fruit. One variety of grafted tree, in particular, boasts 40 different types of stone fruit on the same tree! These botanical masterpieces are created by New York artist Sam Van Aken. He calls them Tree of 40 Fruit. You can find similar stone fruit trees, with four or five types of fruit, available in garden centers and catalogs. These are a great way to make use of a small space.

How Stone Fruits Grow

Members of the *Prunus* genus are all perennial trees and shrubs descended from a Eurasian ancestor. As such, these trees are best suited to northern temperate regions, or climates with four seasons. If you want grow these productive, rewarding trees, be sure to select varieties that have chilling hour requirements that match your microclimate. Otherwise, you might not get any fruit. Adding a stone fruit tree to your landscape is a lovely way to enjoy spring blossoms and summer fruit. There are many dwarf and semi-dwarf varieties that don't take up a lot of room, and some can even be grown in large containers. Properly maintained, *Prunus* trees are classified as low flammability plants, making them a fire-safe addition to your landscape.

Caring for Stone Fruits

Your stone fruits will need the same sort of care as other trees in the rose family. You can prevent corking (dried-out fruit) by making sure that the soil contains enough boron and calcium. Before adding soil amendments, be sure to get a soil test from a local, reputable lab. Over-the-counter kits are not yet effective enough to be useful.

PESTS AND DISEASES OF STONE FRUITS

In addition to all of the garden variety pests and diseases that may attack your fruit and nut trees, members of this group face additional problems. Luckily, there are steps you can take to minimize those risks.

Many beneficial insects, such as braconid wasps, mealybug destroyers, and tachinid flies love to eat peach twig borers and other stone fruit pests. All you have to do is avoid using broad spectrum pesticides and add some flowers to your landscape. You can also dust individual fruits with kaolin clay to protect against several pests.

Apply fixed copper, sulfur, and/or Bordeaux mixture (*Bt*), each in their own way and time, to aid in protecting your stone fruit trees against many pests and diseases. Just don't use sulfur on apricots—they don't play well together.

Prunus Pests & Diseases
- armillaria root rot
- bacterial blast
- brown rot
- blights
- caterpillars
- cucumber beetles
- green fruit beetles
- Japanese beetles
- katydids
- mites
- scale insects
- sharpshooters
- shot hole borers

Netting and tree cages can help protect the fruit from birds, rats, and squirrels. Sticky barriers are an excellent way to thwart crawling insects. While each species has its own set of problems, the better you understand what to look for, the quicker you can nip problems in the proverbial bud.

The sheer volume of fruit that a single fruit or nut tree can produce makes them excellent choices for the home garden. Add some of these stone fruits to your foodscape for years of sweet summer deliciousness and beauty.

Apricots

Zones 5—8
Sun exposure: full sun

Sweet, flavorful apricots, warm from the sun, freshly plucked from the tree, are one of life's perfect moments. In my opinion, they rank right up there with their cousins, peaches and nectarines, as foods that define summer.

While dwarf varieties can be grown in large containers, apricots prefer being planted in the ground, in a sunny location. Plant an apricot tree and you will be treated to lovely spring blossoms and delicious summer fruit. The trunk will, over time, develop a striking gnarled look, too.

HOW TO SELECT AN APRICOT TREE

When selecting rootstock, be sure to match the variety with your microclimate. Chilling hours vary by species, as does disease and pest resistance. If your tree does not accumulate enough chill hours, you won't get any fruit. Most apricots are self-fertile, so it is usually not necessary to have more than one tree. Contact your local Cooperative Extension Office for the best varieties for your area.

Apricots ripening on twig

Unlike other members of the rose family, apricots (*Prunus armeniaca*) grown from seed have a higher chance of being similar to the parent plant. While there are no guarantees, you can take the pit from an apricot, cover it with an inch of soil, keep it watered and in a sunny location, to start your homegrown apricot tree. For faster results, invest in bare root stock. Apricots prefer well-drained soil, but they can tolerate some clay.

APRICOT TREE CARE

Your apricot tree will benefit from the same seasonal care as other stone fruits. Each fall, before the rains begin, remove 20% of last year's growth. This allows more sunlight to reach interior branches, stimulate new spur development, and improve the overall health of the tree. (Spurs are flower-bearing buds). Spray for pest and disease control in winter and again in spring. Feed mature apricot trees 1-2 pounds of urea just before spring irrigation is begun and water it in thoroughly. Young trees should be given the same amount of urea, but spread out in quarters over a four-month period. As fruits reach ½" in diameter, they should be thinned to one fruit every 4"-6", for the best size and flavor. This also reduces the likelihood of pests and diseases. Do not use sulfur on apricots.

IRRIGATING APRICOTS

Begin irrigating in spring by watering every two or three weeks to a depth of 18"-24". This is one of those times where guessing isn't good enough. I use my soil sampler, but you can use a trowel to gently dig down to the appropriate depth. If the soil isn't moist, you need to figure out where the water is going and redirect it. Many times, hydrophobic soil will push water away. Watering more slowly can avoid this problem.

A little space in your yard or on a balcony is all you need to start growing fresh apricots—give them a try!

Cherries

Zones 5—8
Sun exposure: full sun

Fresh, sweet cherries are delicious, but cherry trees can be difficult to grow. According to UC California Backyard Orchard, "cherries are the most difficult trees to keep alive." If you are still determined, let's see what we can learn about these trees.

People have been enjoying cherries since prehistoric times. Cherries are stone fruits, which means the fruit is a drupe. There are two types of cherry trees: sweet (*Prunus avium*) and sour (*Prunus cerasus*). The two cannot cross-pollinate with each other. Both types are native to Europe and western Asia. Sweet cherries are also known as wild cherries or gean.

HOW TO GROW CHERRY TREES

Cherry trees cannot tolerate soggy ground and they need a lot of sunlight. Excellent drainage is critical. So much so, that cherry trees are generally planted on mounds, or berms. Trees should be spaced 14'-20' apart, and you are going to need at least two because most sweet cherry varieties require cross-pollination to bear fruit. Sour cherries, the type used in pies and ries, the type used in pies and preserves, are self-fertile and do not require cross-pollination.

Cherries (Diako1971) CC BY-SA 4.0

While installing bare root stock is preferable, you can grow a cherry tree from a pit. The pit will need to be exposed to cold temperatures (stratification) before it will germinate. When selecting a cherry variety for your landscape, be sure to choose one with a chilling requirement that matches your microclimate. The tree will set fruit in three or four years.

SEASONAL CARE FOR CHERRY TREES

Each winter, you will need to prune out 10% of the previous year's growth, along with the normal stone fruit care. In spring, as blossoms appear, apply a fungicide, such as Bordeaux mixture, to control brown rot, and feed each tree 2 pounds of urea or 70 pounds of aged manure just before a deep watering.

Sweet cherries

Birds will enjoy your cherries long before you do if you do not protect your crop with netting or a tree cage. Trees will need to be drip irrigated every day in summer, or given 3"-5" of water every two or three weeks. After harvesting your cherry crop, feed each tree with 2 pounds of urea and irrigate right away. Keep trees irrigated regularly until autumn, then stop watering altogether. This will help prevent root rot.

CHERRY PESTS AND DISEASES

It is astounding to learn how many diseases and insect pests can interfere with growing cherries. If birds, squirrels, and pocket gophers weren't bad enough, cherry trees are regularly attacked by a wide variety of insect pests and diseases.

Cherries are also susceptible to a genetic disease, called leaf crinkle, and a couple of mysterious diseases, called cherry necrotic rusty mottle and cherry stem pitting, that occur when grafting scions.

Bottom line: cherries are probably best left to the professionals, though you are welcome to try. Hopefully, this information will help you appreciate just how much effort goes into providing these delicious summer treats.

Nectarines and Peaches

Zones 5—8
Sun exposure: full sun

Nothing says summer like sweet, juicy, sun-warmed nectarines and peaches. The good news is, you can probably grow them in your yard, along a fence, or even in a large container.

Nectarines and peaches are delicious fresh, stewed, baked, and sautéed. They freeze well and make excellent jam. A mature peach or nectarine tree can produce up to 65 pounds of fruit each year!

Did you know that peach trees have been around for more than 2.6 million years? Traditionally thought to be from Persia, genetic research shows that peaches and nectarines originated in China. Also, it was thought that peach cultivation started some 6,000 years ago, until some ancient writings

Nectarines

showed that certain kings and emperors, back in the 10th century B.C., favored a delectable peach now and then. So, if you love peaches, you are in good company!

So, WHAT'S THE DIFFERENCE BETWEEN NECTARINES AND PEACHES?

Fur. The only difference between a nectarine and a peach is a single gene that produces fuzzy skin (dominant) or smooth skin (recessive). A nectarine (*Prunus persica* var. *nucipersica* or var.

nectarina) is simply a peach without the furry skin (trichomes). Nectarines and peaches are both members of the rose family, along with apples, pears, blackberries, raspberries, and strawberries. Nectarines and peaches, like apricots, cherries, plums, and almonds, are stone fruits. For simplicity's sake, we will use the word peaches from here forward, but the information refers to both.

If you have ever bitten into a sweet, juicy peach, you may have discovered that the fruit practically fell away from the pit as you neared the center. Or, you may have had to fight for every morsel, leaving behind a ragged, fruit-covered pit. When the fruit comes away from the pit easily, it is called freestone. When the fruit clings to the pit it is, you guessed it, a cling variety. Freestone peaches tend to have firmer fruit, making them better for canning. Clingstone varieties are best for fresh eating, having a sweeter taste, though you can certainly can them, or turn them into a delicious jam or chutney!

Clingstone varieties are harvested earlier in the year, while the freestone harvest extends into autumn There is also a hybrid cross between the two, called a semi-freestone, and flat varieties, called pan-tao. You can find yellow and white peaches. Yellow fruits are more acidic than white fruits.

CHARACTERISTICS OF PEACHES

The main reason you do not see peaches in the store year-round is because they do not ship and store well. While nectarines are usually smaller, firmer, and more aromatic than peaches, they also bruise more easily. (All the more reason to grow your own!) Peaches can also be espaliered, if you only have a narrow space along a wall or fence.

Each spring, your peach tree will produce lovely pink blossoms, followed by a delicious crop of fruit, and then all the leaves fall off (making dormant pruning so much easier!). Before you jump on the peach bandwagon, however, that yummy fruit can only occur if enough chill hours are accumulated each winter.

Most peach trees need 650-850 chill hours.

PEACH SITE SELECTION

Once you have found a variety that matches your garden's chill hours and your personal tastes, you will want to select a site with excellent drainage and plenty of sunshine. Also, peaches prefer a soil pH of 6.5. If your soil is more alkaline than that, acidification may be needed for the best results. Peaches are self-fruiting, so you do not need multiple trees for pollination.

PEACH TREE CARE

Peach trees use a lot more nitrogen than other fruit and nut trees. You can use blood meal or ammonium sulfate to feed your tree. Just be sure to get your soil tested before adding any other amendments. Too much can be just as bad as not enough.

Young trees will need 10-15 pounds of manure or ¼ pound of urea, every month of spring and summer. Mature trees should receive twice that amount. If your peach tree doesn't get enough nitrogen, you will start seeing red areas on the leaves.

These are shallow-rooted trees, so they are susceptible to water stress during summer. You can protect your tree with deep irrigation and a thick layer of mulch, just make sure that the mulch does not actually touch the tree trunk. If your tree becomes too water stressed, it will develop a condition called bitter fruit, which is exactly how it sounds. The problem is, once bitter fruit occurs, the tree will forever after produce fruit that is bitter. So keep your trees well-watered in summer!

Peach trees perform best when trained with what's called the Y system. The Y system features two scaffolding (main) branches, heading in opposite directions, creating a Y shape. You can picture it as a two-dimensional open center system, which also works with peaches and nectarines. These tree training systems leave the trees open in the center, allowing lots of air and sunlight to reach the fruiting wood.

In fall, after harvesting your delicious crop and before the first heavy rain, apply fixed copper to control shot hole fungus, fertilize plants one last time, and give your tree a deep watering. After all the leaves fall, move them away from your peach tree. Destroy or compost the leaves to prevent the spread of apple scab. As always, remove mummies as soon as they are seen.

Bordeaux mixture, dormant oil sprays, and fixed copper sprays should be used in fall and winter to protect against San Jose scale, shot hole disease, and other fungal diseases. You can prevent brown rot with a spring fungicide application. Crawling pests can be blocked from reaching fruit by wrapping the tree trunk with a sticky barrier.

Dwarf nectarine tree in bloom

Each winter, you will want to remove 50% of the previous year's new growth. This stimulates fruit production and maintains a reasonable tree size. One problem that commonly occurs with peach trees is that they produce more fruit than they can support. This can mean broken branches. Proper pruning and fruit thinning can save your tree. Thin fruits to six inches apart when they are the size of a marble. If you think there is too much fruit on a branch, you can always prop the branch up with a board or other support until after the fruit is harvested. Be sure to prune and thin more heavily the next year when this happens.

HARVESTING PEACHES

Color and smell are good ripeness indicators when it comes to peaches. Yellow skin, which may or may not have a red tinge, and that amazing sweet summer aroma of ripe peaches are reason enough to give one a try. Taste, ultimately, is the only true indicator of ripeness, but who can complain about conducting that test? If the fruit comes away from the stem easily, it is ripe. The fruit will bruise easily, so be gentle.

If you install a peach or nectarine tree this spring, you can expect to have a tree for seven to twenty years, depending on where you live. Since each tree can produce up to 65 pounds of fruit each year, or approximately 200 peaches, you will have plenty of delicious fruit to go along with a lovely tree.

Make a place for a peach tree in your yard today for a decade of fresh summer peaches in your pantry!

Plums

Zones 3 —8
Sun exposure: full sun, partial sun

Plum orchards once covered The Valley of Hearts Delight. (What is now known as Silicon Valley.) Many homes are still graced by individual specimens of these prolific fruit producers. It is easy to

Purple plums

add one to your landscape as well.

Plums are cousin to peaches, nectarines, and cherries. One variety of apricot (*Prunus armeniaca*) is so closely related that it is actually a plum!

PLUM VARIETIES

When deciding on a plum variety, keep in mind that plums can be sweet or tart, and early or late blooming and ripening.

Two common varieties are Japanese plums (*Prunus salicina*) and European plums (*P. domestica*), but there are others. Some European plum varieties do not require cross-pollination, but all plum trees produce more if there is a second tree nearby. Japanese plums bloom and mature earlier, but European plums tend to be sweeter.

Commercially, plums grown to be consumed as fresh fruit are called "sugar plums," while the remainder are grown to be dried and sold as prunes. Prunes are almost exclusively made from European plums. You can also find plum-apricot and plum-cherry hybrids! Plums come in skins of many different colors, from yellow, to red and purple, to nearly black. The interior fruit can be yellow, white, red, or green. Or you can try your hand at greengages.

GREENGAGES

Don't let the green skin fool you. Greengages are sugary sweet dessert plums.

While most plums tend to be purple to black, and sometimes yellow, with an edge of tang to their flavor, greengage plums are as sweet as candy!

Greengages were first brought to Europe from Iran in the 1700s. George Washington and Thomas Jefferson both grew greengages on their farms. These garden treats fell out of favor after the 1800s. I do not know why, but I like to think that they are on their way back.

If you want a cultivar that is descended from the original green Iranian plum, you will need to look for a label that reads *Prunus domestica* subsp. *italica* var. *claudiana*. Greengages grow best in Zones 5-9.

Greengages are round or oval, pale green to yellowish freestone fruits with smooth-textured, pale green flesh. You may see some varieties with a pale blue blush. Greengages are smaller than mirabelle prune, or cherry plums, but larger than most other plum varieties. There are also some crossbred greengages that may be reddish-purple. Unlike most modern fruits, greengages

Greengage fruit (Mark Stimson) CC BY-SA 3.0

grow true from seed. This means, if you can find one, you can plant a tree of your own. The original cultivar, now called Reine Claude Verte, remains nearly unchanged from its ancestor.

Not all greengages are self-fertile, so you may need to plant two trees to get fruit, depending on the variety. It is not uncommon to have a bumper crop year followed by a sparser crop, similar to many citrus trees. They simply do not have the energy or resources to crank out huge crops every year.

See if you can make room for these delicious fruits in your foodscape!

How to grow plums

Plums love mild winters and hot, dry summers. While they prefer more sandy soil than your garden may have, they are pretty tolerant of clay, as long as the drainage is good.

Plums are best started from certified disease-free root stock. You can also start a tree from a friend or neighbor's tree by taking one of the many suckers that tend to appear. Suckers root more easily if they are dipped in rooting hormones (auxins), but they will create their own auxins in a day or so. If starting from seed, plums should be planted 3" deep. Be sure to mark the spot so you don't lose track of your new baby!

PLUM TREE CARE

Plum trees grow best when trained into an open center shape. In winter, 20% of the previous year's growth should be removed, along with any dead or diseased limbs, and spray with dormant oil.

Purple plums

In spring, treat with a fungicide, such as fixed copper. Feed mature trees 1-2 pounds of urea or 20-40 pounds of manure. Fruits should be thinned to 4"-6" apart. Young tress receive half the fertilizer given to mature trees, but it is divided up and spread out over several months.

In summer, continue feeding young trees, keep weeds and

grass at least 3 feet away from trunks, mulch, and water deeply every 2-3 weeks. Your harvest should be ready in autumn. After collecting your bounty, be sure to remove any mummies and fallen fruit; feed and water one last time, and treat with fixed copper after all the leaves have fallen off.

Mealy plum aphids (*Hyalopterus pruni*) can be a pain in your plum tree.

Another common problem faced by plum tree owners is overproduction. Overproduction, or overbearing, can cause broken limbs, so it is important to thin fruit to no more than one fruit every 4"-6". Don't be concerned if your plums have a whitish coating on them. This is a protective wax known as "wax bloom" and is easily wiped off.

Add a plum tree to your landscape this spring for decades of delicious summer fruit and year-round jams and jellies.

Nut Trees and Shrubs

The truth about nuts may surprise you.

While you probably already know that peanuts are not nuts (they're legumes), many of the other foods you have come to know as nuts are not true nuts either. Let's begin by learning the botanical definition of nuts.

True nuts are hard-shelled, inedible pods that hold both the fruit and the seed of a plant. These pods do not open of their own accord, which means they are indehiscent. The pod, or shell, of a nut is made from the ovary wall, which hardens over time. Hazelnuts, chestnuts, and acorns are true nuts. So are kola nuts, which gives "cola" soft drinks their signature flavor. (Did you know that small nuts are called "nutlets"? To me, that sounds like the perfect name for a little chihuahua.)

WHEN IS A NUT NOT A NUT?

A nut is not a nut when it is a fruit seed. Fruit seeds can be angiosperm or gymnosperm seeds. Gymnosperm seeds, such as pine nuts and ginkgo nuts, are fruit seeds. Angiosperms, or flowering plants that produce fruit seeds within a carpel, include macadamia nuts, Brazil nuts, peanuts, and soybeans.

Raw mixed nuts

Drupes, such as peaches and cherries, are a type of angiosperm that have hard-shelled pods that hold a seed, but their fruit is on the outside. Almonds, cashews, pecans, pistachios, walnuts, coffee beans, and coconuts are all drupes.

These not-nut nuts are commonly referred to as culinary nuts. Of course, you can call any of these delicious morsels "nuts" whenever you want to. True nut or culinary nut, many of these yummy snacks find their way into our gardens and foodscapes.

NUT FAMILIES

Did you know that cashews are the seeds of an accessory fruit, which means they share characteristics with strawberries and poison ivy? Isn't botany amazing? Most nut producing trees and shrubs share a common ancestor, making them all members of the order Fagales. From there, they diverge into very distinct families. All except almonds and pistachios. Those two are something else entirely.

Ripe cashew apples with seeds hanging below (Abhishek Jacob) CC BY-SA 3.0

Almonds

Zones 7—9
Sun exposure: full sun

Do you have room for an almond tree?
The flowers are lovely, the tree is easy to care for, and who doesn't love almonds? This member of the Rose family produces a lot of food and for much less than almonds cost in the store.

ALMONDS' BITTERSWEET HISTORY

I'm not sure how people started eating almonds because the fruit of wild "bitter" almond trees is poisonous. Bitter almond trees contain a chemical, called glycoside amygdalin, which turns into deadly hydrogen cyanide when the fruit is injured by chewing. All stone fruits have this characteristic, but it takes an awful lot of any of these to get sick. The trees we buy now are called sweet almonds and they are safe to eat. They taste better, too!

Almonds are California's third largest agricultural product. Drought regularly causes prices to skyrocket. Almonds are an incredibly healthful snack and the trees look lovely in a landscape.

THE ALMOND TREE

Almonds are deciduous. They can grow 13'-33' tall, with a 12" diameter trunk. The canopy is 10'-15' wide. Dwarf varieties are being developed, but their productivity is still questionable. Almonds do not grow well in containers. Unlike avocados, which can take 10 years or more to produce, almond trees bear fruit as early as their third year! To improve root development, remove flowers the first couple of years.

Immature almonds

HOW TO GROW ALMONDS

People have been growing almond trees for 6,000 years in South Asia and the Middle East, and you can, too, if you live in Zones 7-9.

Almond tree protected by a tree cage

Unless you get a self-pollinating variety, you will need to plant two or three trees to get any fruit. Truckloads of honey bees are brought to orchards each year to pollinate the almond trees.

Almonds prefer temperatures between 59°F and 86°F. The buds have a chilling requirement of 300-600 hours. Almonds perform best in areas with mild, wet winters and hot, dry summers. They do not like soggy, heavy soil. Almonds are deep-rooted trees and should be planted 20'-25' away from other trees. Almond trees benefit from the same seasonal care as other stone fruits.

Harvest your almonds when the hulls split open and the shells turn brown and dry. Commercial growers use machines specially designed to shake ripe almonds from their trees. Give your almond tree a good shake and see what happens!

Once you've collected your harvest, remove and discard the hulls. Then, freeze your almonds for two weeks to kill any worms that may be present. Store them in airtight containers or plastic bags.

Rather than planting an ornamental tree, almonds can provide 30-40 years of delicious food for you and your family.

Chestnuts

Zones 4—9
Sun exposure: full sun

Plant a chestnut tree today for decades of meaty, delicious nuts.

American chestnut trees are majestic. While young, the bark is a smooth, reddish-brown. As the tree matures, the bark becomes darker and deeply furrowed. Their mature height of over 100 feet equals one-third of a football field. Try picturing that in your yard!

Cousin to beeches and oaks, the roasted chestnuts of holiday fare fame should not be confused with horse chestnuts, which are mildly poisonous, or water chestnuts, which are aquatic tubers. No, chestnuts, or Sardian nuts, as they were called in their native Asia Minor, or Jupiter's nuts, from the Roman Empire, have been cultivated since 2,000 B.C., and they have a rich, delicious history.

CHESTNUTS AS FOOD

Brought to Europe by Alexander the Great and the Roman Empire, chestnut trees thrive in the Mediterranean climate, providing a high carbohydrate food to the masses. Unlike most other nuts, chestnuts are not particularly high in protein or fat. Nutritionally, they are closer to grain or potatoes than nuts, containing 40% carbohydrates.

Ripe chestnuts

Chestnuts were a primary food source for much of southern Europe until the potato was introduced. From the 1500s through the 1700s, Genoan landowners were required to plant four trees each year: olive, fig, mulberry, and chestnut. As a result, that area has rich, productive forests and farmland. (Imagine how productive your yard could be if you planted four food-producing trees each year!)

Being high in calories and carbohydrates, chestnuts were often ground into a flour to make a type of flatbread (chestnut flour does not rise, as it does not contain gluten). Unfortunately, this earned it a reputation as a poor man's food, which lead to a decline in interest. This was unfortunate, because chestnuts are a highly nutritious food.

Across the pond, Native Americans enjoyed local chestnut species long before Europeans arrived. Regions of the Appalachian Mountains were fully one-fourth chestnut trees. Since a mature American chestnut tree can produce 50-100 pounds of fruit each year, that ends up being a lot of food.

EPIC CHESTNUTS

There have been some impressive chestnut trees. The Tortworth Chestnut, also known as the Great Tree of Tortworth, found in South Gloucestershire, has been around since Stephen, King of England (1092-1154). This beast has a circumference of 50 feet! Even larger, the Hundred Horse Chestnut grows on Italy's Mt. Etna and is believed to be the oldest living chestnut tree, at approximately 4,000 years.

Chestnut Species						
Common name	Latin name; other names	Native region	Mature height	Flavor	Peelability	Seeds/burr
American chestnut	Castanea dentata	Appalachian Mts.	100' or more	Sweetest variety	Easy	small; 3 - 4 seeds
Allegheny chinkapin	C. pumila; dwarf chestnut	Southeastern U.S.				
Chinese chestnut	C. mollissima	Northern and western China	40'		Easy	
Chinese chinkapin	C. henryi; Henry's chestnut	China			Easy	
European chestnut	C. sativa; sweet chestnut; Spanish chestnut;	Western Asia, Europe, and North America	100' or more	Sweet	Easy	large
Japanese chestnut	C. crenata; Korean chestnut	Malaysia and SE Asia	50'	Inferior	Difficult	large; 5 - 7 seeds

CHESTNUT SPECIES

There are eight or nine different deciduous trees and shrubs that are called the chestnuts. These are placed into one of four groups: American, Chinese, European, and Japanese, for obvious reasons. Each species has distinct characteristics.

European and American chestnuts tend to grow more tree-like, with a single erect trunk, while the Asian varieties tend to be multilayered and more spread out. Also, the former varieties offer stunning fall foliage. There are hundreds of chestnut varieties to choose from.

CHESTNUT FLOWERS

Like avocados, chestnuts have both male and female flowers. Chestnuts are not self-compatible, which means you will need at least two trees or shrubs to produce fruit. Flowers appear in late spring and early summer. Male (staminate) flowers are shaped like a cat's tail and are called catkins. Catkins mature before the female flowers, and the pollen has a rich, sweet aro-

Chestnut branch

ma. The female, fruit-producing (pistillate) flowers grow together in groups of two or three, which end up forming a prickly, 4-lobed structure called a calybium. The calybium is what ultimately develops into the hull that protects the fruit. Pollen is moved predominantly by wind, though beneficial insects also perform some pollination.

CHESTNUT FRUIT

The fruit of chestnut trees is held in sharp, pokey burrs, called cupules. These burrs tend to be clustered. The burrs of some varieties each contain one nut, while other varieties can hold up to seven. Burrs turn yellowish-brown and split open as the fruit matures. Each fruit has a pointed end, called a flame, and an attachment scar end, called the hilum. Chestnut fruit has two skins: the hard outer pericarpus, called the heel, and an attached, thinner skin, called the pellicle or episperm. Chestnuts are both culinary and botanical nuts, unlike almonds, peanuts, cashews, and walnuts.

CHESTNUT LUMBER

Chestnut lumber is lovely, but larger pieces tend to split. Most chestnut lumber is now produced through coppicing. Coppicing refers to cutting trees back to ground level, forcing new growth. Young chestnut lumber is more durable than oak of the same age. Both species contain high levels of tannins. Chestnut wood was a common source of natural tannins for tanning leather.

HOW TO GROW CHESTNUTS

Chestnuts are in high demand and the supply is limited. This keeps prices high, and is a good argument for growing your own (assuming you are not in a hurry). Going from bare root sapling to mature, productive tree takes about 10 years. Chestnuts need specific chilling hours to produce flowers and fruit. If the dormant period does not get cold enough, you will still have a beautiful tree, but no homegrown chestnuts. Also, if two chestnut trees are planted such that their canopies touch, they produce no fruit. We don't know why.

Allowed to fall to the ground, chestnut seeds germinate right away. You can start them in a cold frame, container, or seedbed outdoors, where they will experience winter temperatures. Seedlings require protection from squirrels and other rodents.

Chestnut trees need good drainage and regular irrigation (31" per year). Once established, they are drought resistant, but do not grow well in heavy clay or alkaline soil. Chestnuts prefer a soil pH of 5.5 to 6.0. If you live in an area where alkaline clay is pretty much the rule, don't despair. Chestnut scions can be grafted onto oak rootstock! Chestnut trees should be trained into a modified central leader scaffold system for the best sun exposure and overall health.

CHESTNUT PESTS AND DISEASES

Squirrels, rabbits, deer, wild boar, livestock, and birds can all take a bite out of your chestnut harvest. You may want to consider a tree cage, at least while the tree is small. Chestnut gall wasps (in southeastern states), some moths, the oak roller weevil, oak aphid, filbert worm, oak leaf mining moth, shot hole borers, and the chestnut weevil are common pests of chestnut, depending on where you live.

In 1904, some Asian chestnut trees that had been planted on Long Island were found to be infected with chestnut blight (*Cryphonectria parasitica*, formerly *Eudothia parasitica*). Over the next 40 years, 4 billion chestnut trees died, nearly wiping out the American chestnut. Reforestation efforts, started in the 1930s using seeds from the few remaining living stumps are giving this majestic tree a new lease on life, but it's a slow process. There are now blight-resistant cultivars. Chestnut trees are also susceptible to Armillaria rot. On the other hand, chestnuts are believed to be naturally resistant to oak rot fungus. You can protect your chestnut tree against sunburn by whitewashing the trunk, and help it stay healthy by mulching under the canopy.

ROASTING CHESTNUTS

Chestnuts have been candied, soaked in wine, and roasted as a holiday tradition throughout Europe for a very long time. To early Christians, chestnuts symbolized chastity, while in modern-day Japan, they symbolize both good times (mastery) and bad times (strength).

You can roast your own chestnuts at home in the oven. Start with raw, unpeeled, chestnuts. Cut an X on the rounded bottom of each nut. Some people soak their chestnuts in water for 30 to 60 minutes before baking, others use wine, and still others don't soak at all. You decide. If you do soak them in water, drain and pat dry before roasting.

Spread the nuts out on a baking sheet. Bake at 425°F for 15 to 20 minutes, or until the skins have pulled away from the cuts and the nutmeats have softened. Take them out of the oven and let them rest for a few minutes. Peel and eat!

Did you know that chestnuts are the only nuts that contain vitamin C? Now you know.

Hazelnuts (Simon A. Eugster) CC BY-SA 3.0

Hazelnuts

Zones 4—8
Sun exposure: full sun, partial sun, partial shade

Hazelnuts, filberts, or cobnuts, whatever you call them, these delicious nuts grow on trouble-free shrubs that make excellent additions to your foodscape.

Since hazelnut shrubs naturally grow alongside creeks and under taller overgrowth, they are a good choice for locations with partial shade.

WHY GROW HAZELS?

The obvious reason for growing a hazel bush is the delicious nuts. Hazelnut plants can produce food for 80 years. Tradition-ally, hazels were planted as hedgerows between properties and grazing fields. They were frequently coppiced, or cut to ground level to stimulate new growth, to provide long, slender poles for basket-making and wattle and daub fencing.

HAZELNUT CLASSIFICATION

Some scientists group the hazels with birch trees, while others claim hazels are their own grouping. All hazels are from the *Corylus* genus and all of their nuts are edible. Worldwide, there are 14-18 species. Only two species are native to North America, with one local variation:

- *Corylus americana* - American Hazelnut; native to Eastern U.S.; up to 16' tall
- *C. cornuta* - Beaked Hazelnut; native to North America; 15'-20' tall
- *C. cornuta* var. *californica* - northern CA native; slow-growing, up to 18' tall

The cornuta varieties are called "beaked hazelnuts" because the nuts' outer covering has a beak shape. Our native varieties are smaller than their European cousins, which can reach a mature height of 30 feet. European varieties tend to produce larger fruit with thinner shells.

HOW HAZELS GROW

Unlike most plants, hazelnuts bloom and pollinate in winter. Yellow pollen-crusted catkins release their bounty to the wind, which carries it to tiny red flowers. There, the pollen stays dormant until summer. That's when the nuts start to form.

Hazels are monoecious, or hermaphroditic, having both male catkins and female flowers on the same plant. Catkins are hanging flower clusters that contain pollen. Hazelnuts are self-infertile, which means you will need more than one plant to produce a crop of edible nuts.

Members of the hazel family are all deciduous. Some are trees and some are suckering shrubs. These suckers can be used to create new shrubs elsewhere on your property or given to family and friends to start their own. Commercially, the suckers are generally removed and the shrub is trained into a tree form to make management and harvest easier. What you do with yours is entirely up to you, but it is nice to have options!

HOW TO GROW HAZELNUTS

If you have access to suckers, use them! Otherwise, you can plant nuts in loose soil and water occasionally. Germination rates and speed can be increased by scarification, or scoring the outer layer of the nut. Once seedlings are 12" tall, they can be transplanted to their permanent location. They will begin producing nuts in their third or fourth year. These nuts grow in clusters called burrs.

Beaked hazelnut

Hazels are shallow-rooted plants that cannot tolerate soggy ground. They are drought tolerant and require little effort on your part, once they are established. Only during the peak of California summers do they need any irrigation.

HAZELNUT PESTS AND DISEASES

One very serious threat to hazelnuts has kept them from being grown commercially in the Eastern U.S. It is called eastern filbert blight. Our native species are resistant, and some are immune. This disease has recently made its way west to Oregon and California. Pests include bud mites, blue jays, and squirrels. Ads claim that floating balloons decorated with giant eyes are a good way to keep birds out of fruit and nut trees, but I was unable to find any research that verified those claims.

HARVESTING HAZELNUTS

Hazelnut harvesting begins in autumn, as the leaves and burrs turn brown. Remove nuts from the burrs and lay them out in a single layer, in a protected area, to dry for a few days. Roasting makes it easy to remove the inner paper, which can taste bitter, and it brings out that rich hazelnut flavor that we all know and love!

Pistachios

Zones 6—9
Sun exposure: full sun

You can grow these tasty nuts in your own backyard, if you have room and patience. The delicious flavor of pistachios doesn't come cheap. They are not inexpensive and they require effort to pry from their shells. That being said, pistachios have a protein-rich flavor that begs us to eat just one more, and another, and another.

WHAT ARE PISTACHIOS?

The meat of a pistachio (*Pistacia vera L.*) is not technically a nut. Like other stone fruits, pistachios are edible seeds held within a hard shell. When these seeds ripen, the shell opens with an audible pop.

Pistachio trees need long, hot, dry summers and gentle winters to produce those hard-shelled nuts. Pistachio trees can tolerate a lot of salinity, but they do not grow well near coasts, due to the lack of adequately hot, dry summers. Soggy soil will kill a pistachio tree, so good drainage is critical. Pistachios are slow-growing, alternate bearing, deciduous trees that need

600-1500 chill hours, depending on variety, to produce fruit. A healthy, mature pistachio tree can produce 110 pounds of seeds every other year. That's a lot of pistachios.

How to grow pistachios

Pistachio trees are dioecious. That means there are both male and female trees. You only need one male for up to 10 females for successful pollination, but these trees get rather large, so you probably won't have room for more than one of each. Mature trees can grow 33' tall and should be spaced 20' apart.

Immature pistachio cluster
(Paulo Galli) CC BY-SA 3.0

Plant pistachio rootstock from January through early May. Be sure to provide support by inserting a large, heavy stake next to the root ball. You will want the wind to push the tree toward the support for the best development. Irrigate the root ball immediately and follow with regular waterings until the root system is established. This may take several months, so be patient. Your pistachio tree will also need to be fertilized regularly. During the first dormant season, cut the top of the main shoot off, just above leaf buds. This heading cut will promote a more solid structure later on.

Pistachio pests and diseases

A disease called panicle and shoot blight, caused by the *Botryosphaeria* fungi, kills flowers and young shoots of pistachio trees. In 2011, 50% of the Australia pistachio harvest was lost to anthracnose. Verticillium wilt can also be a problem. Severe drought has also reduced commercial production in many areas. Common pistachio pests include leaf-footed bugs, mealybugs, nematodes, and late season navel orangeworms.

HARVESTING PISTACHIOS

After waiting for five to seven years, you will finally be able to harvest your very own pistachios. Like almonds, this is done by shaking the tree. Ripe nuts fall and are collected from the ground. If you see any nuts with mold, toss them in the trash. That particular mold is carcinogenic. Also, be sure to dry your pistachios out completely before storing—they have been known to spontaneously combust.

Don't let all those problems discourage you or scare you off. These beautiful trees can produce an edible crop for decades, if cared for properly.

Walnuts

Zones 4—9
Sun exposure: full sun

Growing up in Southern California, I was lucky enough to attend a childcare program that was built on the grounds of a former walnut grove. Scattered throughout the property were dozens of ancient walnut trees that were great for climbing, tire swings, and more delicious walnuts than any of us kids could possibly have eaten. But we sure tried!

Walnut shell inside its green husk
(Böhringer Friedrich) CC BY-SA 2.5

People have been growing walnut trees longer than any other food tree. Nearly 10,000 years ago, in ancient Persia, walnuts were grown for members of the royal family. Traded along the Silk Road, and then via sea trade, Persian walnuts made their way to Rome, where they were called Jupiter's royal acorn, and to England, where the name was changed to English walnuts, even though they were not being grown commercially in England at that time. In the 1700s, missionaries brought walnuts to California.

TYPES OF WALNUT TREES

There are several different trees that qualify as walnut. They are all members of the *Juglans* genus. The familiar English walnut is only one of four types of walnut tree:

- Persian or English walnut (*Juglans regia*) - these trees grow faster than the others, with thinner shells, making it the walnut tree of choice for commercial production
- Black walnut (*J. nigra*) - native to eastern North America; valued for both nuts and extremely hard lumber, they are also grown as shade trees
- Butternut (*J. cinerea*) - also known as "white walnut"
- Heartnut (*J. ailantifolia*) - also known as "Japanese walnut"; these trees produce heart-shaped fruits

THE WALNUT TREE

Walnut is a deciduous hardwood. It is also one of the few trees with a true taproot. (Most tree root systems are fibrous.) Walnut trees can take five to six years before they produce fruit. When selecting a site for a walnut tree, keep in mind that a mature walnut tree can reach 40'-80' in both height and width, and it can live up to 250 years!

Walnut trees, like avocado trees, are monoecious, which means they produce both male and female flowers. Male walnut flowers are catkins that look like hanging cat tails. The female flowers are spiky and short. If you slice open a walnut twig, you will see a series of tan chambers, called pith. This is different from the white pith found in citrus rinds.

FRUITS OF THE WALNUT TREE

The common walnut isn't a nut at all. Botanically, it is a drupe. This means that the walnuts you enjoy eating are a form of fleshy fruit. Almonds are drupes, too. Surrounded by a thick, green rind, the walnuts you see in the grocery store are not what they look like when they are still hanging in the tree. That rind is actually the fruit of a walnut tree, but you wouldn't want to eat it. It tastes nasty.

Walnut fruit

Walnut trees tend to produce heavy crops one year and a light crop the following year. Known as alternate bearing, these fluctuations allow trees to recover from heavy production years.

TOXIC WALNUT

You have probably heard that walnut trees put out toxins that make it impossible to grow other plants nearby. This is only partly true. Many plants use a type of chemical warfare, called allelopathy, to reduce competition. Walnut trees do produce toxins that can cause some other plants to wilt. Tomatoes, potatoes, eggplant, peppers, blackberries, raspberries, blueberries, and asparagus do not grow well when planted near a black walnut tree, according to the University of Illinois Extension. At the same time, according to the Penn State Extension, onions, beets, squash, melons, carrots, parsnips, beans, yarrow, stonecrops, and corn can all be grown near a walnut tree without any problems. In fact, in commercial walnut groves, a type of agroforestry called alley cropping is used to plant other crops, such as corn, between the rows of walnut trees.

PROPAGATING WALNUT TREES

While you can certainly buy a bare root walnut tree, there are other ways. You can plant a raw walnut in the ground, or, if you know of someone with a walnut tree, you can use air layering. Layering is a form of vegetative propagation. Strawberry runners are an example of layering. The nice thing about air layering is that the parent plant continues to feed and care for the newly developing plant, since they are still attached to one another. To air layer a walnut, pull a stem down until it touches the ground at what would have been a leaf node. Instead of developing into a leaf, that bud will start putting out roots.

PRUNING WALNUT

Walnut trees can produce nuts on the same spurs for several years. Because of this, mature walnut trees do not require renewal pruning. The only pruning needed is occasionally thinning branches to maintain overall shape and good health. Young walnut trees are trained using the modified central leader system. In this method, a single, strong shoot is encouraged up the central line of the tree. Two or three lateral branches, spread evenly around the tree both vertically and horizontally, are allowed to grow. All other branches are removed. Eventually, there can be five to seven lateral branches in place before the central leader is removed.

WALNUT PESTS AND DISEASES

Walnuts are susceptible to an astounding number of pests and diseases. Luckily, walnuts are rugged trees that rarely need assistance in fighting off these foes. It's still a good idea to know what your tree might be up against. Many varieties of scale insects, including walnut scale, frosted scale, European fruit lecanium scale, San Jose scale, Kuno scale, and Italian pear scale may be found on walnut. Walnut husk flies, aphids, southern fire ants, walnut twig beetles, fall webworms, Pacific flathead borers, navel orangeworms, false chinch bugs, redhumped caterpillars, American plum borers, and Mediterranean fruit flies prefer walnut, as do tortricid moths, such as the light brown apple moth, which can cause leaf roll of walnut. A type of eriophyid mite, called the blister mite, will also attack walnut trees, as will European red mites and webspinning spider mites. Codling moth larvae will burrow into the nut meat of English walnuts, starting in April. You can monitor your trees for many of these pests by using pheromone traps.

Diseases such as crown gall and walnut blight can be prevented and treated with Bordeaux mixture or fixed copper. Walnut trees may also become infected with anthracnose, armillaria root rot, phytophthora root and crown rot, branch wilt, and several canker diseases. If that weren't trouble enough, squirrels, voles, pocket gophers, rats, and deer will try to get at as much of your walnut crop as they can.

While many trees are treated with horticultural oils during dormancy, oils should not be used on walnut. Dormant oils are phytotoxic (poisonous) to walnut trees. Like apricot trees, walnut trees are also susceptible to Eutypa dieback. This fungal disease can kill a tree. The easiest way to avoid it is to only prune your walnut tree during summer, when there are no rains expected. Also, make sure that your sprinklers are not hitting the tree's trunk.

Walnuts contain high levels of oils that can turn rancid. To keep walnut meats fresh, leave them in their shells and place them in cold storage. If you buy walnuts from a store and plan on using them within one month, store them in your refrigerator. Since walnuts can absorb odors, be sure to keep them away from fragrant foods, such as cabbage, broccoli, and fish. Longer storage should be done in the freezer.

Walnut trees can make a magnificent addition to your foodscape, providing decades of delicious nuts and welcoming shade from the summer sun.

Chapter Sixteen

SHRUBS, VINES, CANES, AND OTHER FAMILIES

These plants are unique to their families. Only distantly related to more common edibles, or not at all, these delicious shrubs, vines, cane fruits, and other plants have their own set of rules for what works for them. These are the outliers of the edible landscaping world. They don't fit neatly into any of the other groups, but they certainly deserve your consideration.

When your house was built, with gingerbread precision, it was designed to offer many of the modern conveniences that we enjoy each day. On the flip side of all that comfort, the soil under and around many homes is often severely compacted during the building process. Most builders install whichever landscaping plants are popular at the time the house was built (or whatever was on sale), without much thought given to invasiveness, native plants, or edibles.

You can, over time, replace many of those ornamentals with raspberry cane borders, hazelnut shrubs, blueberry hedges, and vine-draped pergolas, depending on where you live. These plants can serve the same purpose as their ornamental cousins, with the added benefit of producing food. Because these plants are from a variety of families, their pests and diseases are discussed individually.

Cane Fruits

Zones 4—9
Sun exposure: full sun, partial sun
Ideal soil temperature: above 60°F

Plant some perennial cane fruits this year and juicy berries will be your reward for many years to come. If they ever make their way into the house, these delicious fruits can be used on cereal, to make jam or jelly, in a cobbler, or to make wine. More often than not, you will want to enjoy them as you find them, sweet and warm from the sun.

Blackberries

Blackberries, dewberries, and raspberries are popular cane fruits. Boysenberries, marionberries, and tayberries are cane fruit hybrids. Botanically speaking, blackberries and raspberries are not berries at all. Instead, they are aggregate fruits made up of small drupelets. These plants all have woody stems, called canes, and they're all members of the Rose family (Rosaceae), along with stone fruits, apples and pears, and strawberries.

HOW CANE FRUITS GROW

First- and second-year canes are often covered with numerous sharp prickles, mistakenly called thorns. Prickle-free (thornless) varieties are available. I have heard from several growers that thornless varieties produce bigger fruit, but that varieties with prickles have far better flavor. Personally, I'll take quality over quantity any day!

Cane fruits love water. Sunburned leaves are a common

sign that your cane fruits are not getting enough water. Our raspberries get nearly daily waterings from the bucket of water we collect in the shower as we wait for the water to heat up, at least when it's not raining. Heavy clay soil can also lead to drowning if there is too much water. Since cane fruits have relatively shallow roots compared to other members of the Rose family, regular light watering is better than less frequent, deep watering.

Cane fruits prefer cooler, damp weather, but you can recreate those conditions by adding them to a shade garden or growing them in containers under a pergola or on a shady balcony. These plants need lots of sun but they prefer a little shade in the heat of the afternoon. They grow best in soil with a pH of 5.5 to 7.0, and they thrive in raised beds.

Cane fruits spread by sending suckers up from the roots each year. Roots will also grow any time a stem rests on the ground. Because these plants spread so readily, some people consider them invasive. Rather than looking at this behavior as a negative, you can take advantage of this tenacious fruit producer in your landscape. Worried about someone hopping your fence? Adding a blackberry bramble is likely to change their mind.

Those suckers (the canes, not the burglars) are biennial. New canes emerge from the crown each year. These primocanes are green and flexible and do not produce fruit. They grow and spread and then turn brown and go dormant over the winter, to one degree or another. In spring, these now 2-year-old canes are called floricanes. The fruit is produced on flower clus-

> **Raspberry or Blackberry?**
>
> Do you know how to tell blackberries and raspberries apart?
>
> Hint: It's not the color.
>
> The only way to really tell the difference between blackberries and raspberries is to look at the way the fruit comes away from the torus, or stem. If the torus comes with the fruit, it is a blackberry. If the torus breaks away from the fruit, it is a raspberry.

ters (racemes) found at the tip of lateral buds on the floricanes. After it produces fruit, the cane dies, making room for the next year's crop.

Cane fruits are rugged, as long as they don't get too much scorching sunlight in summer. In the wild, they grow best near creeks, in alluvial soil. They can also be grown in large containers, at least five gallons.

CARING FOR CANE FRUITS

While you can start cane fruits from seed, it is much more satisfying to start with cuttings, dormant bare-root plants, or potted seedlings. To grow your own cane fruits, start by finding a sunny spot with good drainage. Standing water and saturated clay will kill canes. If you are going to use a trellis, install it before planting. Dig a hole that is 4"-6" deeper and wider than the bare roots or potted plants. If your soil is heavy clay, be sure to rough up the edges of the hole to give roots a toe-hold. Remove any damaged roots or stems before planting. Spread the roots out within the hole and cover with aged compost and soil. Make sure that the crown, where the roots meet the stem, is at or slightly above the surrounding soil level. This is important. Planting too deeply is one of the most common causes of plant death.

Resist the urge to tamp the soil down. This damages microscopic root hairs. Those tiny roots absorb the water and nutrients needed for your plants to thrive. Instead, water thoroughly around the plant. This mudding in will help the soil settle without damaging the roots. Plus, it gives the plant the water needed to help it recover from the shock of transplanting. Finally, cut the new canes down so they are only 6" tall. This will encourage strong root growth. Water well but do not feed. Mulch within 12"-18" of each plant to keep weeds down and moisture in. Plants should be spaced 2'-4' apart, with 8'-10' between rows.

If your canes' first summer is hot and dry, water every 7-10 days. Once the plants are established, they will only need 1"-2" of water per week, mid-May through October, generally speaking.

Healthy plants are far less likely to be vulnerable to pests and diseases, so you will want to feed your plants each time they start a new bloom cycle. According to UC Davis, 3-6 pounds of blood meal, feather meal, or fish meal should be applied for every 100 feet of row. Most of us don't have a 100 feet of row of raspberry or blackberry plants. I did the math and it works out to approximately 1-2 ounces per plant. You will need a lab-based soil test to see if anything else is needed.

If you train your cane fruits up a trellis or cattle panel, pinch them off when they reach the top. This will encourage more lateral growth. This also makes the plants more manageable and less prone to fungal diseases or mite damage. Be sure to remove any dead or damaged canes whenever you are working your cane fruits. Canes left to grow a third year may produce some fruit on the lower part of the canes, but they should be pruned out after that to make room for new canes and to reduce the spread of disease. It is a good idea to wear long sleeves, long pants, and heavy gloves when working with cane fruits. Those prickles are sharp!

Cane fruits are very low-maintenance once established. After a cane has produced fruit, it can be removed. This cuts down on the thicket effect and encourages the root system to generate new canes that will produce even more fruit.

Blackberries

People have been enjoying blackberries (*Rubus fruticosus*) for thousands of years. These North America natives can be allowed to grow wild, creating giant mounds, or they can be grown up a fence or trellised. The mounding habit common to blackberries is what earns them the name bramble.

There are two basic cultivars of blackberries: erect and trailing. Erect blackberries have stiff canes that arch. While not completely self-supporting, erect blackberries tend to grow into huge thickets if not pruned. Trailing cultivars, also known as dewberries, will spread horizontally across the ground. If you live in a cold area, there are even late-season blackberry varieties that can produce late summer crops.

Blackberries are green when they are red.

This old saying reminds blackberry growers that unripe fruits are red. They become ripe two or three weeks later, when the fruits are black, but still firm.

Blackberries

British folklore warns against picking blackberries after Old Michaelmas Day (October 11). That's because the devil is said to have spit on them! This tradition has a reasonable explanation in science. As cooler, moist weather kicks in, several types of mold can begin to grow on the fruit, which can make it toxic. So, enjoy your blackberries before October 11th and leave the rest for the birds!

Raspberries

Nothing compares with the sun-warmed sweetness of a raspberry freshly picked and popped into your mouth.

Raspberries do not ship well, so the specimens we find at the grocery store, like most tomatoes, are simply not up to par with fresh from the garden varieties. The nice thing about raspberries is that they can grow in some unusual places.

When I first moved into our San Jose home, I wasn't sure where I wanted my container raspberries to end up, so I heeled them in (laid them down on the ground and covered the roots with some soil) in the unlikeliest of places—a six-inch strip of soil next to a concrete slab, where the property line fence was installed. And then I forgot all about them.

Six months or so later, after unpacking, settling in, and beginning to work the garden and landscape, I came around the corner of my house and BAM! There, in the shade of my garage, the neglected raspberries had thrived and were climbing the fence! All in a six-inch strip of what was probably construction soil.

What made that dubious location work was afternoon shade and a ready supply of water. It was winter in San Jose, California, and a rain gutter downspout pointed directly their way. You may not want to try growing your berries in such a questionable location, but it shows how tenacious these cane fruits can be. Once the plants are established, they can produce fruit for decades. In addition to traditional red raspberries, you can also find cultivars that are golden, purple, and black.

Raspberries are self-fertile, which means you can get fruit from a single plant. Fruit production varies between everbearing and summer-bearing varieties. Summer-bearing raspberries bear one crop in summer on two-year-old canes, while everbearing cultivars have two crops, one small crop in summer on new canes and one

Raspberries

heavier crop in fall on two-year-old canes. Everbearing cultivars are sometimes called fall-bearing. It is a good idea to check with your local Cooperative Extension Office to find the best cultivar for your location.

Raspberry pruning methods will vary, depending on the cultivar. Fruit-producing canes of summer-bearing red and yellow raspberries should be cut to ground level after harvest and removed. Thin primocanes to no more than four or five per foot. Fall-bearing raspberries can be treated the same as everbearing varieties, if you want both the summer and fall crops. Otherwise, leave the canes in place for an extra year.

Raspberries can survive in unlikely places

If you are growing black or purple raspberries, you will need to pinch the canes when they reach 2'-2½' in height and then again two or three times during the summer. This will promote lateral cane growth for more fruit.

Note: If you have never grown raspberries before, you may be surprised to learn that they ripen unevenly. One part of a berry will look ripe days before the rest of it does. This is okay, simply wait (if you can!) for the entire berry to ripen before picking.

Grapes

Zones 4—10
Sun exposure: full sun
Ideal soil temperature: above 45°F

California is famous for its wine grapes, but did you know it is easy to grow your own grapes at home?

Not only will you get sweet, luscious grapes, but the vines

can be trained over a patio or pergola, providing a nice shady spot in summer!

How to Grow Grapes

First, select a site with full sun and good drainage. Then, build and install a sturdy trellis to support the vines and ensure good sun exposure. You will want to start with one-year-old bare root grape vines or healthy cuttings. If you get bare roots, be sure to trim off any broken or damaged bits and then soak the vines in a bucket of water for one to six hours, depending on how dried out they feel.

Grapes

Dig planting holes that are two to three times the diameter of the plant, but only as deep as the roots. No deeper. Place the vines six to ten feet apart with two bud spurs at soil level. Water well at planting time to help the soil settle around the roots.

During the first two years, allow vertical and horizontal shoots to grow so the leaves can produce energy for a strong root system. You may need to provide a vertical stake to help the shoots reach the trellis.

Once the vine is established, select the strongest vertical

shoot to become the trunk and remove all the others. Start training vines during winter, when they are dormant. The main trunk should be "headed" (trimmed) when it reaches the top trellis wire. Canes should not be cut during the growing season.

PRUNING GRAPE VINES

The variety of grapes being grown determines which of two pruning methods to use. Grapes are either spur-pruned or cane-pruned. This is because different grape varieties produce fruit on different bud spurs.

Cane pruning refers to removing everything except the trunk and two to four shoots from the previous year's growth to be trained along support wires. New buds will emerge from these canes to produce leaves and fruit. 'Thompson Seedless' and 'Concord' are cane-pruned grapes.

Spur pruning leaves the bilateral cordons, or horizontal branches, permanently in place. In spring, new growth will emerge from this old wood. 'Flame Seedless', 'Tokay', and 'Ribier' are spur-pruned grapes.

In either case, you will want to trim each cane to have no more than 14 spurs. Otherwise, all the plant's energy will go into vegetative growth, rather than producing grapes.

IRRIGATING GRAPES

While most of a grape vine's roots are in the top 3' of soil, some of those roots can go down as much as 15' deep! Grapes perform best when they are watered deeply and allowed to dry out between waterings. The amount of water needed depends on the type of soil, the depth of the roots, and the weather. At the peak of summer, grape wines may need a deep watering every 2-3 weeks. During cooler or wet weather, little or no water is needed. Once your vines have bloomed, it is important to water regularly. As fruit develops, erratic watering can lead to water-stress and cracked fruit.

FEEDING GRAPE VINES

If you are growing grapes in rich soil, nothing needs to be added. Too many nutrients can reduce or eliminate fruit production. Remember, in the plant world, it's all about reproduction. Grapes are the reproductive part of the vine. If the plant doesn't feel the need to reproduce, it won't.

Princess seedless white grapes

Assuming your soil isn't perfectly rich, nitrogen and potassium can be added before berry set. ("Berry set" is when the grapes are ¼" in diameter.) Zinc should only be added before the vines bloom. The only way to know if these additives are needed is to have your soil tested by a reputable lab.

HARVESTING GRAPES

To reduce the chance of pest problems, harvest grapes as soon as they taste ripe. Unripe grapes will not ripen off the vine. Grape clusters should be cut, not pulled, from the vine, and then cooled after being harvested. Do not rinse grapes off before storing them. Do that just before eating.

PESTS AND DISEASES OF GRAPES

Spider mites, aphids, mealybugs, cutworms, thrips, click beetles, leafhoppers, branch and twig borers, and ants can infest grape vines. Diseases such as Eutypa Dieback and Pierce's Disease can infect grape vines, and powdery mildew is a common problem. Birds and rodents can also wreak havoc on your harvest. Monitor grape vines regularly for these pests and diseases to ensure timely control. Contact your local County Extension office for information specific to your region.

While grape vines take some time to become productive, an established grape vine can produce fruit for fifty to one hundred years! Only one or two vines are needed to provide a family with an abundance of grapes. Get yours started.

Gooseberry Family

Zones 3—8, with a couple of exceptions
Sun exposure: full sun, partial sun, partial shade
Ideal soil temperature: below 85°F

Members of the Gooseberry family (Grossulariaceae). This group only has one genus (*Ribes*), which includes currants and gooseberries.

Currants

Not to be confused with the tiny black raisins made from black Corinth grapes, currants are something else entirely. Currants are close cousins to gooseberries. If you cross currants with gooseberries, you get jostaberries.

Berries and leaves of white currants

Most Americans are unfamiliar with currants because they were banned in 1920. This ban was put in place because currants are co-hosts, along with white pine, of white pine blister rust (*Cronartium ribicola*). This fungal disease was devastating to white pines on the East Coast. That ban was lifted, in 1966, as resistant cultivars were developed. The small, pea-sized fruits can be red, pink, white, or black and are produced in clusters called "strig". Currants are tart, so they are not usually eaten fresh. They are more commonly used for jams, jellies, pies, syrups, wine, and brandy. The flowers are also edible.

Currant plants are thornless, deciduous shrubs. They are drought tolerant and provide food and shelter to many indigenous birds. Native Americans frequently used currants as both food and medicine. In particular, they used currant roots to treat menstrual and menopausal problems. Scientists have found that currant roots and seeds contain high levels of gamma-Linolenic acid, a chemical known to be effective for those same issues.

CURRANT VARIETIES

Scientists are still sorting out the *Ribes* family, and currants, in particular. According to some, there are black currants, red currants, and white currants. According to the University of Massachusetts, "Species are *Ribes rubrum* (most red currants and some whites), *R. petraeum* (white), *R. vulgare* (pink, white, and red), and *R. nigrum* and *R. ussurienses* (black). Native currants belong to the species *R. odoratum*.

I ordered Golden Currants (*Ribes aureum*). Clearly, there is some confusion. Here's the bottom line, as well as I can figure:

- *Ribes rubrum* - red and white currants are really the same plant with different colored fruit; an upright shrub from northern Europe
- *R. sativum* (*R. vulgare*) - a large-fruited spreading shrub from western Europe

- *R. petraeum* - a vigorous shrub from Europe and north Africa
- *R. aureum* (*R. odoratum*) - native to North America (except southeastern U.S.); drought tolerant; smaller shrub with yellow flowers; loses its leaves in late August

HOW TO GROW CURRANTS

Traditionally, currants grow in cool climates with fertile, well-drained soil. They can grow in full sun or partial shade. In areas with hotter summers, currants prefer heavier soil and more shade. Mulch can be used to keep roots cool and moist in summer. Most currant bushes grow 3'-5' tall, but they can go as tall as 9', under ideal conditions. Currents can also be grown in large containers.

Currants are normally purchased as bare root stock or young saplings that were propagated from hardwood cuttings. These young currant bushes need a lot of water to get established, but are very drought tolerant later on. Currents also need a lot of potassium. Get your soil tested every few years, so you know what you and your plants are working with. Most currant plants are self-pollinating, but production is significantly higher per plant with multiple plants nearby.

PRUNING CURRANTS

Currants can be pruned as shrubs or trees, depending on your preferences and the plant's location. Currants should be pruned once a year in winter using a method called renewal pruning. Renewal pruning ensures that there are fruit-producing 2- and 3-year-old stems each year. Use the following pruning schedule on currants:

- Year One - remove all but three stems, at ground level
- Year Two - remove all but two or three of the previous season's new stems
- Year Three - repeat Year Two

- Year Four and ever after - remove any stems that are more than three years old and trim back any low-hanging branches

PESTS AND DISEASES OF CURRANTS

Aphids, mites, currant borers, and the larva of some moths and butterflies are really the only pests that bother currants. Problems are more commonly caused by mineral imbalances in the soil or improper irrigation. Rust, powdery mildew, anthracnose, and leaf spot can sometimes appear on currants.

Since currant flowers tend to appear early in the growing season, they provide pollen and nectar to our earliest pollinators. This helps set the stage for a more productive year overall. Each bush can produce up to 10 pounds of fruit, so it won't hurt to leave some behind for the birds.

Gooseberries

Gooseberries may be the perfect addition to your foodscape or pollinator garden.

Native to Europe, gooseberries are now commonly found in North America. Cousin to currants and jostaberries, gooseberries can be eaten fresh or used to make delicious pies, jams, and jellies. Gooseberry flowers also attract many pollinators and other beneficial insects.

GOOSEBERRY DESCRIPTION

Gooseberries (*Ribes uva-crispa* also *R. grossularia*) grow on bushes that can reach five feet tall and wide. These shrubs have spiny branches and stems that can make working with them a little tricky. Berries can be hairy or smooth. They are usually green, but can also be white, yellow, or a reddish-purple. Gooseberries are categorized as either culinary or dessert varieties.

HOW TO GROW GOOSEBERRIES

Gooseberries are self-pollinating, so you only need one. They can be propagated from seed or cuttings. You may also find them available as bare root stock. Gooseberries can be planted from late fall through early spring.

CARING FOR GOOSEBERRIES

Gooseberries perform best when pruned for good air flow. This is best done in winter, while the plant is dormant. Gooseberries can be grown in large containers or trained along a fence or up a trellis. This also makes it easier on your arms when harvesting. When pruning gooseberries, start by removing any dead, diseased, or rubbing branches and any suckers. Then prune to reduce crowding. Finally, prune back any remaining growth by one-half. Lateral branches should also be cut back, leaving one to three buds.

Ripening red gooseberries

Being native to alpine regions and other areas with poor soil, gooseberry plants don't need extra nitrogen, which often results in too many leaves and not enough fruit. Gooseberries should be given a top dressing of aged compost at the end of each winter to help them grow in spring. Mulching is a good idea, too.

Both because of the spines and the need for significant pruning, heavily laden branches should be removed completely, once the fruit is ripe. This allows light to reach new growth next year.

Gooseberry Pests and Diseases

Gooseberry plants are susceptible to several common fungal diseases as well as American gooseberry mildew, so avoid overhead watering and be sure to provide good drainage. In North America, gooseberry sawflies (*Nematus ribesii*), also known as currant sawflies and imported currantworms, are the most common pest. Aphids, brown marmorated stinkbugs, currant borers, gooseberry fruitworms, and clearwing moths may also cause problems. And birds.

Note: If you live in New Hampshire, North Carolina, or West Virginia, you are not allowed to grow gooseberries or other *Ribes* plants. If you live in Massachusetts, New Jersey, Rhode Island, or Delaware, you'll need a permit. These bans are in place because *Ribes* can carry white pine blister, an imported Asian rust fungus that has devastated high elevation pine forests.

If you are lucky enough to live where you can grow gooseberries, give them a try. These shrubs are very prolific and the fruit is delicious!

Heather Family

Scottish moors and marshes are the favorite habitats of blueberries, bilberries, cranberries, huckleberries, lingonberries, and loganberries. Members of the Heather family (*Ericaceae*) thrive in acidic, infertile areas where many others plants cannot survive.

Blueberries

Zones 5—9
Sun exposure: full sun
Ideal soil temperature: above 55°F

Lucious fresh blueberries in your own backyard? Maybe… While blueberries traditionally grow in colder climates, now there are varieties that grow in warmer places, too.

There are three main types of blueberry plant: southern highbush, northern highbush, and rabbiteye. Southern high-bush and rabbiteye varieties often perform well in warmer areas. Northern highbush varieties need colder weather.

Blueberries

HOW TO GROW BLUEBERRIES

Blueberry plants are sold as one-gallon yearlings. As with all new plants, place them in quarantine while they get used to their new surroundings.

Be sure to keep the soil moist but not soggy. Blue-berry root systems should never be allowed to dry out completely. If they do, they die. At the same time, too much water sets the stage for fungal disease. Yeah, I know—picky, picky, picky! Of course, once you start picking

Blueberry Pests
Asian longhorn beetles
blueberry bud mites
citrus thrips
cranberry weevils
katydids
light brown apple moths
masked chafers
plum curculio
spotted wing drosophila
span worms

sweet blueberries off your very own edible hedge, you'll realize it's worth the effort.

Plants should be placed with the crown at soil level. Since blueberries have a shallow root system, mulch is a good idea. They can also be grown in containers. Blueberries prefer a soil pH of 4.5 to 5.5.

Even though most blueberry plants are self-pollinating, you will get a substantial increase in both fruit quantity and quality through cross-pollination with multiple plants. Plants should be spaced 4'-6' apart.

FEEDING BLUEBERRIES

Blueberries seem to prefer ammoniacal nitrogen-based fertilizers over nitrate-based. I have heard tell that blueberries do not take up the nitrogen in nitrate-based fertilizers. Too much nitrogen can burn blueberry plants, so do not feed until leaves have emerged, and then feed sparingly.

BLUEBERRY PROBLEMS

Blueberry plants are subject to many of the more common pests and diseases, along with a few extras, but birds will probably cause the most damage. Caging your blueberry helps. Removing dead or diseased canes and treating with dormant oil can also

Blueberry Diseases
blueberry stunt disease
canker
mummy berry
stem blight
twig blight

go a long way toward protecting your blueberry plants.

Your blueberry plants can live for 20 years, producing fruit after the third year.

<u>Lingonberries</u>

Zones 3—8
Sun exposure: full sun, partial sun, partial shade
Ideal soil temperature: 40°F to 80°F

Native to boreal and arctic forests, lingonberries are close cousins to cranberries. Used to make jam, syrup, and sauce, lingonberries are very tart, tasting like a cross between cranberries and raspberries.

Ripening red gooseberries

Lingonberries (*Vaccinium vitis-idaea*) are also known as cowberries, mountain cranberries, partridgeberries, cougarberries, beaverberries, and several other animal-berry combinations, depending on where they are found.

TOUGH SHRUBS

Lingonberries are tough, short evergreen shrubs. They rarely grow more than 18" in height. Plants produce white to pink bell-shaped flowers and bright red edible berries. Fruit is bitter early in the season but sweetens somewhat through winter. Even at their sweetest, lingonberries are very tart.

Plants spread out using underground stems, or rhizomes. Lingonberry plants are self-pollinating, but crops are larger and ripen earlier when more than one plant is nearby. Each plant blooms twice a year, creating the potential for two crops. Flowers are not frost-hardy, so the first crop is often lost to a late frost, but these tiny shrubs are very prolific.

There are two regional subspecies of lingonberry. The Eurasian lingonberry (*V. vitis-idaea* subsp. *vitis-idaea*) has larger leaves that can be more than one inch long. The North American lingonberry (*V. vitis-idaea* var. *minus*) has much smaller leaves, usually less than a half inch long. Sadly, some North American populations and subspecies of lingonberry are now in trouble. Specifically, the Michigan lingonberry is endangered and the Connecticut lingonberry is believed to be extinct.

How to Grow Lingonberries

Lingonberry plants need cold weather and good drainage. They can tolerate temperatures as low as -40°F but cannot grow well in areas with hot summers. They grow best in moist, acidic soils (pH 4.2-5.2) in the type of shade one would find under a forest canopy, which certainly rules out my yard.

Most people start with potted seedlings. You can also grow lingonberries from cuttings or divided roots. At planting time, dig a hole that is large enough to allow the roots to spread out, making sure that the planting depth remains the same. Plants should be spaced 12" apart.

Weeds are the biggest threat to your lingonberry plants. A thick mulch of wood chips can reduce that problem. Your lingonberries will not require much in the way of fertilizer. In fact, adding too much nitrogen increases the odds of your plant dying in winter. A better choice would be to top dress around your lingonberry plants with a little bit of aged compost or fish emulsion and leave them alone.

Lingonberries perform well in raised beds and containers. You should protect your lingonberry plants from severe winds. Lingonberry plants are sensitive to chlorides, which means your need to keep them away from chlorinated pool water, de-icing salts, and fertilizers containing potassium chloride.

LINGONBERRY PESTS AND DISEASES

Birds, bears, and foxes love lingonberries. So do many common garden pests. Bacterial leafspot and gray mold may occur, but these diseases can often be prevented by not watering from above. Instead, use soaker hoses or furrow irrigation to keep water off the leaves.

Not everyone lives where lingonberries grow. If you do, you owe it to yourself to give them a try.

Okra

Zone 2—11
Sun exposure: full sun
Ideal soil temperature: above 60°F

While it is okra pods that we normally think of eating, okra leaves and flowers are also edible. Cousin to hollyhocks, cocoa, cotton, hibiscus, and mallow, okra is a simple addition to your garden.

Okra (*Abelmoschus esculentus*) is an attractive plant. Large flowers tend to be white or yellow with red or purple spots at the base. These are big, impressive plants, similar to artichokes. They can reach five feet in height and two or three feet wide.

HOW TO GROW OKRA

Okra prefers hot, sunny weather and warm soil (at least 75°F). It will tolerate clay soil but grows best in soil with lots of organic material. Okra can be planted in large containers.

Okra is a heavy feeder, so top dressing with some aged compost when plants are eight inches tall and again when pods set and when plants are four feet tall. This will ensure they have all the nutrients they need. (Of course, it is always a good idea to get a soil test, so you know what your plants are growing in.) Over-fertilization of okra creates huge, beautiful leaves and zero pods.

Okra plant with blossoms and immature pods (Delince.J) CC BY-SA 3.0

Once pod-formation begins, be sure to harvest pods every other day, while they are less than four inches long. Larger pods are tough and inedible. If pods are allowed to ripen on the plant, pod production will stop.

OKRA PESTS AND DISEASES

Okra is frequently attacked by aphids, cutworms, flea beetles, and whiteflies. You can protect young okra plants from earwigs and cutworms by using brassica collars. Being susceptible to Fusarium wilt and Verticillium wilt, okra should not be planted where tomatoes or peppers have been grown recently.

Okra is a drought-tolerant plant, but it grows best with regular irrigation. Some people are sensitive to okra leaves, so you might want to wear gloves. Just in case.

The roots of okra seedlings are very delicate and easy to damage. Seedlings can be difficult to find, depending on where you live. Okra can be started from seeds, but it is a slow growing plant. Seeds should be sowed ¾" deep in mounds.

Rhubarb

Zones 3—8
Sun exposure: full sun, partial sun, or partial shade
Ideal soil temperature: above 45°F

What summer picnic would be complete without the tang of rhubarb pie?

While purists may enjoy their rhubarb raw, dipped lightly in sugar, many others prefer rhubarb pie with luscious strawberries. However you eat rhubarb, it is a sturdy perennial that can provide shape, color, and food in a garden or landscape for decades.

Rhubarb stalks

Rhubarb (*Rheum rhabarbarum*) is generally a cool season plant. It needs temperatures below 40°F in the winter and prefers temperatures below 75°F in the summer. That being said, I have had excellent success with rhubarb in San Jose where our peak summer heat can reach well above 100°F.

You may be surprised to learn that rhubarb is related to buckwheat and sorrel. If you look at the seeds, you can see the similarity. Rhubarb is believed to have started in Asia, some 5,000 years ago. Marco Polo is cited as the one who brought it to Europe and Benjamin Franklin carried rhubarb to North America, way back in the 1700s!

HOW TO GROW RHUBARB

When selecting a site for rhubarb, keep the plant's mature size in mind. Rhubarb plants can reach three feet in height and four feet in diameter. Rhubarb generally prefers full sunlight, but I grow mine under a small tree, which probably protects the rhubarb from our summer heat. In temperate regions, the rhubarb harvest begins in April and continues until September.

Rhubarb

Individual plants will be productive for 8-20 years, but, since they grow from rhizomes, the plants will replace themselves over time. Many years ago, my mother purchased a 200-year-old farmhouse in Upstate New York and decided to plant rhubarb along the southern side of an outbuilding.

Apparently, the original owners felt the same way because, come spring, not only did the new plants come up, but so did the offspring of the original plants! Needless to say, Mom had plenty of rhubarb!

Rhubarb can be grown in large containers, but it will do much better in the ground. Start by selecting a site large enough for the plants, where they will get plenty of sunlight. Clear out all the weeds and top dress the bed with aged compost. Rhubarb prefers nutrient-rich, well-drained soil.

In early spring (or fall), dig a large hole for each plant, spacing plants four feet apart. Plant one-year crowns two to three inches below the soil surface and cover with aged compost or manure, or straw, and water well. Rhubarb plants are heavy feeders and will need repeated applications of compost throughout the year. Do not apply chemical fertilizers to rhubarb in the first year. Chemical nitrates can kill young rhubarb plants. Mature plants can be fed one cup of 10-10-10 fertilizer each spring.

Be sure to water regularly during summer to prevent bolting. If flower stalks do appear, remove them. Flowering and going to seed will use up nutrients better spent producing roots and edible stalks. Also, rhubarb grown from seed is often not as tasty as plants grown from crowns.

Do not harvest rhubarb stalks the first year. This gives the root system time to get established. Mature plants should be dug up, separated, and replanted every three to four years while they are dormant (early spring or fall). When you do, be on the alert for crown rot, the only real problem for rhubarb. Most insects do not bother rhubarb, probably due to the oxalic acid* in the leaves.

* While rhubarb leaves are mildly toxic, they are not the poison we have been led to believe. You would have to eat several pounds of rhubarb leaves to cause problems. In fact, spinach has more oxalic acid than rhubarb. That being said, I do not feed them to my chickens.

After the harvest has ended, remove any dead plant material and cover the plants with two to four inches of mulch. Underneath this protective cover, the plants will rest and prepare for the next growth season.

One easy way to keep weeds down in a rhubarb patch is to simply take a few of the large rhubarb leaves and lay them on the ground. The leaves block sunlight needed by the weeds and then they break down, adding organic matter to the soil.

Get your rhubarb crowns in today for a lifetime of red-stalked deliciousness!!

Strawberries

Zones 4—8
Sun exposure: full sun
Ideal soil temperature: 65°F to 75°F

Strawberries may surprise you as members of the rose family. Like others in this genetic line, strawberries love sunny days and cool nights. And homegrown strawberries taste amazing! Commercially grown strawberries are treated like annuals, but these plants are perennial.

Botanically, strawberries are not berries at all. Strawberries are aggregate fruits, along with raspberries and blackberries. And those tiny seeds are a special variety known as achenes, which are actually dried fruits!

Strawberries

HOW TO GROW STRAWBERRIES

Strawberries make excellent container plants. They grow very well in towers, raised beds, narrow planter boxes, and even rain gutters. Containers should be 6"-8" deep and at least 18" long.

Potting soil mixed with aged compost or organic fertilizer should be used to provide plenty of nutrients.

Select a sunny location where members of the tomato family have not been planted in the past three years and clear the planting area of all weeds. Amend the soil with aged compost or manure and fertilize with alfalfa meal or other nitrogen-rick treatment.

Build rows that are 6" tall and 10" wide, with each row being 28" apart and cover the planting area with straw. Place plants 10"-14" apart. Crowns should be at or just above the soil line after watering. Keep the roots moist as they become established. Drip irrigation or soaker hoses work well for strawberries. Prune any runners the first year to encourage fruit and root development.

Strawberries growing in a tower

STRAWBERRY VARIETIES

Strawberries are classified as either "day neutral" or "short-day" varieties. Day neutral strawberries, also known as "everbearing," flower and produce fruit year-round, peaking April through October. Aptos and Fern are popular everbearing strawberry plants. Short-day varieties, such as Pajaro, Seascape, Tioga, and Chandler, produce more as days become shorter, in fall, through early spring.

Strawberry Pests and Diseases

Slugs and snails, earwigs and sowbugs will eat fruit that is lying on the ground, which is why a barrier of straw is used to cover strawberry beds. Keeping fruit off the ground will also reduce berry rot. Powdery mildew, Botrytis fruit rot (gray mold), Verticillium wilt, and leaf spot diseases are common on strawberries.

Strawberries occasionally undergo a process called vivipary, in which each tiny seed sprouts a leaf.

Chapter Seventeen

CONCLUSION

If you've gotten this far, you have what it takes to garden. Assuming, of course, your yard or balcony gets enough sunlight. Or, you enjoy learning about plants. In either case, I hope you feel inspired to see which edible plants will grow in your yard.

Growing food isn't out of reach. It isn't even difficult. You can do this. Just give yourself permission to learn from your mistakes and to enjoy the process.

Happy gardening!

Kate

RESOURCES

How to compost

Creating and applying compost is one of the very best things a gardener can do for their soil.

Composting is the natural process by which organic materials are broken down, making them available to plants and microorganisms. It is a major component of pedogenesis, or soil creation. Without healthy soil, we begin to lose our food, water, and air. Yeah, it's kind of important.

More benefits of composting include:

- Less biodegradable materials in landfills
- Improved soil structure
- Reduced water consumption
- Reduced compaction and need for aeration
- Improved permeability
- Reduced use of carbon fuels
- Promotion of soil fertility
- Stimulation of healthy root development
- Reduced erosion
- Reduced need for chemical fertilizers

One of the nicest things about composting is that bacteria and fungi do most of the work for you. Other organisms, such as worms and insects, will pitch in, too. Now, it is possible to simply dump everything in a pile and wait for nature to takes its course. Eventually, there would probably be a nutrient rich soil amendment, but it might take years. It might also turn into a stinky, rotten mess. Follow these tips for successful composting in a reasonable amount of time.

SELECTING A SITE FOR COMPOSTING

Put your compost close enough to be convenient, but not bothersome. Don't put it up against a house, fence, or other structure. Moisture and bugs do happen. The location can be on dirt or cement, in shade or sun. (If the compost pile is on dirt, that spot is going to provide some excellent growing in the future!) The ideal size is a 3' cube. Anything smaller than that and it won't get warm enough. Anything larger than that, and it can't breath.

Composting bins

BINS, DRUMS, OR PILES?

Catalogs and garden centers urge you to try their latest and greatest rolling drums. Those bins rarely work as well as advertised and you still need to move the materials around. Closed drums are also more prone to excess moisture, which can lead to rot.

Wire bins work well and are highly mobile. You simply move the wire away to flip the pile and pitch the material back in, watering as you go. If you look online or in your local library, there are many DIY compost bin instructions available for free and these simple structures do not require a contractor's license or skill set to build. For me, I find that simple piles work the best. I keep my regular compost pile near my chicken coop, for convenience. Occasionally, I move it to an exhausted bed for a season to supercharge it with nutrients and organic material.

UNDERSTAND THE PROCESS: ORGANIC MATTER + AIR + WATER = COMPOST

Organic matter consists of yard and kitchen waste that has been cut into two-inch or smaller sized pieces. Smaller pieces compost faster because there is more surface area for decomposers to reach. Organic matter is considered either green or brown. Green matter includes cut grass, pulled weeds, kitchen scraps and manure, and it is rich in nitrogen. Brown matter is rich in carbon and includes dried leaves, straw, and shredded newspaper. The ratio of green to brown is a major factor in how long it takes compost to break down. "Hot" piles work fastest and use a 30:1 carbon-to-nitrogen ratio, while slower piles can have a 2:1 carbon-to-nitrogen ratio. If material is continually added to a single pile, it will slow the process. A better choice is to have two or three piles, at various stages of decomposition.

MEAT AND DAIRY IN THE COMPOST PILE?

Most recommendations warn against using meat, dairy, and grease in compost piles. Other people have no problems with it. Personally, I use the majority of my kitchen "waste" to make soup stock. The solids are then fed to my chickens. Whatever they don't eat (along with what they did eat) ends up in the compost pile, bones and all. I have had few problems and my plants seem to appreciate the calcium. Of course, my dogs help keep opossums, rats, and raccoons out of my yard. It's your call.

DECOMPOSITION

Decomposition is an aerobic process, which means it needs air. Air helps break down organic matter, and those tiny workers need it, too! Air enters a compost pile by turning it every few days. [Read: good exercise]

Compost pile

Water is needed for the same reasons as air: it aids in decomposition and keeps microorganisms and other decomposers alive. Keep the compost as damp as a wrung-out sponge and avoid simply watering the top, as this tends to cause runoff. Watering as the piles are turned works the best. If the pile gets too wet, spread it out and let it dry, or it will rot.

Temperature is another factor in decomposition. As materials break down, especially the green ones, energy is released in the form of heat. If you've ever watched a big pile of freshly cut grass, you know exactly what I mean. Under the right conditions, a pile of grass clippings can burst into flames. (And it stinks to high heaven). Ideally, the right conditions will generate temperatures between 122°F and 131°F. If temperatures remain above 140°F for at least 10 days, weed seeds and pathogens will be killed. If temperatures stay above 160°F for too long, decomposers will die and the process will stop.

Because temperature is a factor, do not expect much out of a compost pile in winter. Material can still be added, or another pile started. In spring, the whole process will begin again. Also, if an area is especially hot or wet, cover the compost pile to maintain desirable moisture levels.

STOP WASTING YOUR YARD!

COMPOSTING MANURE

Animal bedding and manure are reasonably good sources of nitrogen and organic material, but they can make you sick. To be safe, manure must be composted for at least 45 days, 15 of which must be at temperatures between 131°-170°F, and turned at least five times, assuming it hasn't been recontaminated by air-dropped bird poop or other pathogens. Raw manure should never be applied to the soil while plants are growing. If it is, be sure that the manure does not touch the plants.

WHEN IS COMPOST READY?

Compost is called "finished" when it is ready to use. There is simply no way to say how long finishing will take because of the factors already mentioned. Generally speaking, under reasonably good conditions, a compost pile is ready for use in 45-60 days. Finished compost takes up 25%-40% of the original occupied space, depending on its ingredients. Compost can be dug into beds before planting or it can be used as mulch or top dressing.

COMPOSTING WITH WORMS

For those who do not have space for a compost pile, bin, or drum, try composting with worms. This is called vermiculture. Worm bins can compost an amazing amount of yard and kitchen scraps pretty quickly. Did you know that worms can eat their body weight in scraps every single day? Learn how to build worm bins and compost with worms at the UC Agriculture and Natural Resources page about worms.

Remember, composting is easy and it provides a powerful boost to the garden. Start composting today!

How to plant seeds

Plant your seeds too deeply and they will either rot or use up all their resources, struggling to reach the surface. These plants may grow, but they will rarely thrive. Plant them too shallowly and they won't have the time or moisture they need to grow properly.

The basic rule of thumb for the planting depth for any seed is to use the longest length measurement of the seed and bury it that deep. This means that your large, one-inch-long bean seeds should be buried one inch deep, while your minuscule lettuce and carrots seeds are barely covered with soil.

The following planting chart template provides average seed planting depths and mature plant sizes. Since there are so many variations in the plant world, it's always a good idea to read and use the information on seed packets and plant labels.

Traditionally, gardeners used a tool called a dibble to ensure uniform seed planting depths. I use my finger. Just take a ruler and a marker or pen and calibrate your finger to depths of ¼", ½", 1", and 2". That should cover it. Before long, you'll know what those measurements look and feel like.

HOW TO USE THE PLANTING CHART

As you acquire seeds and seedlings, you can enter them in your planting chart for easy reference. I keep a copy of mine taped to the inside of my seed box. I urge you to make copies of the template for ease of use.

Start with the type of plant you have, and then enter the variety. You'll want this information later on, as you learn which varieties perform well in your yard and which do not.

Next, add the year for which the seeds were produced. Most seeds lose their spark after a year or two. It's always better to use seeds before they get too old. Check the package to see if the recommended sun exposure, seed planting depth, mature size, and days to harvest match the average information I've included. Make any necessary corrections. The seed packet will tell you the best time of year to plant. You can use the calendar boxes to mark the best time of year to direct sow (D), start seeds for transplanting (S), transplant seedlings (T), and expected harvest dates (H) to help you plan the best use of your growing season. It will also help you keep track of where you got your seeds and seedlings.

As you become a better gardener, your friends and neighbors are sure to ask where you got those amazing tomatoes or that stunning purple kale. If you've written it down, it will be easy to share that information. It makes shopping for next year's seeds easier, too.

Taking notes about your experiences with each plant can help you learn to be a better gardener. Garden journals are another good tool. You can keep a notebook or journal that will help you remember what you did, what happened, and what you'd like to try. It's a good way to note when seasonal changes occur in your yard, too.

Seed planting chart

Seed Planting Chart

Plant	Variety	Year	Bed/Location	Date placed	Seed depth	Mature size (")	Jan	Feb	Mar	Apr	May	Jun	Jul	Aug	Sep	Oct	Nov	Dec	Seed to transplant (weeks)	Days to maturity	Notes	Rooting depth	Source
Arugula					1/2"	12x12													4	40		S	
Basil					1/4"	6x6													6	75		S	
Beans					1-1/2"	6x6													3	60		M	
Beans, chickpea					1/2"	6x6													3	60		M	
Beans, cowpea					1"	4x4													N/A	80		D	
Beets					1/2"	12x12													6	55		M	
Broccoli					1/2"	18x18													6	90		M	
Brussels Sprouts					1/4"	24x24													6	90		M	
Cabbage					<1/4"	24x24													6	50		M	
Carrot					1/4"	4x4													N/A	70		M	
Cauliflower					1/2"	24x24													6	75		S	
Cilantro					1/4"	8x8													4	55		S	
Corn					2"	10x10													N/A	80		D	
Cucumber					1"	36x36													4	65		M	
Dill					1"	12x12													N/A	90		D	
Eggplant					1/4"	24x24													8	110		M	
Endive					1/2"	12x12													N/A	85		S	
Garlic					2"	12x12													N/A	220		S	
Groundcherry					1/4"	24x24													6	60		D	
Kale					1/2"	12x12													4	60		M	
Leeks					1/2"	4x4													8	110		M	
Lettuce					1/4"	12x12													4	30		S	
Melon					1"	36x36													4	80		M	
Onions					1/4"	6x6													8	65		S	
Peas					1"	4x4													3	60		D	
Peppers					1/4"	18x18													8	80		M	
Potatoes					N/A	12x12													N/A	80		S	
Shallots					1/2"	3x3													N/A	90		S	
Spinach					1/2"	4x4													4	45		S	
Squash, Summer					2"	36x36													3	50		M	
Squash, Winter					2"	36x36													3	100		M	
Swiss Chard					1/2"	6x6													4	60		S	
Tomato					1/8"	24x24													6	60		M	
Watermelon					1"	36x36													4	80		M	

Recipes

Growing your own food provides you with the freshest produce and herbs possible. Here are just a few of my favorite recipes for all that produce.

Chocolate Zucchini Cake

Sometimes you just need to give yourself a treat and this is one of my all-time favorites. (Thanks, Jo!) The zucchini provides a refreshing balance to the sweetness of the chocolate cake. This is one of those recipes that, once you try it, you will want to make it again and again. Even the kids and sworn Zucchini Haters end up loving this one!

Difficulty: Easy
Total time: 55 minutes
Yield: 20 squares

Ingredients
½ c. butter
½ c. olive oil*
1¾ c. sugar
2 eggs
1 tsp. vanilla
½ c sour milk
2½ c. flour
¼ c. cocoa
1 tsp. baking soda
½ tsp. baking powder
½ tsp. cinnamon
½ tsp. cloves
2 c. diced zucchini

Chocolate Zucchini Cake

*Make this recipe even better by using one-half regular olive oil and one-half blood orange or other citrus infused oil. It's amazing!

Instructions
Preheat oven to 325°F.
Grease and flour a 9" x 13" pan.
Sift together all dry ingredients and set aside.
Combine all wet ingredients except zucchini.
Combine everything and blend gently.
Spread in pan and bake 40-45 minutes.

Lettuce Wraps

Refreshing and nutritious, these snacks make every day just a little bit special.

Difficulty: Easy
Total time: 1 hour
Yield: 4 servings

Lettuce wraps with noodles

Ingredients
½ Tbsp. olive oil
1 lb. ground sausage
4 cloves garlic, minced
½ onion, minced
2 pinches Chinese five spice
1 Tbsp. soy sauce
1 tsp. rice wine vinegar
1 Tbsp. freshly grated ginger (or minced candied ginger)
1½ Tbsp. garlic red pepper sauce
¼ cup dry roasted peanuts, crushed
2 scallions, thinly sliced
Kosher salt
Freshly ground black pepper
1 head butter lettuce

Instructions
Brown ground sausage in a heavy skillet.
Add garlic and onion, stirring until caramelized.
Whisk together Chinese five spice, soy sauce, rice wine vinegar, ginger, peanuts, and garlic pepper sauce.
Add to the skillet and cook until warmed through.
Season with salt and pepper, to taste.
Spoon mixture into lettuce leaves.
Sprinkle with sliced scallions.

Serve next to Ramen cooked normally, drained, and then stirred up with peanut butter and garlic pepper sauce.

Pear Feta Bites

These are always a party favorite, but there's no reason why you can't treat yourself every once in a while.

Difficulty: Easy
Total time: 15 minutes
Yield: 8 to 12 servings

Ingredients
3 medium heads endive
¾ c. feta cheese
2 c. small-dice pear
1½ tsp. lemon juice
1 Tbsp. olive oil
¾ tsp. ground coriander
salt and pepper

Pear feta bites

Instructions
Trim the ends off the heads of endive and remove the leaves; set aside.
Gently toss the feta, pear, lemon juice, olive oil, and coriander in a medium bowl until evenly coated.
Season with salt and pepper and toss to coat well.
Place 1 tablespoon of the cheese-pear mixture in each endive leaf and serve immediately or cover with plastic wrap and chill.

Spicy Orange Beef Stir-Fry

Winter oranges help you recall the warm days of summer with this high protein, high fiber meal. Fast, easy, and packed with nutrients, this meal quickly becomes a family favorite!

Difficulty: Easy
Total time: 55 minutes
Yield: 4 servings

Ingredients
1 lb. trimmed ribeye, cut into strips
Grated peel from two oranges
Juice from four oranges
1 Tbsp. corn starch
1 Tbsp. honey
2 Tbsp. cooking oil
2 carrots, cut on the diagonal
½ onion, diced
2 Tbsp. soy sauce
4 stalks of celery
4 scallions
Red pepper flakes or Ghost Peppers, to taste

Spicy orange beef stir-fry

Instructions
Stir the grated orange rind into the meat and allow to reach room temperature.
Cut carrots, celery, and scallions on the diagonal.
Place carrots, onion, and soy sauce in a large wok or skillet and simmer until carrots begin to lose their crunch. Add celery and stir occasionally.
Whisk together orange juice, corn starch, honey, spices, and oil.
Crank up the heat and add the ribeye. After the meat begins to cook, move everything to the sides of your pan. Pour the juice mixture into the center, stirring constantly, until it thickens.
Remove from heat and stir everything together.
Serve over rice, garnish with shredded scallions and enjoy.

Zucchini Wraps

These tasty bites are ridiculously easy to make and surprisingly satisfying.

Difficulty: Easy
Total time: 10 minutes
Yield: 4 servings

Ingredients
1-2 medium zucchini
1 apple
1 pear
2 slices cheddar cheese, cut into 1" strips
Dried figs
Sunflower seeds
Cherry tomatoes

Zucchini wraps

Instructions
Slice the zucchini lengthwise, as thinly as is manageable.
Cut the apple and pear into wedges, removing the cores.
Roll each wedge with a slice of cheese in a zucchini slice.

Serve with dried figs, cherry tomatoes, and a sprinkling of sunflower seeds for a tasty snack or a nice light lunch.

Soil Tests

1. Collect 2 cups of soil, removing all rocks, roots, and debris.
2. Spread the soil out on a newspaper to dry, crushing any clumps.
3. Finely pulverize the soil sample after it is dry.
4. Shake the soil through the smallest screen you can find. (Labs use 2 mm. This soil residue is called fine earth.)
5. Fill a tall, slender, lidded jar ¼ full of the sifted soil.
6. Add water until it is ¾ full.
7. Put on a tight-fitting lid and shake hard for 10-15 minutes. (Some people use a blender for this, but their margaritas may end up being a tad gritty…)
8. Place the jar in a location where it will not be disturbed for two or three days.
9. After one minute, you can mark the sand level on your jar.
10. After two hours, you can mark the silt level on the jar.
11. Once the water clears, which may take one to three days, or weeks, you can mark the clay level.
12. Using a ruler, measure the thickness of each layer and the total sample.

13. Calculate the percentage of sand, silt, and clay by dividing each individual layer by the total sample depth.

For example, say your sample ends up being 5″ deep, with 2½″ of clay, 1″ of silt, and 1½″ of sand. You would use these calculations:

2½ / 5 = 50%
1 / 5 = 20%
1½ / 5 = 30%

You would then draw lines on the soil texture triangle (right) to show that your soil is 50% clay (blue line), 20% silt (pink line), and 30% sand (green line). Where those three lines intersect, you can see that the sample should be classified as sandy clay loam.

If your soil is too sandy, you can improve its texture by adding organic matter to help it retain water and nutrients. If your soil contains too much clay, adding organic matter will improve soil structure and porosity, and to speed the breakdown of organic matter. If you are lucky enough to have silty soil, you will still want to add organic matter to help maintain the inorganic mineral and organic matter balance.

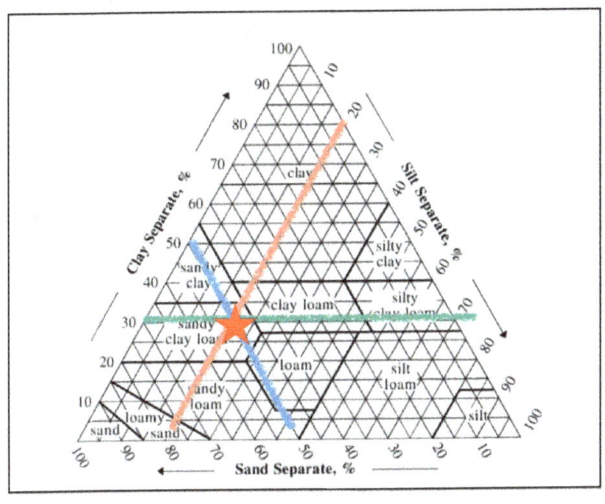

Soil texture triangle

375

CONDUCT YOUR OWN PERC TEST

Follow these steps to conduct your own permeability test.

1. Dig a few holes six inches wide and one foot deep.
2. Fill the holes with water.
3. After the holes drain completely, refill with water.
4. If the total drainage time is longer than four hours, your soil has poor permeability.

Ideally, you will want the water to drain at a rate of one to two inches per hour. Of course, sandy soil will drain much faster, taking valuable nutrients with it. You can improve the holding capacity of sandy soils by adding aged manure or compost. If your soil contains more clay, you can improve permeability by adding...you guessed it—aged manure or compost! Compost and aged manure add organic material to the soil, creating a wider variety of sizes of both soil and spaces. This variety allows for healthier growth and drainage.

Paved areas can lead to drainage and permeability problems. Permeable paving materials solve this problem by creating a firm surface for walking and parking while still allowing water to seep through. Permeable paving materials are affordable and attractive. They can also eliminate weeds growing up between paving stones!

ABOUT THE AUTHOR

Kate Russell, gardening columnist and science-based garden blogger, grows hundreds of pounds of food in her 4,000-square-foot landscape each year and delights in sharing her love of gardening with anyone who will listen.

Her blog, The Daily Garden (www.thedailygarden.us), is the basis for this and future books.

Soon to follow in The Daily Garden series: Common Plant Diseases, Garden Design, Insects and Other Garden Critters, Plant Care, Plants 101, Soil, and Weeds.

DETAILED CONTENTS